THE
AMERICAN
COOKBOOK

THE
AMERICAN
COOKBOOK

A fresh take on classic recipes

CAROLINE BRETHERTON
ELENA ROSEMOND-HOERR

LONDON NEW YORK MUNICH
MELBOURNE DELHI

DK UK

Senior Editor Bob Bridle
Senior Art Editor Lucy Parissi
Editorial Assistant Elizabeth Clinton
Managing Editor Dawn Henderson
Managing Art Editor Christine Keilty
Senior Jacket Creative Nicola Powling
Jacket Design Assistant Rosie Levine
Senior Pre-Production Producer Tony Phipps
Senior Producer Oliver Jeffreys
Art Director Peter Luff
Publisher Peggy Vance

DK INDIA

Senior Editor Dorothy Kikon
Senior Art Editor Balwant Singh
Editor Arani Sinha
Art Editor Simran Kaur
Assistant Editor Aditi Batra
Assistant Art Editor Pooja Verma
Managing Editor Alicia Ingty
Managing Art Editor Navidita Thapa
Production Manager Pankaj Sharma
Pre-Production Manager Sunil Sharma
DTP Designers Rajesh Singh Adhikari,
Rajdeep Singh Rawat

Studio photography Stuart West
Additional photography Elena Rosemond-Hoerr

First published in Great Britain in 2014 by
Dorling Kindersley Limited,
80 Strand, London, WC2R 0RL

A Penguin Random House Company

2 4 6 8 10 9 7 5 3 1

001 – 197059 – Feb/2014
Copyright © 2014 Dorling Kindersley Limited

A CIP catalogue record for this book is available from
the British Library.

ISBN 978-1-4093-4517-6

Printed and bound in Italy by L.E.G.O. S.p.A.

Discover more at
www.dk.com

CONTENTS

Introduction   6

STARTERS, SOUPS, AND SALADS   **8**

A taste of the Northeast   40

BREAKFASTS AND LIGHT BITES   **52**

A taste of the Southeast   72

MAINS AND SIDES   **92**

A taste of the Southwest   116

A taste of the Midwest   154

DESSERTS   **170**

BAKING, CANDY, AND PRESERVES   **200**

A taste of the Pacific Northwest   216

Index   250

Acknowledgments   256

INTRODUCTION

For too long, American cuisine has been characterized (at least overseas) as consisting of mainly fried foods and baked goods. However, having moved to the States just over a year ago, it has quickly become apparent to me that America's foods are as interesting and diverse as its people.

There are many different food cultures around the country, and you can trace the history of each one right back to the settlers that first colonized the regions. The Midwest, for example, home to many Central and Eastern European settlers, is full of dishes that would be just as at home on a table in Germany as they are in Ohio. Equally, in the South, the influence of the French settlers in Louisiana is heavily reflected in its food. Right across the nation, the major cities are a melting pot of cultures – with cuisines to match. In fact, some of the country's most interesting fusion foods have sprung from urban centres such as New York and Los Angeles.

America is a big country, and as such has a unique ability to grow, fish, and farm a wide range of high-quality produce. From the wild salmon caught in the icy waters off Alaska to the sweet and sour, yellow-tinged Key limes grown in sub-tropical Florida, the bounty is delicious and vast.

In this book, we have tried to encapsulate the classic recipes that hold pride of place in American homes, and also reflect the culinary innovations that have allowed those recipes to adapt to the colourful, diverse, and ever-changing landscape of modern America.

Caroline

Caroline Bretherton

STARTERS, SOUPS, AND SALADS

GRILLED PEACH SALSA WITH CORN CHIPS

Full of vibrant colours and flavours, this salsa is great by itself or as an accompaniment to grilled fish.

★ **SERVES** 4

★ **PREP TIME** 20 mins, plus chilling

★ **COOK TIME** 15 mins

Ingredients

2 large peaches, not too ripe, halved and stoned

1 tbsp olive oil

2 ripe tomatoes, skinned, deseeded, and finely chopped

1 large spring onion, trimmed and finely chopped

½ jalapeño or other mild green chilli, deseeded and finely chopped

2 tbsp finely chopped coriander

2 tbsp finely chopped mint

1 tbsp extra virgin olive oil

1 tbsp lime juice

1 tsp hot chilli sauce

salt and freshly ground black pepper

For the corn chips

8 x 15cm (6in) corn tortillas

1 tbsp olive oil, or some olive oil spray

4 tsp spice mix, such as Old Bay or Cajun spice, or smoked paprika

1 Heat a griddle pan or a barbecue on a high heat. Griddle or grill the peach halves for 2–3 minutes on each side, until they blacken in places and start to soften. Cool, peel, and finely dice the peaches.

2 Transfer the peaches to a medium bowl and add the remaining salsa ingredients. Season to taste. Chill the salsa in the fridge for 1 hour to allow the flavours to develop.

3 Preheat the oven to 230°C (450°F/Gas 8). Brush or spray the corn tortillas on both sides with a little oil, then sprinkle ½ tsp spice mix on each. Pile the spiced tortillas in a stack, then cut them into 6 equal wedges. Lay out the spicy wedges in a single layer on several baking sheets, taking care that they do not touch each other.

4 Bake in the oven for 5 minutes, checking them after 3 minutes, as they can burn easily. They should be brown and crispy in places, but still chewy in the middle. Remove from the oven and tip out onto a wire rack to cool and crisp up further. Serve with the peach salsa, brought to room temperature before serving.

COOK'S TIP Many oils and fats are now available in spray form. While many are artificial, and should be avoided, a natural olive oil spray is ideal here for coating the tortillas with a thin, even layer of oil.

CHUNKY GUACAMOLE FETA SALSA

More substantial than a guacamole dip, this salsa is perfect with barbecued lamb or beef.

★ **SERVES** 4
★ **PREP TIME** 10 mins
★ **COOK TIME** 15 mins

Ingredients

1 sweetcorn cob
1 tbsp olive oil
2 ripe avocados, halved, stoned, and cut (see technique, below)
12 cherry tomatoes, halved or quartered, if large
2 large spring onions, trimmed and finely chopped
2 heaped tbsp chopped coriander
juice of 1 lime
1 tsp hot chilli sauce
salt and freshly ground black pepper
60g (2oz) feta cheese

1 Rub the sweetcorn cob with oil and grill under a hot grill for 5–10 minutes, turning occasionally, until lightly charred in places. Alternatively, griddle it on a griddle pan over a high heat, or grill it directly over a gas flame or on a barbecue. Set it aside to cool.

2 When cool enough to handle, rest it vertically on a chopping board and, with a sharp knife, cut downward to shear off the kernels (see technique, p152).

3 In a large bowl, place the corn, avocados, tomatoes, and all but 1 tbsp each of the spring onions and coriander. Toss them together with the lime juice and hot chilli sauce, and season well.

4 Place the guacamole in a large bowl and crumble over the feta cheese. To serve, top with the remaining spring onions and coriander.

STONING AND PEELING AN AVOCADO

1 Slice the avocado lengthways in half, cutting all the way round the central stone, then separate the two halves by twisting gently.

2 Strike the stone with the blade of a large knife to embed it, then twist and lift the knife to remove the stone.

3 Cut each avocado half in half again. Use a paring knife to lift off the skin gently. Cut into 1cm (½in) chunks to use in the recipe.

BUFFALO CHICKEN WINGS

Hailing from Buffalo, New York, these sweet, spicy wings are served with a salty blue cheese dressing.

★ **SERVES** 6

★ **PREP TIME** 20–30 mins, plus resting

★ **COOK TIME** 40–50 mins

Ingredients

130g (4¾oz) plain flour
150g (5½oz) breadcrumbs
1 tsp paprika
½ tsp cayenne pepper
½ tsp salt
500ml (16fl oz) buttermilk (or to make your own, see Cook's tip, right)
24 bone-in chicken wings
1 litre (1¾ pints) peanut or sunflower oil, for frying
250ml (9fl oz) hot chilli sauce
2 garlic cloves, chopped
2 tbsp honey
115g (4oz) butter

For the cheese dressing

50g (1¾oz) mayonnaise
100g (3½oz) soured cream
90ml (3fl oz) buttermilk
115g (4oz) blue cheese, crumbled
30ml (1fl oz) cider vinegar

1 In a large bowl, combine the flour, breadcrumbs, paprika, cayenne pepper, and salt. Pour the buttermilk into a separate bowl. Dip the chicken wings in the buttermilk and toss them in the flour mixture, coating each one evenly. Refrigerate the coated chicken wings for at least 1 hour.

2 In a large, heavy-based saucepan or deep-fat fryer, heat the oil to 190°C (375°F), as shown in the technique on p144.

3 Meanwhile, in another saucepan, combine the hot chilli sauce, garlic, honey, and butter and place over a low heat. Let the butter melt, then simmer for 5 minutes.

4 When the oil is hot, fry the chicken pieces in batches, 4–5 pieces in each batch, for 8–10 minutes, or until golden brown. Remove the fried pieces from the oil with a slotted spoon and dip them in the sauce mixture. Turn the pieces through the mixture to coat them on all sides. Place on a wire rack to cool.

5 For the blue cheese dressing, process the mayonnaise, soured cream, buttermilk, blue cheese, and vinegar in a food processor. Serve the dressing in a small bowl alongside the chicken.

COOK'S TIP If buttermilk isn't available, you can make your own buttermilk substitute by combining 1 tbsp of lemon juice or vinegar with 250ml (9fl oz) of semi-skimmed milk. Let it stand for 10 minutes before using.

NOW TRY...

HONEY & CHIPOTLE

For a honey chipotle glaze, combine 140g (5oz) **runny honey**, 30g (1oz) **hot chilli sauce**, and 1 tbsp **chipotle paste**.

RANCH DRESSING DIP

Mix 50g (1¾oz) **mayonnaise**, 90ml (3fl oz) **buttermilk**, 100g (3½oz) **soured cream**, ½ tsp each of **onion powder**, freshly ground **black pepper**, **garlic powder**, and **dried thyme**, and 1 tbsp chopped **parsley**.

BAKED WINGS

For a sweet and salty baked variation, add 75g (2½oz) crushed **sweet potato crisps** to the breading and bake on a parchment-lined rack at 200ºC (400ºF/Gas 6) for 40 minutes, glazing with the sauce mixture every 10 minutes.

SMOKY BACON POTATO SKINS

Loaded with moreish fillings, these stuffed potato skins would make a welcome addition to any Super Bowl party.

★ **MAKES** 12
★ **PREP TIME** 20 mins
★ **COOK TIME** 1 hr 20 mins

Ingredients
6 baking potatoes, about
    7cm (2¾in) long, scrubbed
1 tbsp peanut or sunflower oil,
    plus extra for brushing
3 smoked streaky bacon rashers
3 tbsp soured cream
1 tsp smoked paprika or ancho
    chilli powder
salt and freshly ground
    black pepper
60g (2oz) finely grated red
    cheese, such as Red Leicester
2 spring onions, trimmed and
    finely chopped
soured cream, to serve
snipped chives, to serve

1 Preheat the oven to 200°C (400°F/Gas 6). Put the potatoes in a bowl and drizzle over 1 tbsp of oil. Rub the potatoes all over with the oil, then prick them with a fork and set them on a baking tray. Bake for about 45 minutes, turning once, until they are cooked through and golden brown. Set aside to cool.

2 Meanwhile, put the bacon on a baking tray and cook in the oven for about 10 minutes, turning once, until crispy. Drain on kitchen paper and set aside to cool, then dice it very finely.

3 Turn the oven up to 230°C (450°F/Gas 8). When the potatoes are cool enough to handle, cut them horizontally in half. Scoop out the insides, leaving a small amount of potato attached to the skin to make a sturdy shell. Brush the potato shells all over with a little oil, then put them back on the baking tray, skin-side up. Bake them for 10 minutes, then turn them over and bake for a further 5 minutes. Remove from the oven.

4 While the shells are crisping, place the scooped-out cooked potatoes in a bowl, add the soured cream and smoked paprika, and season well. Mash until smooth.

5 Set aside a little of the grated cheese and add the rest to the mashed potato mixture, along with the chopped crispy bacon and the spring onions. Mix well and stuff the filling into the crisped shells, mounding it up slightly in the centre.

6 Top the loaded potato skins with the remaining cheese and bake for a further 10 minutes, until they are golden brown and hot right through. Serve with a teaspoon of soured cream and a sprinkling of snipped chives, if desired.

COOK'S TIP Cook the potatoes up to 3 days in advance – when using the oven for another dish perhaps – and chill them until needed.

Spring onions add bite to the rich filling and cook quickly, too.

SPICY CHICKEN NACHOS WITH JALAPEÑOS

Tender shredded chicken makes a healthy alternative
to the more traditional pulled pork.

★ **SERVES** 4
★ **PREP TIME** 30 mins
★ **COOK TIME** 25–30 mins

Ingredients

175g (6oz) skinless boneless
  chicken breast
salt and freshly ground
  black pepper
pinch of chilli flakes
220g bag tortilla chips
400g can black beans, drained

For the pico de gallo

2 red tomatoes, deseeded
  and diced
1 red onion, diced
handful of coriander, chopped,
  plus extra for garnishing
juice of 1 lime

For the quick pickles

1 red onion, thinly sliced
1 jalapeño or other mild green
  chilli, cut into 5mm (¼in) slices
250ml (9fl oz) cider vinegar
1 tsp sea salt

For the queso

125ml (4½fl oz) single cream
225g (8oz) grated Spicy Jack
  cheese or mozzarella
olive oil
1 onion, diced
2 garlic cloves, crushed
1 jalapeño or other mild green
  chilli, finely chopped

1 For the pico de gallo, mix the tomatoes and onion with the coriander and lime juice. Season to taste and set aside.

2 For the quick pickles, combine the onion and jalapeño in a non-reactive saucepan (not aluminium or cast iron) with the vinegar and sea salt and cook over a low heat. Simmer for 5 minutes until the jalapeño turns dark green and the onion is translucent. Remove from the heat and set aside.

3 For the queso, put the cream and cheese in a small heatproof bowl over a saucepan of simmering water, making sure the bowl does not touch the water. Cook for 10 minutes, stirring occasionally as the cheese melts.

4 Meanwhile, heat some oil in a small pan over a medium heat and sauté the onion and garlic. Add the jalapeño. Once the jalapeño has softened slightly and the onion is translucent, stir in the melted cheese. Reduce the heat and stir occasionally.

5 Sprinkle the chicken with salt, pepper, and chilli flakes and griddle for 5–6 minutes on each side. Let it cool slightly, then shred with a fork.

6 Lay out half of the tortilla chips on a large plate, then pour over half the queso, followed by the black beans. Add a second layer of chips and the remaining queso. Top with the chicken, pico de gallo, and drained pickles. Garnish with coriander before serving.

COOK'S TIP If time is short, try using shop-bought salsa and thinly sliced red onions for a quick but tasty alternative to the pico de gallo and the quick pickles.

TROPICAL TEXAS CAVIAR

This healthy, zesty dish is equally delicious as a simple dip with tortilla chips, or served alongside grilled meat or fish.

★ **SERVES** 4-6
★ **PREP TIME** 15 mins, plus resting

Ingredients

1 jalapeño or other mild green chilli, deseeded and finely chopped

1 mango, peeled and roughly chopped

½ pineapple or 200g (7oz) canned pineapple, cut into cubes

2 garlic cloves, crushed

1 red pepper, deseeded and roughly chopped

1 green pepper, deseeded and roughly chopped

1 red onion, roughly chopped

1 tomato, roughly chopped

340g can sweetcorn, drained

400g can black-eyed beans, drained

juice of 4 limes

salt and freshly ground black pepper

tortilla chips, to serve

1 In a large bowl, mix the jalapeño, mango, pineapple, garlic, peppers, onion, and tomato. Combine well with the sweetcorn and black-eyed beans.

2 Add the lime juice, season well, and cover. Leave to rest for 1 hour to allow the flavours to develop.

3 Serve chilled or at room temperature with tortilla chips for dipping.

WHAT'S THE STORY?

Texas caviar is a cold dish of cooked black-eyed beans soaked in vinaigrette and enhanced with various chopped vegetables and herbs. Black-eyed beans are a heat-loving plant widely grown in Texas, where Helen Corbett, a chef and cookbook writer who advocated the use of fresh ingredients, popularized the dish in the 1950s.

Mangoes, with their vivid colour and sweet flavour, contrast well with many savoury salads.

DEVILLED DUCK EGGS WITH SMOKED SALMON

Adding lemon, dill, and smoked salmon can turn a simple boiled egg into an indulgent starter, picnic dish, or sandwich filling.

★ **MAKES** 8 egg halves

★ **PREP TIME** 15 mins, plus cooling

★ **COOK TIME** 15 mins

Ingredients

4 duck eggs
1 heaped tbsp soured cream
1 tbsp chopped dill, plus extra to garnish
1 tbsp chopped chives
grated zest of ½ lemon
1 tsp lemon juice
salt and freshly ground black pepper
30g (1oz) smoked salmon, finely diced

1 Place the eggs in a medium, heavy-based saucepan and cover with cold water. Bring the water to the boil, then reduce to a simmer and cook the eggs for 15 minutes until hard-boiled. Remove the pan from the heat, rinse the eggs under cold running water, and leave them to cool.

2 When the eggs are cold, peel off the shells, cut them in half horizontally and, using a teaspoon, carefully scoop out the egg yolks into a small bowl, leaving the egg whites intact. Cover the egg whites with cling film and chill until needed.

3 Mash the egg yolks well with the back of a fork. Add the rest of the ingredients, except the smoked salmon, and mash them together until smooth. Season to taste.

4 Pile the filling into the centre of the reserved egg whites with a spoon. Alternatively, transfer the filling into a piping bag and pipe into each egg half. Top with the diced salmon and garnish with dill.

Duck eggs have a rich flavour and an attractive dark yellow yolk.

PIGS IN BLANKETS WITH PARMESAN PASTRY

These simple appetizers are a family favourite and can be made with whatever sausages you prefer.

★ **MAKES** 12
★ **PREP TIME** 30 mins, plus chilling
★ **COOK TIME** 25-30 mins

Ingredients

150g (5½oz) plain flour, plus extra for dusting
½ tsp paprika
½ tsp salt
freshly ground black pepper
115g (4oz) unsalted butter, chilled
15g (½oz) finely grated Parmesan cheese
12 chipolata sausages
1 tbsp Dijon mustard
1 egg, beaten, for glazing
ketchup and hot chilli sauce, or a crème fraîche and mustard dip, to serve

1 Sift the flour, paprika, salt, and a good grinding of pepper into a large mixing bowl. Coarsely grate the chilled butter directly into the flour mixture (dipping the butter in the flour first will stop it from sticking to the grater). Add the Parmesan cheese and mix well so that the butter is evenly distributed throughout the flour.

2 Make a well in the centre of the flour mixture and add 3–4 tbsp of iced water. Bring the mixture together to form a rough dough, wrap in cling film, and chill for 30 minutes.

3 Preheat the oven to 200°C (400°F/Gas 6). On a lightly floured surface, roll out the dough to a 30 x 25cm (12 x 10in) rectangle. Cut the rectangle into 12 strips, each measuring 2 x 30cm (¾ x 12in). If you do not get 12 strips, bring the trimmings together, re-roll, and cut until you have the required number of strips.

4 Brush the surface of the sausages with a little of the Dijon mustard, then wrap the pastry strips around the sausages in a spiral fashion, overlapping the pastry slightly and pressing lightly at each end to seal it. The ends of the sausages may stick out of the pastry. Lay the finished sausages on an oven tray. Brush them lightly with a little egg wash and bake for 25–30 minutes, until golden brown.

5 Leave to cool on a wire rack for at least 5 minutes before serving hot, warm, or at room temperature. A little ketchup mixed with hot chilli sauce, or a crème fraîche and mustard dip would be an ideal accompaniment to these moreish snacks.

FRIED SHRIMP WITH LEMON AÏOLI

Japanese panko breadcrumbs give these shrimp a real crunch. Day-old breadcrumbs work well, too.

★ **SERVES** 4
★ **PREP TIME** 10 mins
★ **COOK TIME** 12–16 mins

Ingredients

500ml (16fl oz) peanut or sunflower oil, for frying
1 egg
130g (4¾oz) plain flour
1 tsp paprika
½ tsp cayenne pepper
½ tsp salt
75g (2½oz) panko breadcrumbs or day-old breadcrumbs
24 king prawns, peeled and deveined

For the lemon aïoli

110g (3¾oz) mayonnaise
juice of ½ lemon
3 spring onions, chopped
2 garlic cloves, crushed
salt and freshly ground black pepper

1 In a large, heavy-based saucepan or deep-fat fryer, heat the oil to 190°C (375°F), as shown in the technique on p144.

2 Break the egg into a bowl, add 1 tbsp water, and whisk with a fork. In a separate large bowl, mix the flour, paprika, cayenne pepper, salt, and breadcrumbs.

3 Dip the prawns in the egg wash and toss them in the breadcrumb mixture, coating each one evenly. Fry the prawns in batches of 6 for 3–4 minutes each, or until golden brown.

4 For the aïoli, whisk the mayonnaise, lemon juice, spring onions, and garlic in a small bowl and season to taste. Serve with the prawns.

COOK'S TIP When deep-frying, make sure you do not overcrowd the pan as the prawns will not brown well.

Prawns come in all shapes and sizes, but look for wild-caught prawns if possible.

NOW TRY...

HOT & SPICY SAUCE

Mix together 110g (3¾oz) **mayonnaise**, 2 tbsp **hot chilli sauce**, 1 tbsp **soy sauce**, and 1 tsp **red chilli paste**. Toss the prawns in the sauce and serve with cocktail sticks.

ASIAN-STYLE DIP

Combine 2 tbsp **runny honey**, 2 tbsp **soy sauce**, and ½ tbsp **ground ginger** for an Asian-style dipping sauce.

BAKED OPTION

For a lighter alternative to frying, add 75g (2½oz) grated **Parmesan** to the breading and bake the coated prawns at 230ºC (450ºF/Gas 8) for 5-7 minutes, or until golden brown, turning once so they are evenly browned.

LEMON SHALLOT CRAB CAKES

Fresh crabs, fished from the Chesapeake Bay, are traditionally used to make these famous Maryland crab cakes.

★ **MAKES** 4
★ **PREP TIME** 15 mins
★ **COOK TIME** 6-10 mins

Ingredients

300g (10oz) cooked white and
   brown crabmeat (to extract
   crabmeat from shell, see p25)
1 egg
100g (3½oz) crushed crackers
   or dried breadcrumbs
juice of 1 lemon, plus extra
   to serve
zest of 2 lemons
salt and freshly ground
   black pepper
1 shallot, finely chopped
2 garlic cloves, crushed
peanut or sunflower oil,
   for frying

For the aïoli

220g (7¾oz) mayonnaise
juice of 1 lemon
bunch of spring onions,
   finely chopped
1 garlic clove, crushed

1 Rinse and pick over the crabmeat, removing any pieces of shell, then drain well. In a bowl, mix together the crab, egg, crackers, lemon juice and zest, and season to taste. Add the shallot and garlic, and mix well.

2 Take a quarter of the mixture and form a cake 7.5cm (3in) in diameter and set aside on a plate. Repeat to make 3 more cakes.

3 Pour the oil into a large, heavy-based frying pan to a depth of at least 2.5cm (1in). Heat the oil to 190°C (375°F), and fry the cakes for 3–5 minutes on each side, or until golden.

4 Meanwhile, make the aïoli. Mix together the mayonnaise, lemon juice, spring onions, and garlic in a bowl. Season to taste. Serve the crab cakes hot with the aïoli and a squeeze of lemon.

COOK'S TIP Add a finely chopped jalapeño or other mild green chilli to step 1 for a spicy twist.

Lemon, freshly squeezed, adds a bright tartness to the rich flavour of seafood.

NEW ENGLAND CRAB DIP

Adding Greek yogurt to the mayonnaise gives a light, fresh taste to this dip, enhanced here with lemon and herbs.

★ **SERVES** 6

★ **PREP TIME** 5 mins

Ingredients

450g (1lb) white crabmeat, cooked or canned (drained)

4 tbsp thick Greek yogurt

2 tbsp good-quality mayonnaise

1 tbsp finely chopped dill

1 tbsp finely chopped chives

finely grated zest of ½ lemon

¼ tsp cayenne pepper

salt and freshly ground black pepper

crackers or home-made baguette bruschetta, to serve

1 If using crabmeat from a cooked crab, extract the white meat, as shown in the technique below. Place the crabmeat in a bowl and mash it finely with the back of a fork to break up any large pieces.

2 Whisk together the yogurt and mayonnaise until well combined, then fold it into the crabmeat.

3 Add the dill, chives, lemon zest, and cayenne pepper and mix well. Season to taste. Serve with crackers or home-made baguette bruschetta (see Warm artichoke and spinach dip, p26).

EXTRACTING MEAT FROM A COOKED CRAB

1 Twist off the claws and legs and set them aside. Twist off the tail flap and discard. Break and separate the body from the shell. Discard the gills and stomach sac.

2 Cut the body into quarters and pick out the white meat with a fork. Using a nut cracker, break the shell of the claws and the legs across their narrowest part, and extract the white meat.

3 Using a spoon, scoop out the white meat from the shell. Remove and reserve the brown meat for another time and discard any pieces of shell or membrane from the crabmeat.

SPICY SWEETCORN FRITTERS WITH SALSA

If you're using young, tender sweetcorn, there is no need to cook it before making these flavour-loaded fritters.

★ **SERVES** 4
★ **PREP TIME** 20 mins
★ **COOK TIME** 10 mins

Ingredients

2 sweetcorn cobs, about
  250g (9oz) kernel weight
100g (3½oz) self-raising flour
1 tsp baking powder
2 large eggs
4 tbsp milk
1 tsp smoked paprika
  or ancho-chilli powder
2 spring onions, finely
  chopped, green and white
  parts separated
4 tbsp chopped coriander
1 red chilli, deseeded and
  finely chopped (optional)
salt and freshly ground
  black pepper
2 tbsp peanut or sunflower oil
2 ripe tomatoes, skinned and
  roughly chopped
2 tbsp extra virgin olive oil
dash of Tabasco or chilli sauce

1 Hold the corn cobs upright on a chopping board and, using a sharp knife, cut downwards to shear off the kernels (see technique, p152).

2 Sift the flour and baking powder into a bowl. Mix the eggs and milk together in a jug and gradually whisk them into the flour to make a thick batter. Add the corn, paprika, the white parts of the spring onions, 2 tbsp of the coriander, and the chilli (if using). Mix well and season.

3 Heat the peanut or sunflower oil in a large frying pan and add tablespoonfuls of the batter mixture. Use the back of the spoon to spread the fritters out slightly, and fry for 2–3 minutes on each side until puffed up and golden brown. Fry in batches until all the mixture is cooked, adding a little more oil as necessary.

4 Put the tomatoes, the remaining coriander and spring onion, olive oil, and Tabasco or chilli sauce into a food processor and process until blended but still quite chunky. Check the salsa for seasoning and serve the hot fritters with the salsa on the side.

WARM ARTICHOKE AND SPINACH DIP

This rich, creamy dip is delicious served warm with home-made bruschetta or simple sliced baguette.

- ★ **SERVES** 4-6
- ★ **PREP TIME** 15 mins
- ★ **COOK TIME** 30 mins, plus cooling

Ingredients

1 day-old baguette, thinly sliced
1 tbsp olive oil, plus extra for brushing
25g (scant 1oz) unsalted butter
2 garlic cloves, crushed
175g (6oz) baby spinach
175g (6oz) artichoke hearts preserved in oil, drained weight
200g (7oz) cream cheese
50g (1¾oz) finely grated Parmesan cheese
100g (3½oz) soured cream
1 tbsp plain flour
150g (5½oz) grated Gruyère cheese
freshly ground black pepper

1 Preheat the oven to 180°C (350°F/Gas 4). Spread out the slices of baguette in a single layer over 1 or 2 baking trays and brush them on both sides with a little oil. Bake them in the top of the oven for about 5 minutes on each side, until they are golden brown and crispy. Set aside to cool.

2 Melt the butter and oil in a large saucepan over a medium heat. Add the garlic and cook for 2 minutes, until golden. Add the spinach and continue to cook for 2–3 minutes, stirring constantly, until the spinach wilts. Place the spinach in a sieve and press down with the back of a spoon to remove any excess liquid. Let it cool, then roughly chop it.

3 Rinse the artichokes under cold running water and pat them dry. Roughly chop them and set them aside. Place the cream cheese, Parmesan, soured cream, flour, and 100g (3½oz) of the Gruyère cheese in a food processor and process until smooth.

4 Add the spinach and artichokes to the mixture, season with pepper, and pulse briefly until the mixture is well combined, but with small chunks of vegetables still visible.

5 Pour the mixture into individual ramekins or a 20cm (8in) ovenproof baking dish. Scatter with the remaining Gruyère cheese and bake at the top of the oven for 25–30 minutes, until the top is golden brown and the cheese is bubbling on the sides. Allow to cool for 10 minutes before serving with the baked baguette.

Artichokes, even when canned or frozen, add a rich, luxurious taste to this dip.

NOW TRY...

MIDDLE EASTERN DIP

For a Middle Eastern twist, add ½ tsp each of ground **cumin** and **coriander** to the cheese, and serve with **tortillas** brushed with olive oil, scattered with **sesame seeds**, and baked in a hot oven until crispy.

SAUTÉED KALE

Spinach can be easily replaced with **sautéed kale**, which has a stronger flavour, although it will need to be cooked for 1 or 2 minutes longer.

GREEK YOGURT

For a simple, fresh dip, omit the Gruyère cheese, replace the soured cream with an equal amount of **Greek yogurt**, and serve without baking.

SPICY PIMIENTO CHEESE DIP

This versatile dip can be processed smooth as a dip for crackers or potato chips, or coarse for a sandwich filling.

★ **SERVES** 6

★ **PREP TIME** 10 mins, plus chilling

Ingredients

250g (9oz) grated strong
  Cheddar cheese
4 tbsp soured cream
4 tbsp good-quality mayonnaise
4 tbsp finely diced roasted red
  peppers (pimientos), from
  a can or jar
2 large spring onions, trimmed
  and finely chopped
1 tsp smoked paprika
1 tsp cayenne pepper
salt and freshly ground black
  pepper, to taste
crackers or home-made
  baguette bruschetta,
  to serve

1 Put all the ingredients into a food processor and pulse until the mixture is well combined, but rough in texture.

2 Place the mixture in an airtight container and chill for at least 1 hour to allow the flavours to develop.

3 Serve with crackers or home-made baguette bruschetta (see Warm artichoke and spinach dip, p26).

COOK'S TIP This tasty dip makes a delicious alternative filling for a Grilled cheese sandwich (see p90), layered with crispy, grilled prosciutto or applewood smoked bacon.

SERVE WITH

BUFFALO CHICKEN WINGS
SEE PAGE 12

CHEDDAR CHEESE STRAWS
SEE PAGE 230

ASIAN CHICKEN AND RICE NOODLE SOUP

Make this with home-made chicken stock to get a second delicious meal from a simple roast chicken.

★ **SERVES** 4
★ **PREP TIME** 20 mins
★ **COOK TIME** 25 mins

Ingredients

2 tbsp olive oil
2 stalks of lemongrass, trimmed
bunch of spring onions, trimmed
 and roughly chopped
2 red chillies, deseeded
 and halved
5cm (2in) thumb of ginger,
 cut into slices
small bunch of coriander,
 leaves and stalks separated
1.2 litres (2 pints) hot
 chicken stock
200g (7oz) cooked
 chicken, shredded
150g (5½oz) soup noodles,
 such as vermicelli
salt and freshly ground
 black pepper

1 Heat the oil in a large saucepan. Roughly bruise the lemongrass with a rolling pin. Add the lemongrass, spring onions, chillies, ginger, and coriander stalks to the saucepan and fry over a medium heat for 2 minutes to release their flavours.

2 Add the stock and bring to the boil. Reduce the heat to a gentle simmer and cook for about 20 minutes, until the vegetables are soft. Take the saucepan off the heat and pass the stock through a sieve to remove the vegetables. Wipe the saucepan clean and return the flavoured stock to the heat.

3 Add the chicken and noodles, and continue to cook until the noodles are ready (according to the packet instructions). Check the seasoning. Roughly chop the coriander leaves and scatter over the hot soup before serving immediately.

COOK'S TIP If you have extra stock, double the quantities and cook up to step 3. Add the chicken, but leave out the noodles. Freeze it in portions. Then, when needed, defrost the portions, bring to the boil, add the noodles, and cook until tender.

WHAT'S THE STORY?

Chicken noodle soup is a deeply comforting soup traditionally made from the long, slow simmering of a whole chicken. Although versions of this soup appear in several cuisines worldwide, the Jewish kitchens of America's East Coast have a special claim. The soup has attained the almost mythical (yet unproven) status as a cure for the common cold, amongst other ailments.

TORTILLA CHICKEN SOUP

Full of the vibrant flavours of the Southwest, this colourful, hearty soup is a meal in itself.

★ **SERVES** 6
★ **PREP TIME** 20 mins
★ **COOK TIME** 45 mins

Ingredients
3 tbsp olive oil
2 garlic cloves, crushed
1 jalapeño or other mild green
　chilli, finely chopped
1 green pepper, deseeded
　and roughly chopped
1 red pepper, deseeded
　and roughly chopped
340g can sweetcorn, drained
400g can black beans, drained
3 tbsp fine polenta or cornmeal
2 x 400g can chopped tomatoes
salt and freshly ground
　black pepper
2 tsp chipotle paste
1.25 litres (2 pints)
　hot chicken stock
2 chicken breasts, 350g (12oz)
　in total

To garnish
3 tortillas, cut into 1cm
　(½in) strips
handful of coriander, chopped
115g (4oz) grated
　Cheddar cheese
juice of 1 lime

1 Heat 1 tbsp of the oil in a large soup pot over a medium heat. Add the garlic, jalapeño, and onion, and cook over a medium heat for 3–4 minutes. Add the peppers with the sweetcorn, beans, and polenta. Simmer, stirring occasionally, for 2–3 minutes.

2 Stir in the tomatoes with their juices, a little salt, 1 tsp of the chipotle paste, and the stock. Reduce the heat to low and simmer for 35 minutes.

3 Meanwhile, season the chicken on both sides with salt and black pepper, and smear all over with the remaining chipotle paste. Heat 1 tbsp of the oil in a frying pan and cook the chicken breasts for 8–10 minutes per side, then cut them into 1cm (½in) slices and add to the soup.

4 Heat the remaining oil in a large frying pan over a low-medium heat. Sauté the tortilla strips for 2–3 minutes, or until crisp and browned. Serve the soup hot, garnished with the coriander, cheese, lime juice, and tortilla strips.

Chipotle chillies, common in Mexican cuisine, are smoke-dried jalapeños.

SPICY CHORIZO MINESTRONE

A classic Italian minestrone is given added spice with the use of chorizo, a Spanish cured pork sausage.

- ★ **SERVES** 8–10
- ★ **PREP TIME** 20 mins
- ★ **COOK TIME** 2 hrs

Ingredients

1 tbsp olive oil
3 garlic cloves, crushed
250g (9oz) red onion, chopped
225g (8oz) green pepper, deseeded and chopped
250g (9oz) celery sticks, chopped
200g (7oz) carrots, sliced
225g (8oz) courgettes, roughly chopped, skin-on
2 x 400g can chopped tomatoes
400g can chickpeas
750ml (1⅓ pints) hot chicken stock
225g (8oz) cherry tomatoes
salt and freshly ground black pepper
600g (1lb 5oz) chorizo
100g (3½oz) Parmesan rind
60g (2oz) kale, de-ribbed and chopped
225g (8oz) dried orecchiette pasta
175g (6oz) Portobello mushrooms, sliced

1 Heat the oil in a large soup pot over a medium heat and add the garlic. Stir in the onion, pepper, celery, carrots, and courgettes. Cook for 5 minutes. Add the chopped tomatoes, chickpeas with their juices, stock, and cherry tomatoes. Season and bring to the boil.

2 Remove the skin from the chorizo and crumble the sausagemeat into a frying pan. Cook for 5–7 minutes, until browned. Reserve the drippings and transfer the chorizo to the soup pot, along with the Parmesan. Stir to incorporate, reduce the heat, and simmer, uncovered, for 1 hour 45 minutes.

3 Stir in the kale and pasta. Cook for a further 15–20 minutes, or until the pasta is tender.

4 Meanwhile, cook the Portobello mushrooms in the frying pan with the chorizo drippings over a medium heat for 3–5 minutes, until browned. Season to taste. Serve the soup hot, topped with the Portobello slices.

Carrots are loaded with vitamins, and make a good addition to almost any soup or stew.

CREAMY TOMATO SOUP WITH CORN AND PEPPERS

This delicate soup brings together the best of the summer's vegetable harvest in one creamy bowlful.

★ **SERVES** 8

★ **PREP TIME** 20 mins

★ **COOK TIME** 1½ hrs

Ingredients

3 tbsp olive oil
2 garlic cloves, crushed
1 onion, chopped
salt and freshly ground
   black pepper
175g (6oz) tomato purée
4 x 400g can chopped tomatoes
1 red pepper, deseeded
   and diced
340g can sweetcorn, drained
250ml (9fl oz) double cream
crusty bread or a Grilled cheese
   sandwich (see p90), to serve

1 In a large soup pot, heat 1 tbsp of oil over a medium heat. Add the garlic and onion, and season. Add the tomato purée and stir for 2–3 minutes.

2 Add 500ml (16fl oz) of water, the tomatoes, and salt. Cover and simmer for 45 minutes.

3 Toss the pepper in the remaining oil. Grill on a very low heat for 3–4 minutes, or until the pepper has roasted.

4 Using a hand-held blender, purée the tomato mixture in the pot. Stir in the sweetcorn and pepper, reserving a little of both to garnish, then add the cream. Simmer, uncovered, for a further 30–45 minutes. Remove from the heat, garnish with the reserved sweetcorn and pepper, and serve hot with crusty bread or a Grilled cheese sandwich.

COOK'S TIP In high summer, use the kernels from 2 fresh sweetcorn cobs instead of using canned.

NEW ENGLAND CLAM CHOWDER

Once plentiful on the New England coast, clams were widely used as a source of cheap protein.

★ **SERVES** 4
★ **PREP TIME** 15 mins
★ **COOK TIME** 1 hr

Ingredients

350g (12oz) thick-cut bacon, chopped
3 garlic cloves, crushed
1 large onion, roughly chopped
3 tbsp plain flour
1 celery stick, sliced
500g (1lb 2oz) fingerling potatoes, such as Anya, cut into thirds
1 litre (1¾ pints) hot chicken stock
2 x 300g can clams
250ml (9fl oz) double cream
juice of 1 lemon
salt and freshly ground black pepper
flat-leaf parsley, to garnish
crusty bread, to serve

1 In a large, heavy-based pan or soup pot, cook the bacon for 3–5 minutes, until sizzling and softened. Add the garlic, onion, flour, and celery. Cook until the onions are translucent.

2 Add the potatoes, along with the stock, clams, and cream. Simmer for 50–60 minutes, or until the potatoes are soft.

3 Add the lemon juice and season to taste. Garnish with the parsley and serve hot with crusty bread.

Clams should be treated in the same way as mussels – any left unopened after cooking should be discarded.

NOW TRY...

CORN CHOWDER

For a vegetarian version, use **vegetable stock** instead of chicken; substitute the bacon with 200g (7oz) **button mushrooms**, halved; and swap the clams for 340g can **sweetcorn**.

FRESH SEAFOOD

Make this an authentic seafood soup with 225g (8oz) **fresh clams**, 450g (1lb) **lobster tail**, and 12 cooked **king prawns**. Add for the last 10 minutes of cooking in step 2, with the lid on and slightly open.

SEMI-SKIMMED MILK

For a lighter soup, try substituting the cream with **semi-skimmed milk** or **rice milk** and blending with a food processor to incorporate.

SMOKY SPLIT PEA SOUP

The croutons and crispy bacon garnish add a satisfying crunch to this hearty, warming soup.

★ **SERVES** 6-8

★ **PREP TIME** 5 mins

★ **COOK TIME** 1 hr 10 mins

Ingredients

10 smoked streaky
bacon rashers
1 onion, roughly chopped
2 garlic cloves, roughly chopped
2 carrots, thickly sliced
2 potatoes, such as Desiree,
quartered
3 celery sticks, chopped
1 tbsp chopped rosemary
1 tbsp chopped thyme
1 tbsp chopped oregano
2 litres (3½ pints) hot
chicken stock
450g (1lb) dry split peas
salt and freshly ground
black pepper

For the croutons

2 tbsp olive oil
2 garlic cloves, crushed
2-3 slices of day-old bread,
cut into cubes

1 Brown the bacon in a heavy-based soup pot or flameproof casserole over a medium heat. Take out a small amount of bacon and set aside for garnishing.

2 Add the onion and garlic to the pot. Stir in the carrots along with the potatoes, celery, and the herbs. Cook over a low heat until the onions turn translucent, then add the stock and peas. Cover and cook over a low heat for 45 minutes to 1 hour, or until the peas are soft.

3 Transfer the mixture to a food processor or use a hand-held blender and blend to a smooth purée. Season to taste.

4 For the croutons, heat the oil in a small pan over a medium-high heat. Add the garlic and the bread and toss until brown. Crumble or finely chop the reserved bacon. Serve the soup hot, topped with the croutons and crumbled bacon.

BLACK BEAN AND CHIPOTLE SOUP

Black beans are a good source of protein and fibre, and this soup makes a healthy and satisfying lunch in itself.

- ★ **SERVES** 4
- ★ **PREP TIME** 15 mins
- ★ **COOK TIME** 2–3 hrs

Ingredients

250g (9oz) bacon, chopped
3 garlic cloves, crushed
1 onion, diced
2 x 400g can black
  beans, unsalted
175g (6oz) cherry
  tomatoes, halved
700ml (1¼ pints) hot
  chicken stock
1 tbsp ground cumin
½ tsp chipotle paste
salt and freshly ground
  black pepper

For the topping

2 smoked streaky
  bacon rashers
4 tbsp soured cream
1 avocado, halved,
  stoned, and sliced
  (see technique, p11)
bunch of coriander leaves,
  roughly chopped

1 Put the bacon, garlic, and onion in a large soup pot and place over a medium heat. Cook, stirring frequently, until the bacon begins to fry and the onions begin to soften.

2 Stir in the beans with their juices, tomatoes, chicken stock, ground cumin, and chipotle paste. Season to taste and bring to the boil. Reduce the heat and simmer, uncovered, for 2–3 hours, or until the soup has thickened and reduced by half.

3 In a frying pan, dry-fry the bacon rashers until crisp. Remove from the pan and leave to cool, then crumble them into pieces.

4 Serve the soup hot, topped with the bacon, a dollop of soured cream, avocado, and coriander.

CAESAR SALAD WITH SEARED SALMON

This salad uses an easy version of the classic Caesar dressing, replacing the traditional recipe made with raw egg.

★ **SERVES** 4
★ **PREP TIME** 20 mins
★ **COOK TIME** 20 mins

Ingredients

2 salmon fillets, each
150g (5½oz)
1 tbsp olive oil
salt and freshly ground
black pepper
peanut or sunflower oil,
for frying
3 heaped tbsp capers,
drained and rinsed
1 large romaine lettuce,
leaves torn
2 avocados, halved,
stoned, and sliced
(see technique, p11)

For the dressing

100ml (3½fl oz) extra
virgin olive oil
1 tbsp Dijon mustard
3 tbsp good-quality mayonnaise
4 anchovy fillets, chopped
½ tsp Worcestershire sauce
1 garlic clove, crushed
2 tbsp finely grated
Parmesan cheese
pinch of caster sugar

1 Put a griddle pan on a high heat, or preheat the grill on its highest setting. Rub the salmon with the olive oil, season well, and either griddle in the griddle pan or grill under the hot grill for 3–4 minutes on each side. Set aside to cool, then flake the salmon into large pieces using your hands.

2 Pour the peanut or sunflower oil into a small, heavy-based saucepan to a depth of 1cm (½in) and heat over a high heat. Meanwhile, dry the capers well on a piece of kitchen paper. When the oil is hot, drop the capers in (be careful, they will spit) and fry for a minute until puffed up and crispy. Remove from the oil with a slotted spoon and leave to cool on clean kitchen paper.

3 To make the dressing, put all the ingredients into the bowl of a mini food processor, or into a suitable container for a hand-held blender, and process or blend until the mixture has emulsified into a thick, creamy dressing. Season with pepper.

4 To serve, put the lettuce leaves in a large bowl and toss them in the dressing. Carefully toss through the sliced avocados, then arrange the flaked salmon over the top of the salad and scatter over the deep-fried capers.

Avocados are packed with monounsaturated fats, which are essential for a healthy diet.

A taste of the
NORTHEAST

The cuisine of this corner of the United States reflects both its cultural heritage as the landing point for the early British and European settlers, as well as its varied and fertile geography.

Despite harsh winters and an inhospitable coastline, the Northeast has long been a place of plenty. For hundreds of years, the Native Americans tapped the maple tree – a local mainstay – for its sweet, sticky sap, which they boiled down to make syrup. This soon became a widespread practice among the early farmers, who also made good use of the region's fertile soils, growing the beans and squash favoured by the Native Americans, as well as their own European imports. Hunters soon learned how best to capture the area's indigenous wild turkeys, and fishermen flocked to the waters around Cape Cod to fish the abundant seas. Although less bountiful than they once were, the shorelines of New England are still a rich source of oysters, clams, and lobsters.

In New York City, global immigrants have added to the vast array of foodstuffs available, from the layered sandwiches of the Jewish delis, to the spicy delights of Chinatown.

FOODS AND FLAVOURS

★ Chesapeake Bay, Maryland, is renowned for its **blue crabs**, as well as for seafood of all kinds. **Crab cakes** (see p22) are just one of the area's famous dishes.

★ **New England clam chowder** (see p34) marries rich **cream** from the dairy farms of Vermont with the simply prepared fresh **clams** caught off the coast.

★ **Boston baked beans** (see p146), created by the early settlers, is an interpretation of a Native American dish. Traditionally cooked on a Saturday and kept overnight in a brick oven, the beans would stay warm until the following morning, allowing the settlers to enjoy them while still adhering to strict Sabbath rules.

★ A typical **Thanksgiving dinner** in New England will include **succotash**, a mixed corn and bean dish traditionally made by the Native Americans. There are many vibrant, modern variations of the recipe (see p145).

The Reuben is the archetypal New York deli sandwich, packed with tasty fillings.

Sweet, sour, and crunchy, the Waldorf salad originated in New York and is popular the world over.

Maryland crab cakes are traditionally made using the fabulous fresh crabs of the region.

Fresh clams are often used in chowder, but canned ones, or smoked fish, are also good.

Chinatown, in New York City, offers a vast array of succulent fresh seafood.

Camden Harbour is one of the many places in Maine that produces outstanding seafood.

Best when small and sweet, the lobsters of the Eastern seaboard, sometimes known as Maine lobsters, are a regional delicacy.

WALDORF SALAD

Created at the Waldorf Astoria Hotel in New York, this salad has been a favourite for over 100 years.

★ **SERVES** 4

★ **PREP TIME** 15 mins

Ingredients

2 large apples

4 celery sticks, thinly sliced

25 red seedless grapes, halved

2 tbsp toasted and crushed walnuts

60g (2oz) mayonnaise

juice of 1 lemon

salt and freshly ground black pepper

2 hearts of romaine lettuce

1 Remove the cores of the apples by using a corer. Then, using a sharp knife, cut the apples into slices of an even thickness. Stack the slices, a few at a time, and cut lengthways through the pile and then crossways, making equal-sized cubes.

2 Put the apples, celery, grapes, and walnuts in a bowl. Add the mayonnaise and lemon juice and toss well to combine. Season to taste.

3 Roughly chop the lettuce and divide between 4 plates. Serve the fruit and nut mixture on each bed of lettuce with a squeeze of lemon.

Red apples, with their bright colour and crisp texture, make a great addition to any salad.

NOW TRY...

FRUIT & PECANS

Instead of using apples, celery, grapes, and walnuts, try combining 2 **pears**, 350g (12oz) **blackberries**, and 30g (1oz) **toasted pecans**.

GREEK YOGURT

For a lighter take on this salad, simply substitute the mayonnaise with an equal amount of **Greek yogurt**.

SMOKY BACON

Add **maple-cured smoked bacon bits** for a sweet and smoky flavour. Dry-fry 8 **smoked streaky bacon rashers** in a frying pan until crisp. Remove and allow to cool, then break them up into pieces and mix into the salad.

FRIED CHICKEN COBB SALAD

This main course salad is served with a sharp, salty buttermilk and blue cheese dressing.

★ **SERVES** 4

★ **PREP TIME** 20 mins, plus soaking

★ **COOK TIME** 20 mins

Ingredients

2 skinless boneless chicken breasts
1 tsp cayenne pepper
salt
250ml (9fl oz) whole milk
8 smoked streaky bacon rashers
75g (2½oz) plain flour
75g (2½oz) breadcrumbs
1 tbsp chipotle paste
1 litre (1¾ pints) peanut or sunflower oil, for frying
bunch of baby spinach or rocket leaves
300g (10oz) cherry tomatoes, halved
1 avocado, stoned, peeled, and chopped (see technique, p11)
4 hard-boiled eggs, roughly chopped

For the blue cheese dressing

60g (2oz) mayonnaise
100ml (3½fl oz) soured cream
90ml (3fl oz) buttermilk (or to make your own, see p12)
115g (4oz) blue cheese, crumbled
2 tbsp cider vinegar

1 Put the chicken in a pan along with the cayenne pepper and 1 tsp salt. Pour in the milk and leave the chicken to soak for 2 hours in the fridge.

2 In a frying pan, dry-fry the bacon over a medium heat until crispy. Remove from the pan and cool on a wire rack, then set aside.

3 In a shallow bowl, mix together the flour, breadcrumbs, chipotle paste, and 1 tbsp salt. Drain and discard the milk and turn the chicken in the bread mixture until well coated.

4 Pour the oil into a large, heavy-based saucepan or deep-fat fryer. Heat it to 190°C (375°F), as shown in the technique on p144. Fry the chicken for 5–7 minutes, or until golden brown. Remove with a slotted spoon and cool on a wire rack. Set aside.

5 Spread the spinach evenly in a large, wide serving dish. Place the tomatoes in a row across the greens. Add the avocado, placing it next to the tomatoes, then add a row of the eggs. Chop the chicken into bite-sized pieces and distribute evenly around the salad. Crumble the bacon and scatter it over the top.

6 For the dressing, mix together the mayonnaise, soured cream, buttermilk, blue cheese, and vinegar. Serve the salad, while the chicken is still warm, with the buttermilk dressing on the side. Any leftover dressing will keep in the fridge for up to 3 days, tightly sealed.

WHAT'S THE STORY?

It is widely accepted that the first Cobb salad was made at The Brown Derby restaurant in Hollywood in the early 20th century, and was named in honour of the then owner, Bob Cobb. Exactly who created it, and when, is less clear, but there is no doubt that the eponymous salad, with its distinctive stripes of fresh, colourful ingredients, is a true Tinseltown classic.

EGG SALAD WITH CELERY, CAPERS, AND DILL

A step up from traditional egg mayonnaise, try this spread on wholemeal toast for a quick, delicious lunch.

★ **SERVES** 2–3
★ **PREP TIME** 10 mins, plus cooling
★ **COOK TIME** 10 mins

Ingredients

6 eggs
6 tbsp good-quality mayonnaise
1 tbsp lemon juice
1 celery stick, finely chopped
1 heaped tbsp finely chopped dill
1 heaped tbsp Dijon mustard
1 large spring onion, finely chopped
1 heaped tbsp capers, drained and roughly chopped
pinch of salt and freshly ground black pepper
pinch of smoked paprika, to serve

1 Bring a saucepan of water to the boil, lower the eggs into the water using a large spoon, and boil for 8 minutes. Remove with a slotted spoon, run under cold water, and leave to cool. When cool enough to handle, peel the shells from the eggs.

2 In a large bowl, beat the remaining ingredients, except the paprika, until well combined.

3 Finely chop the boiled eggs and gently mix them into the mayonnaise mixture, being careful not to break up the eggs too much. Serve sprinkled with paprika.

COOK'S TIP Try using this as a filling for a light, flavoursome packed lunch for children. It also serves as a good source of protein.

Smoked paprika, known in Spain as pimentón, has a dark, smoky spiciness that is hard to beat.

SHRIMP, CORN, AND AVOCADO SALAD

This healthy main course salad is packed with colour and flavour. Try it with baby spinach or finely shredded raw kale.

★ **SERVES** 2
★ **PREP TIME** 15 mins, plus marinating
★ **COOK TIME** 20 mins, plus cooling

Ingredients

1 large sweetcorn cob
200g (7oz) raw prawns, peeled and deveined
5 tbsp finely chopped coriander
juice of 1 lime
3 tbsp extra virgin olive oil
2 tbsp pumpkin seeds
1 tbsp Thai sweet chilli sauce
salt and freshly ground black pepper
mixed salad greens, about 100g (3½oz)
12 cherry tomatoes, halved
1 avocado, halved, stoned, peeled, and thickly sliced (see technique, p11)

1 Heat a griddle pan on a high heat. Rub the corn with a little oil and griddle it in the pan for 5–10 minutes, turning occasionally, until it is blackened in places and the kernels are tender. Set it aside. When it is cool enough to handle, cut the kernels off the cob with a sharp knife, as shown in the technique on p152.

2 Meanwhile, put the prawns in a small, non-reactive bowl (not aluminium or cast-iron), along with 1 tbsp each of the coriander, lime juice, and oil and toss well to combine. Chill for 30 minutes.

3 Heat a heavy-based frying pan over a medium heat and add the pumpkin seeds. Toast them for 2–3 minutes, stirring frequently, until they begin to colour and make a popping sound. Set aside to cool.

4 For the dressing, put the sweet chilli sauce and the remaining coriander, lime juice, and oil in a blender or food processor. Season well and blend until it has emulsified to a thick, vivid green dressing.

5 Reheat the griddle to a high heat and griddle the marinated prawns for a minute or two on each side until pink all over and charred in places. Set aside to cool.

6 When everything has cooled down, assemble the salad. Put the mixed leaves into a bowl and toss with the dressing. Add the cherry tomatoes and corn kernels, and toss again. Arrange the avocado slices and griddled prawns on the top, and scatter with the toasted pumpkin seeds to serve.

Sweetcorn is best eaten very fresh – milky kernels are a sign of freshness.

SALAD DRESSINGS

From a rich and herby Green Goddess to a light and elegant raspberry walnut vinaigrette, these dressings enhance any salad.

Green Goddess

★ **MAKES** 300g (10oz)
★ **PREP TIME** 10 mins

3 anchovies from a can,
  or 2 tsp anchovy paste
2 garlic cloves, crushed
110g (3¾oz) mayonnaise
110g (3¾oz) soured cream
30g (1oz) chopped parsley
15g (½oz) chopped tarragon
3 tbsp chopped chives
juice of 1 lemon
salt and freshly ground
  black pepper

Put all the ingredients in a food processor and blend until smooth. Season to taste.

Thousand Island

★ **MAKES** 300g (10oz)
★ **PREP TIME** 10 mins

110g (3¾oz) mayonnaise
2 tbsp tomato ketchup
2 tbsp pickle relish (see
  Spicy chow chow, p246)
2 tsp finely chopped red onion
salt and freshly ground
  black pepper

Put all the ingredients in a food processor and blend until smooth. Season to taste.

Buttermilk ranch

★ **MAKES** 300g (10oz)
★ **PREP TIME** 10 mins

50g (1¾oz) mayonnaise
90ml (3fl oz) buttermilk
100g (3½oz) soured cream
½ tsp onion powder
½ tsp freshly ground
  black pepper
½ tsp garlic powder
½ tsp dried thyme
1 tbsp chopped parsley

Put all the ingredients in a food processor and blend until smooth. Season to taste.

Raspberry walnut

★ **MAKES** 300g (10oz)
★ **PREP TIME** 10 mins

½ tsp honey mustard
1 tsp sugar
60ml (2fl oz) red wine vinegar
5-7 raspberries
1 shallot, about 60g (2oz)
120ml (4fl oz) walnut oil
salt and freshly ground
  black pepper

Put the mustard, sugar, vinegar, raspberries, and shallot in a food processor and pulse to a purée. Blend on a high setting, while pouring the oil in a thin stream through the opening (in the top) of the processor, until light and fluffy. Season to taste.

Catalina

★ **MAKES** 300g (10oz)
★ **PREP TIME** 10 mins

1 large onion, about
  350g (12oz), chopped
3 tbsp ketchup
1 tbsp sugar
2 tbsp light soft brown sugar
60ml (2fl oz) red wine vinegar
1 tsp Worcestershire sauce
1 tsp smoked paprika or
  ancho chilli powder
120ml (4fl oz) light olive oil
  or vegetable oil
salt and freshly ground
  black pepper

Put the onion, ketchup, both the sugars, vinegar, Worcestershire sauce, and smoked paprika in a food processor. Blend on a high setting, while pouring the oil in a thin stream through the opening (in the top) of the processor, until light and fluffy. Season to taste.

HOME-STYLE POTATO SALAD

There are many ways to prepare a potato salad, and this tasty version is a Midwestern classic.

★ **SERVES** 6
★ **PREP TIME** 10 mins
★ **COOK TIME** 20-25 mins, plus cooling

Ingredients
1kg (2¼lb) waxy potatoes, such as Charlottes, peeled
salt and freshly ground black pepper
4 heaped tbsp good-quality mayonnaise
2 tsp Dijon mustard
1 celery stick, finely chopped
bunch of spring onions, white and pale green parts only, finely chopped
1 tbsp capers, drained or rinsed, and finely chopped
1 tbsp lemon juice

1 Cook the potatoes whole in a large pan of boiling salted water for 20–25 minutes until tender. Drain and set aside to cool. When cold, peel and cut the potatoes carefully into 3cm (1¼in) cubes.

2 In a bowl, mix together the mayonnaise, mustard, celery, spring onions, capers, and lemon juice, and season well.

3 Place the potatoes into a large serving bowl and gently toss the mayonnaise mixture through the potatoes, being careful not to break them up.

Celery, with its strong, fresh flavour, brightens up a simple potato salad.

NOW TRY...

FRENCH STYLE

Try making a warm new potato salad in the French style by tossing 1kg (2¼lb) still-warm **new potatoes**, halved, in a **vinaigrette**, along with a bunch of finely chopped **spring onions**.

SWEET POTATO

Substitute Charlotte potatoes for the same amount of **sweet potatoes** for an interesting variation. Cook as per the main recipe. However, they will need a shorter cooking time (around 10 minutes) and should be used while still slightly undercooked.

EGG & TUNA

Adding 2 roughly chopped hard-boiled **eggs** and 1 small can good-quality **tuna**, drained, will turn this side dish into a star attraction.

BREAKFASTS AND LIGHT BITES

WAFFLES WITH BACON MAPLE SAUCE

These easy-to-make and versatile cornmeal waffles are perfect for breakfast, a light snack, or dessert.

- ★ **MAKES** 6-8
- ★ **PREP TIME** 5 mins
- ★ **COOK TIME** 20-25 mins

Ingredients

125g (4½oz) plain flour
50g (1¾oz) fine polenta
   or cornmeal
1 tsp baking powder
2 tbsp caster sugar
300ml (10fl oz) milk
75g (2½oz) unsalted butter,
   melted
1 tsp vanilla extract
2 large eggs, separated
4 smoked streaky bacon rashers
100ml (3½fl oz) good-quality
   maple syrup
jam, fresh fruit, sweetened
   cream, or ice cream,
   to serve (optional)

1 Place the flour, polenta, baking powder, and sugar in a bowl. Make a well in the centre and pour in the milk, butter, vanilla extract, and egg yolks. Gradually whisk together.

2 Preheat the waffle maker or iron. In a clean, large bowl, whisk the egg whites until soft peaks form. Fold into the batter with a metal spoon.

3 Preheat the oven to 130°C (250°F/Gas ½). Pour a small ladleful of the batter onto the waffle maker or iron and spread almost to the edge. Close the lid and bake until golden. Keep warm in a single layer in the oven while you make the rest of the waffles.

4 In a frying pan, dry-fry the bacon until crispy. When cool enough to handle, crumble the bacon. Gently heat the maple syrup in a small, heavy-based saucepan over a low heat. Add the bacon to the warm syrup before pouring over the waffles. Serve immediately with jam, fresh fruit, sweetened cream, or ice cream, if desired.

COOK'S TIP Although best eaten as fresh as possible, you can make waffles 24 hours in advance and reheat them in a toaster.

Maple syrup, when pure, has a strong, dark, almost smoky sweetness.

STRAWBERRY-STUFFED FRENCH TOAST

French toast is always a treat, but this cream cheese and strawberry version would be the pride of any brunch table.

★ **MAKES** 4
★ **PREP TIME** 10 mins
★ **COOK TIME** 30 mins

Ingredients

8 tbsp cream cheese
8 slices of challah bread
   or brioche, each
   4cm (1½in) thick
8-12 strawberries, hulled
   and thickly sliced
4 eggs
100g (3½oz) light soft
   brown sugar
125ml (4½fl oz) milk
1 tsp vanilla extract
1 tsp ground cinnamon
4 tbsp butter
honey, to serve

1 Preheat the oven to 190°C (375°F/Gas 5). Spread 1 tbsp of the cream cheese over each slice of bread. Top 4 bread slices with 2–3 strawberries each, then cover with the remaining bread slices to make 4 sandwiches.

2 In a bowl, whisk together the eggs, sugar, milk, vanilla extract, and cinnamon with a hand whisk. Dip the sandwiches in the egg mixture, submerging them completely.

3 In a frying pan, melt 1 tbsp of butter over a medium heat. Pan-fry the sandwiches for 3–4 minutes on each side, or until golden brown. Add the remaining butter to the pan, as needed, while frying the remaining sandwiches. Transfer to a baking sheet and put the sandwiches in the preheated oven for 5 minutes. Serve hot, drizzled with honey.

PREPARING STRAWBERRIES

1 To prepare a strawberry, hold the fruit on its side on a chopping board. Using a sharp knife, cut off the stalk without removing too much fruit.

2 Cut the strawberry in half. Lay each half cut-side down, then cut into slices of even thickness. Repeat for the remaining strawberries.

BUTTERMILK PANCAKES

You can make these pancakes with whole milk, but using tangy buttermilk makes them lighter.

- ★ **MAKES** 10
- ★ **PREP TIME** 5 mins
- ★ **COOK TIME** 20 mins

Ingredients

300g (10oz) self-raising flour
60g (2oz) caster sugar
1 tsp baking powder
250ml (9fl oz) buttermilk (or to make your own, see p12)
2 eggs
60g (2oz) unsalted butter, melted and cooled, plus extra for frying and serving
3-4 tbsp milk (optional)
maple syrup, to serve
fresh berries or diced fruit, to serve

1 Put the flour, sugar, and baking powder into a large bowl and mix well with a balloon whisk. In a separate bowl, whisk together the buttermilk, eggs, and melted butter. Make a well in the centre of the flour mixture and gradually whisk in the buttermilk mixture to a smooth, thick batter. If the batter is not quite a thick pouring consistency, stir in 3–4 tbsp milk.

2 In a 15cm (6in) non-stick frying pan, heat a knob (about ½ tbsp) of butter over a medium heat until the butter begins to sizzle. Pour in just enough batter to coat the base of the pan.

3 Cook the pancake over a medium heat until the edges are set and small bubbles appear on the surface of the pancake, burst, and leave small "holes".

4 Turn the pancake and cook for 1–2 minutes on the other side. Serve immediately, or keep warm in a low oven while you cook the remaining pancakes. Serve with unsalted butter, maple syrup, and a bowl of fresh berries or diced fruit for an indulgent weekend breakfast treat.

NOW TRY...

CINNAMON & BANANA

Add 1 tsp of **ground cinnamon** to the flour. Once you have poured the batter into the pan, thinly slice half a **banana** and arrange it on top of the pancake, then cook as directed in the main recipe.

BLUEBERRY COMPOTE

For the ultimate blueberry pancakes, make a thick compote to serve alongside. Cook down 150g (5½oz) of ripe **blueberries** with 2 tbsp **water** and 1 tbsp **sugar** for 5 minutes, or until they burst.

SOUTHERN TWIST

For a Southern-inspired variation, replace 150g (5½oz) of the self-raising flour with **fine polenta or cornmeal**.

BISCUITS AND CREAMY SAUSAGE GRAVY

Traditionally served with a thick, milk-based gravy, using cream here makes this Southern favourite rich yet light.

- ★ **SERVES** 4
- ★ **PREP TIME** 15 mins
- ★ **COOK TIME** 20 mins

Ingredients

300g (10oz) self-raising flour, plus extra for dusting
1 tsp baking powder
1 tsp smoked paprika or ancho chilli powder
½ tsp salt
85g (3oz) unsalted butter, chilled
60g (2oz) coarsely grated strong red cheese
freshly ground black pepper
225ml (7½fl oz) buttermilk (or to make your own, see p12)
1 egg, beaten with 1 tbsp cold water

For the sausage gravy

1 tbsp peanut or sunflower oil, for frying
about 250g (9oz) spicy gourmet sausages
1 tbsp plain flour
250ml (9fl oz) hot good-quality chicken stock
125ml (4½fl oz) single cream

1 Preheat the oven to 230°C (450°F/Gas 8). Sift the flour, baking powder, smoked paprika, and salt into a food processor. Add the butter and process until the mixture resembles fine breadcrumbs. Add the grated cheese and a good grinding of pepper, and pulse briefly to combine. Tip out the mixture into a large bowl and add the buttermilk. Stir with a wooden spoon, until the mixture is soft and sticky.

2 Turn the mixture out onto a lightly floured surface and gently pat the mixture into a smooth block, then gently pat or lightly roll it out to a thickness of 3cm (1⅛in). Cut rounds out of the mixture with a 6cm (2½in) biscuit cutter and place them on a baking sheet. Gather the trimmings and gently squeeze them together. Pat it out again, or re-roll, and continue to cut out more rounds until all the dough is used up.

3 Brush the tops of the biscuits lightly with a little of the egg wash. Bake in the preheated oven for 10–12 minutes, until risen and golden brown. Remove the biscuits from the oven and allow them to rest on the baking sheet for 5 minutes before transferring them to a wire rack to cool completely.

4 Meanwhile, make the gravy. Heat the oil in a heavy-based frying pan. De-skin the sausages and crumble the meat into the pan. Fry over a high heat for 3–5 minutes, turning frequently, until the meat is brown and crispy. Reduce the heat and sprinkle the flour over the sausagemeat. Stir, then add the stock, a little at a time, stirring constantly. Finally, add the cream and reduce the heat to a low simmer. Cook for 5 minutes until the sauce has thickened. Pour it over the biscuits to serve.

GRANOLA WITH DRIED FRUIT COMPOTE

Making your own granola is a cost-effective way of ensuring that your cereal contains exactly what you like.

★ **SERVES** 4-6

★ **PREP TIME** 10-15 mins

★ **COOK TIME** 45 mins, plus cooling

Ingredients

125g (4½oz) porridge oats

50g (1¾oz) mixed seeds, such as sunflower, sesame, pumpkin, and golden linseed

50g (1¾oz) mixed unsalted nuts, such as cashews, almonds, hazelnuts, and walnuts

1 tbsp light olive oil, plus extra for greasing

2 tbsp runny honey

3½ tbsp maple syrup

25g (scant 1oz) dried blueberries

25g (scant 1oz) dried cranberries

25g (scant 1oz) dried cherries

15g (½oz) desiccated coconut

Greek yogurt or milk, to serve

For the compote

100g (3½oz) dried apples

100g (3½oz) dried figs

100g (3½oz) dried prunes

1 cinnamon stick

½ vanilla pod, halved lengthways

finely grated zest and juice of 1 orange

1 tbsp demerara sugar

1 Preheat the oven to 150°C (300°F/Gas 2). Place the oats, seeds, and nuts in a large mixing bowl. Add the oil, honey, and maple syrup and stir well to combine.

2 Tip the mixture into a large, lightly oiled roasting tin and spread out into an even layer. Bake for 15 minutes. Mix together the berries, cherries, and coconut. Stir into the tin and bake for a further 15 minutes. Leave in the tin to cool completely. When cool enough to handle, break the granola into small pieces and transfer to an airtight container.

3 For the compote, place all the dried fruits in a mixing bowl. Add the cinnamon, vanilla pod, and orange zest and juice. Pour in 200ml (7fl oz) of boiling water. Cover the bowl and set aside overnight.

4 Transfer the contents of the bowl to a saucepan. Add the sugar and 150ml (5fl oz) of cold water and bring to the boil. Reduce the heat and simmer very gently, uncovered, for 15 minutes. Remove the vanilla pod and cinnamon stick.

5 Put the granola into individual bowls, pour over the compote, and serve with Greek yogurt or milk.

COOK'S TIP Any combination of dried fruits works well – try using apricots, peaches, or dates, or a mixture of dried berries. For a warming winter compote, add 2 finely chopped balls of stem ginger in syrup, plus 2 tbsp of the syrup.

SOUTHERN-STYLE BREAKFAST CASSEROLE

A classic American brunch dish, but a relative newcomer to European tables, this is quick to assemble, and delicious.

★ **SERVES** 4-6

★ **PREP TIME** 15 mins, plus resting

★ **COOK TIME** 40 mins

Ingredients

1 tbsp olive oil
200g (7oz) thick spicy chorizo-style pork sausages, casings removed
butter, for greasing
100g (3½oz) stale baguette or other coarse white bread, crusts removed and cut into 1cm (½in) cubes
4 spring onions, finely sliced
1 large ripe tomato, skinned, deseeded, and chopped
1 jalapeño or other mild green chilli, deseeded and finely chopped
75g (2½oz) grated strong cheese, such as Cheddar
6 eggs
100ml (3½fl oz) single cream
100ml (3½fl oz) whole milk
1 tsp smoked paprika or ancho chilli powder
salt and freshly ground black pepper

1 Heat the oil in a non-stick frying pan. Add the sausagemeat to the pan and cook, chopping it up with a spatula, turning it over, and stirring until it is broken into large lumps and is well browned on all sides. Remove the pan from the heat.

2 Preheat the oven to 180°C (350°F/Gas 4). Grease a 25cm (10in) flameproof casserole with the butter. Spread out the bread in a single layer in the dish, then evenly scatter over the sausagemeat. Sprinkle over the onions, tomato, and jalapeño, then top with the cheese.

3 In a bowl, lightly beat together the eggs, cream, milk, and smoked paprika and season well. Pour the egg mixture evenly into the dish, then set aside to rest for about 15 minutes.

4 Bake the casserole in the oven for 30–40 minutes until puffed up and golden brown and a skewer, when inserted, comes out clean.

HUEVOS RANCHEROS ON TORTILLA

This all-in-one Mexican breakfast is full of fresh and vibrant flavours, and is good to eat at any time of the day.

★ **SERVES** 4
★ **PREP TIME** 20 mins
★ **COOK TIME** 15–30 mins

Ingredients

400g can black beans
1 tsp smoked paprika or ancho chilli powder
pinch of chilli flakes
salt and freshly ground black pepper
olive oil, for drizzling
4 large flour tortillas
225g (8oz) grated Cheddar cheese
4 eggs
1 avocado, halved, stoned, and thickly sliced (see technique, p11)

For the pico de gallo

3 large tomatoes, deseeded and diced
1 jalapeño or other mild green chilli, finely chopped
1 small red onion, chopped
2 garlic cloves, crushed
2 tbsp chopped coriander
juice of 2 large limes

1 For the pico de gallo, put the tomatoes, jalapeño, onion, garlic, coriander, and lime juice in a bowl. Season, mix well, and set aside.

2 In a medium saucepan, gently heat the black beans in their own liquid. Stir in the smoked paprika and chilli flakes, and season well.

3 Meanwhile, heat the oil in a large, non-stick, heavy-based pan over a medium heat. When the oil is hot, place a tortilla in the centre of the pan. Using one-quarter of the grated cheese, make a ring inside the tortilla and crack an egg into the centre, making sure that it is contained within the cheese ring.

4 Cover and cook for 3–4 minutes until the egg starts to set and the cheese melts, then use a spatula to flip the tortilla along with the egg. Cook for 1–2 minutes for a runny yolk, and 3–4 minutes for a firm yolk. Use a spatula to lift the tortilla and the egg, flipping them egg-side up onto a plate. Clean any cheese from the pan and repeat to make the remaining tortillas.

5 Remove the black beans from the heat and drain. Serve the tortilla and egg topped with the black beans, pico de gallo, and sliced avocado.

COOK'S TIP Use a wide spatula to flip the tortilla so that the egg is cradled in the middle. This will help to keep everything together. Flip quickly and confidently.

EGGS BENEDICT WITH SMOKED SALMON

The combination of salty protein and rich, creamy sauce is irresistible in this classic breakfast dish.

★ **MAKES** 4
★ **PREP TIME** 15 mins
★ **COOK TIME** 10 mins

Ingredients

4 eggs
2–4 English muffins
150g (5½oz) smoked
　salmon

For the sauce

100g (3½oz) unsalted
　butter
1 large egg yolk
½ tbsp lemon juice
salt and freshly ground
　black pepper

1 To make the hollandaise sauce, melt the butter over a gentle heat, taking care it does not split. Put the egg yolk, lemon juice, and seasoning into a blender and process briefly. With the motor running, pour in the melted butter drop by drop, accelerating to a thin stream, until it has emulsified to a thick sauce.

2 Boil a large saucepan of salted water, then reduce the heat to a low simmer. Crack an egg into a teacup and gently slip the egg out of the cup and into the bubbling water. Repeat for all the eggs. Poach for 3 minutes, until the white is set but the yolk is still runny. Remove with a slotted spoon.

3 At the same time, toast the muffins. If you like thick muffins use 4, cutting a thin slice off each one to add the egg, otherwise split 2 muffins horizontally to make 4 halves. When they are toasted, divide the salmon between them and top each with a poached egg and a little hollandaise sauce.

★ ★ ★
WHAT'S THE STORY?

The origins of the familiar bacon version of this dish are far from clear. Two different cookery books, both published in the 1890s, feature recipes for poached eggs and ham on a toasted muffin, smothered in hollandaise sauce. Other sources claim either the famous New York eatery Delmonico's or the Waldorf Hotel as the birth place of the dish.
★ ★ ★

NOW TRY...

SOURDOUGH BREAD

For a more rustic feel, serve 2 eggs, side by side, on a piece of griddled **sourdough bread**, topped with rashers of **crispy bacon** and hollandaise sauce.

EGGS FLORENTINE

For Eggs Florentine, wilt down 250g (9oz) of **baby spinach** in 1 tbsp of **olive oil**, then drain well. Mix with a spoonful of the hollandaise sauce before using it in place of the salmon.

POTATO RÖSTIS

For a gluten-free alternative, serve the eggs and hollandaise sauce on **potato röstis**. Follow the recipe for the hash brown nests on p66 but use the mixture to form 8 pancakes. Fry in 2 tbsp peanut or sunflower oil over a medium heat for 5 minutes on each side, until crispy and cooked through.

BAKED EGG HASH BROWN NESTS

Perfect for brunch, these hash brown nests can be part-baked, then filled and finished at the last minute.

★ **MAKES** 8
★ **PREP TIME** 20 mins
★ **COOK TIME** 25-35 mins

Ingredients

175g (6oz) potatoes, such as Maris Piper or King Edward, grated weight

75g (2½oz) sweet potato, grated weight

1 small red onion, finely chopped

50g (1¾oz) pancetta, finely chopped

50g (1¾oz) Cheddar cheese, coarsely grated

2 tbsp olive oil, plus extra for greasing

salt and freshly ground black pepper

8 eggs

1 Preheat the oven to 200°C (400°F/Gas 6). Place the grated potatoes in a large bowl of cold water and soak them for 5 minutes to get rid of the excess starch. Drain, then put in a clean tea towel and wring to remove as much moisture as possible.

2 Place the potatoes, onion, pancetta, and cheese in a large bowl and toss them all together. Add the oil, season well, and toss again.

3 Lightly oil a 12-hole muffin tin. Divide the mixture evenly between 8 of the holes. Use the back of a tablespoon to push the mixture down into the tin, then up the sides. Make sure that there is enough mixture at the bottom to form a base for the eggs. The sides need to be as high as possible, as the nests will shrink slightly as they cook.

4 Bake in the centre of the oven for 15–20 minutes, until the edges are browned and a little crispy. Remove from the oven and reduce the oven temperature to 180°C (350°F/Gas 4).

5 Carefully crack an egg into each of the nests, sprinkle a little pepper on top, and return to the oven for 10–15 minutes (depending on whether you like your eggs soft or hard). Remove from the oven and leave to cool in their tins for 2 minutes (the eggs will continue to cook a little more). Run a knife around the edge of each nest to loosen and remove from the tin. Serve immediately.

COOK'S TIP These delicious nests can also be filled with fried mushrooms, wilted spinach, or chopped crispy bacon before being topped with the eggs.

Pancetta, an Italian cured bacon, can be replaced with thick-cut smoked streaky bacon.

EGG WHITE, SPINACH, AND SALMON OMELETTE

Packed with protein and low in fat, these quick and easy egg white omelettes are a healthy breakfast choice.

★ **SERVES** 1
★ **PREP TIME** 10 mins
★ **COOK TIME** 4–7 mins

Ingredients
3 egg whites
15g (½oz) unsalted butter
50g (1¾oz) baby spinach, roughly chopped
small grating of nutmeg, or a pinch of dried nutmeg
freshly ground black pepper
30g (1oz) smoked salmon, roughly torn

1 Put the egg whites in a large bowl and whisk with a balloon whisk or an electric hand whisk until light and frothy (see the technique below). In a large, heavy-based frying pan or omelette pan, melt the butter over a medium heat. Add the spinach, season with a little grated nutmeg and pepper, and cook for 2–3 minutes, stirring frequently, until it has wilted and any moisture has evaporated.

2 Distribute the spinach evenly around the pan and pour over the whisked egg whites. Using a heatproof spatula, move them around slightly to incorporate the spinach into the egg whites. Allow the omelette to cook over a low heat for 1–2 minutes, until the edges are set and the underside is brown. Don't worry if the top still looks frothy.

3 Arrange the smoked salmon over half of the omelette. Using a spatula, gently fold the omelette in half, so that the salmon is covered. Cook the omelette for another minute on each side, pressing down gently with the spatula, until the centre is light and fluffy, but just set.

WHISKING EGG WHITES

1 Place the egg whites in a large, clean, dry mixing bowl and start whisking them slowly, using a small range of motion.

2 Continue whisking, using larger strokes, until the whites have lost their translucency and start to foam.

3 Incorporate as much air as possible, increasing your speed and range of motion until the whites turn light and frothy.

BREAKFAST BURRITOS

Stuffed with spicy and filling ingredients, these wraps are perfect for breakfast on the go.

- ★ **SERVES** 4
- ★ **PREP TIME** 20 mins
- ★ **COOK TIME** 50 mins

Ingredients

2 red potatoes, such as Desiree
1 tsp olive oil
1 onion, cut into large chunks
1 red pepper, cut into large chunks
1 green pepper, cut into large chunks
1 jalapeño or other mild green chilli, finely chopped
salt and freshly ground black pepper
450g (1lb) chorizo, casings removed and thickly sliced
8 eggs
1 tsp chipotle paste
175g (6oz) grated Cheddar cheese
4 large tortillas
60ml (2fl oz) soured cream

For the guacamole

1 avocado, halved, stoned, and sliced (see technique, p11)
juice of 2 limes
12 cherry tomatoes, halved
handful of chopped coriander

1 Cook the potatoes in a saucepan of boiling water for 10 minutes. Drain and leave to cool. Leaving the skin on, cut each potato into chunks and set aside.

2 Heat the oil in a large, heavy-based frying pan. Add the onion, peppers, and jalapeño and toss over a medium heat for about 10 minutes until starting to soften. Add the potatoes and season well. Cook, stirring occasionally, for 15–20 minutes until tender or they can be easily pierced with a fork.

3 Meanwhile, in a separate large frying pan, cook the chorizo over a medium heat for 4–5 minutes, or until browned. Remove from the pan with a slotted spoon and combine with the potatoes at the end of their cooking time.

4 Put the eggs in a bowl, along with 60ml (2fl oz) water and the chipotle paste. Season well. Using a balloon whisk or an electric hand whisk, beat the mixture until well blended. Transfer the egg mixture to the frying pan used for the chorizo. Fry the mixture, scrambling it and moving it around the pan occasionally, for 3–4 minutes or until firm. Add the cheese and stir as it melts, so that it is well incorporated.

5 For the guacamole, mash the avocado and stir in the lime juice, tomatoes, and coriander.

6 Lay each tortilla on a plate and spread a spoonful of soured cream along the centre line of each tortilla. Top with the potato hash, scrambled eggs, and guacamole. To make the burritos, fold the shorter ends in over the filling. Press down and fold the longer ends up over the filling, flipping the burrito over so that the shape is preserved. Serve hot.

NOW TRY...

VEGGIE TWIST

Substitute the chorizo with 400g can drained **black beans** and 1 sliced **Portobello mushroom**. Toss the mushroom and beans in 1 tbsp oil, season well, and cook in a frying pan, as directed in step 3.

JALAPEÑO HUMMUS

Blend 400g can drained **chickpeas**, 1 chopped **onion**, 2 **garlic cloves**, 4 tbsp **tahini**, 1 deseeded and chopped **jalapeño**, bunch of **coriander**, pinch of **salt**, and the juice of 2 **limes**. Spread liberally over the tortillas.

FRIED EGGS

Fry the eggs instead of scrambling. For each serving, fry 2 **eggs**, sunny side up, for 5-7 minutes, then season. Alternatively, for a classic American diner breakfast, try the potato hash without the tortilla, served with a fried egg and **bacon**.

GRILLED BANANA PBJ

A classic PBJ (peanut butter and jelly or jam sandwich) is a childhood favourite. Add bananas and grill for an adult treat, too.

★ **MAKES** 4
★ **PREP TIME** 10 mins
★ **COOK TIME** 20 mins

Ingredients

300g (10oz) blackberry jam
8 slices of crusty bread
250g (9oz) peanut butter
2 bananas, cut into
    5mm (¼in) slices
4 tbsp butter

1 Pour the blackberry jam into a saucepan and place it over a low heat until warm. Then remove from the heat and set aside.

2 Generously spread the slices of bread with peanut butter. Top 4 bread slices with 4 banana slices each, then cover with the remaining bread slices to make 4 sandwiches.

3 Melt 1 tbsp of butter in a frying pan. Pan-fry the sandwiches for 2–3 minutes on each side over a medium heat until crisp. Add the remaining butter to the pan, as needed, while frying the remaining sandwiches. Transfer the sandwiches to a serving plate and top with the warm jam. Serve hot.

Bananas sweeten on cooking, and you should choose slightly underripe ones to cook with.

BLT WITH FRIED GREEN TOMATOES

For a gourmet BLT (bacon, lettuce, and tomato) sandwich, add crunchy fried tomatoes and this zesty lemon and basil mayo.

★ **MAKES** 1

★ **PREP TIME** 5 mins

★ **COOK TIME** 10 mins, plus 15 mins for the fried green tomatoes

Ingredients

3 slices of applewood or other good-quality bacon

2 thickly cut slices of good-quality white bread

2 tbsp unsalted butter, softened

2 large cos lettuce leaves, de-ribbed and roughly chopped

4 slices of Fried green tomatoes (see p164)

For the lemon and basil mayo

2 tbsp good-quality mayonnaise

2 tsp lemon juice

1 tbsp finely chopped basil leaves

salt and freshly ground black pepper

1 Preheat the grill on its highest setting. To make the lemon and basil mayo, mix together the mayonnaise, lemon juice, and basil. Season well and set aside.

2 Preheat a griddle pan or a large, cast-iron frying pan. While it is heating, grill the bacon under the grill for 2–3 minutes on each side until crispy. Drain on kitchen paper and keep warm.

3 Spread a little butter on both sides of the bread slices and griddle them in the pan for 2 minutes on each side, until nicely toasted.

4 Remove the bread slices from the heat. Spread one side of the toast with a little of the mayonnaise, then top it with the lettuce, fried green tomatoes, and the bacon. Finish with a final layer of mayonnaise and top with the second piece of bread. Cut in half to serve.

Basil, a sweet, fragrant herb, can be used to flavour oils and mayos.

A taste of the
SOUTHEAST

Encompassing coastal and mountain cooking – and with strong influences from Africa, the Caribbean, and Cuba – this region has one of the most complex and varied cuisines in the country.

The warm, damp climate of the Southeast allows for two distinct growing seasons – one in spring and a second in the autumn. This double harvest is further boosted by extremely fertile soils that encourage the growth of everything from sweet potatoes and sugar cane to limes and persimmons.

The Southeast, historically a centre for the slave trade, has adopted many of the culinary traditions brought to the region from Africa and the Caribbean in the 18th century. In the great culinary city of New Orleans, for example, sophisticated Creole cooking (a mixture of Spanish, French, and African cuisines) jostles for attention alongside simpler Cajun fare.

More recently, in the 1950s, immigrants from Cuba brought their own distinct foods and flavours to Florida.

Brunswick stew – a dish with its roots firmly in the Southeast – is traditionally made with cheap, readily available meats such as squirrel and rabbit. Modern variations (see p131) are more likely to include chicken instead.

FOODS AND FLAVOURS

★ **Barbecued meat** is synonymous with the Southeast, and each state has its own classic dish; the Carolinas, for example, specialize in **pulled pork** (see p130).

★ **Gumbo**, a stew-like dish made with seafood or meat (see p112), has come to symbolize the rich culinary heritage of New Orleans.

★ **Seafood**, such as the **shrimp** found in Pamlico Sound in the north, and the Florida stone crabs caught further south, is integral to the food traditions of the region.

★ **Corn**, an important crop for the Southeast, can be eaten raw when young in salads, cooked in fritters (see p25), and, when ground into cornmeal, made into cornbread (see p228) or grits (see p110).

★ **Biscuits**, a true Southern dish, can accompany any meal but are traditionally served for breakfast (see below and p58).

Fried chicken, a staple of the southern food scene, tastes fantastic when home made.

Creamy grits, made with either white or yellow cornmeal, are perfect with East Coast shrimp.

Light and delicate, beignets derive their name from the French version of doughnuts.

Key limes, although not native to Florida, are a speciality crop now grown throughout the region.

The vast Mississippi River runs all the way from northern Wisconsin to the Gulf of Mexico.

New Orleans, a melting pot of Creole and Cajun cultures, has a diverse and vibrant food scene.

FRIED SHRIMP PO' BOYS

Shrimp or oysters are the star ingredients in this tasty and filling recipe from New Orleans.

★ **SERVES** 4
★ **PREP TIME** 10 mins
★ **COOK TIME** 18–24 mins

Ingredients
2 loaves of French bread
8 leaves of round lettuce
1 ripe red tomato, sliced

For the prawns
500ml (16fl oz) peanut or
    sunflower oil, for frying
1 egg
130g (4¾oz) plain flour
1 tsp paprika
½ tsp cayenne pepper
½ tsp salt
75g (2½oz) panko
    breadcrumbs or
    day-old breadcrumbs
48 king prawns, peeled
    and deveined

For the remoulade
220g (7¾oz) mayonnaise
125g (4½oz) mustard
juice of ½ lemon
30ml (1fl oz) pickling
    vinegar or cider vinegar
1 tsp paprika
1 tbsp creamed
    horseradish

1 In a large, heavy-based saucepan or deep-fat fryer, heat the oil to 190°C (375°F), as shown in the technique on p144.

2 Break the egg into a bowl, add 1 tbsp water, and whisk with a fork. In a separate large bowl, mix together the flour, paprika, cayenne pepper, salt, and breadcrumbs. Dip the prawns in the egg wash and toss them in the breadcrumb mixture, coating each one evenly.

3 Fry in the hot oil in batches of 8 for 3–4 minutes each, or until golden brown. Remove the fried prawns from the pan with a slotted spoon and let them cool on a wire rack.

4 For the remoulade, combine the mayonnaise, mustard, lemon juice, vinegar, paprika, and horseradish in a bowl.

5 Slice each loaf in half lengthways, without cutting through the bottom, and spread the remoulade on either side. Layer each bottom half with the lettuce, sliced tomatoes, and fried prawns. For a truly New Orleans experience, serve with potato chips tossed in Cajun seasoning.

WHAT'S THE STORY?

The po' boy (short for "poor boy") was created by New Orleans restaurant owners and former streetcar drivers Clovis and Benjamin Martin. When streetcar drivers went on strike in 1929, the brothers served the sandwich free to unemployed workers and the cry "here comes another poor boy!" would go up in the kitchen each time.

NOW TRY...

BLACKENED FISH

Try making this recipe with blackened white fish, such as the **mahi-mahi** from p106, instead of prawns.

VEGGIE OPTION

Make vegetarian po' boys by chopping and sautéeing 1 **aubergine**, 1 **red pepper**, 1 **onion**, and a handful of fresh **porcini**, **button**, or **cremini mushrooms**, and season with the paprika, cayenne pepper, and salt.

FISH & CORNMEAL

Use a white firm-fleshed fish, such as **cod**, instead of the prawns, and substitute the breadcrumbs with 150g (5½oz) **fine polenta or cornmeal** for a polenta crust.

SUMMER VEGETABLE PHILLY CHEESE STEAK

Give a lighter twist to the classic steak sandwich from Philadelphia by adding pan-fried summer vegetables.

- ★ **SERVES** 4
- ★ **PREP TIME** 10 mins, plus chilling
- ★ **COOK TIME** 30 mins

Ingredients

2 tbsp butter
1 onion, chopped into large pieces
1 green pepper, chopped into large pieces
1 small aubergine, roughly chopped into large pieces
12 cremini or button mushrooms
½ tsp chilli flakes
2 garlic cloves, crushed
salt and freshly ground black pepper
500g (1lb 2oz) sirloin steak, chilled for 45 minutes to make slicing easier
4 sub rolls
8 slices of provolone or Jarlsberg cheese
mustard, to serve

1 In a heavy-based frying pan, melt 1 tbsp of the butter over a medium-low heat. Add the onion, green pepper, aubergine, mushrooms, chilli flakes, and garlic. Season well. Cook the vegetables, stirring occasionally, for 15–20 minutes, or until tender.

2 Meanwhile, cut the steak into paper-thin slices. In a separate heavy-based frying pan, heat the remaining butter and cook the steak over a medium-high heat. Add a pinch of salt and cook the meat, stirring occasionally, for 3–5 minutes, or until browned.

3 Slice each sub roll in half lengthways, without cutting through the bottom, and line each roll with 2 slices of cheese. Add the vegetables and top with the steak. Serve hot with mustard.

Aubergines are at their best when the skin is very smooth and they feel heavy for their size.

PRAWN AND SWEET POTATO QUESADILLAS

These Mexican inspired hot tortilla sandwiches are quick and easy to prepare – and incredibly moreish.

★ **MAKES** 4
★ **PREP TIME** 20 mins
★ **COOK TIME** 45 mins

Ingredients

2 large sweet potatoes
3 tbsp olive oil
1 garlic clove, crushed
600g (1lb 5oz) king prawns,
   cooked and peeled
8 x 30cm (12in) large tortillas
225g (8oz) Monterey Jack
   or Cheddar cheese, grated
salt and freshly ground
   black pepper
1 tsp smoked paprika or
   ancho chilli powder
1 avocado, halved, stoned, and
   peeled (see technique, p11)
115g (4oz) soured cream
juice of 1 lime
bunch of coriander, chopped

1 Cook the potatoes in a pan of boiling water, skin-on, for 20 minutes. Drain the potatoes and set them aside to cool. When cool enough to handle, peel, cut into cubes, and set aside.

2 Heat 1 tbsp of the oil in a deep, straight-sided frying pan. Add the garlic, along with the potatoes, and cook over a medium heat for 5–10 minutes, or until the potatoes have browned. Add the prawns and reduce the heat. Stir to incorporate.

3 Lay out 4 tortillas and spread equal portions of the prawn and potato mixture on them and top with the grated cheese. Sprinkle each tortilla with salt, pepper, and smoked paprika. Top with the remaining tortillas to create 4 "sandwiches" or quesadillas.

4 Heat another tbsp of oil in a large, non-stick, heavy-based pan. Cook the quesadilla for 2–3 minutes on each side, or until browned and the cheese has melted. Add the remaining oil to the pan, as needed, while cooking the remaining quesadillas.

5 In a bowl, mash the avocado with the back of a fork to the desired consistency. Mix together the soured cream, avocado, lime juice, and coriander. Top the quesadillas with the avocado cream, slice into quarters, and serve hot.

Tortillas, either wheat- or corn-based, are a great alternative to more traditional breads.

FLANK STEAK AND CHEDDAR BURRITOS

Bursting with meat, vegetables, rice, beans, and cheese, these burritos are the ultimate meal in one simple package.

★ **MAKES** 4
★ **PREP TIME** 20 mins
★ **COOK TIME** 20 mins

Ingredients

150g (5½oz) green pepper, deseeded and sliced
250g (9oz) onion, sliced
1 tbsp olive oil
450g (1lb) flank or bavette steak
salt and freshly ground black pepper
1 tbsp chipotle paste
4 x 30cm (12in) large tortillas
200g (7oz) white rice, cooked
200g (7oz) black beans, cooked
200g (7oz) strong Cheddar cheese, crumbled
2 avocados, halved, stoned, and peeled (see technique, p11)

For the salsa verde

200g (7oz) green tomatoes, roughly chopped
1 onion, about 150g (5½oz), diced
40g (1¼oz) coriander
30g (1oz) jalapeño or other mild green chilli, deseeded and chopped
2 garlic cloves, roughly chopped
juice of 2 limes

1 First, make the salsa verde. In a food processor, pulse the tomatoes, onion, coriander, jalapeño, garlic, lime juice, and seasoning to make a smooth purée. Set aside.

2 In a large frying pan, sauté the pepper and onion in ½ tbsp of oil over a high heat. Cook for 5–7 minutes, stirring frequently, or until tender and crisp. Remove from the pan and set aside.

3 Sprinkle both sides of the steak with salt and pepper and spread the chipotle paste evenly all over. Cook over a medium-high heat in the remaining oil for 4–10 minutes on each side, depending on how you like your meat. For rare, allow 4–6 minutes on each side; for medium, 6–8 minutes; and for well done, 8–10 minutes. Remove from the pan and let it rest for 5 minutes before cutting into slices.

4 Lay out the tortillas. Layer each one with the rice, beans, sautéed vegetables, steak, Cheddar cheese, and salsa verde, keeping the ingredients piled in the middle of the tortilla. To make the burritos, fold the shorter ends in over the filling, then press down and roll the longer ends over each other, flipping the burrito over so that the shape is preserved. Return the burritos, seam-side down, to the pan and cook for 2–3 minutes on each side.

5 In a griddle pan, griddle the avocados over a medium-high heat for 3–4 minutes. Serve the burritos hot with the salsa verde and avocado on the side.

DELI-STYLE REUBEN

This sandwich is piled high with classic deli fillings, contrasting sweet, sour, and salty flavours.

- ★ **SERVES** 4
- ★ **PREP TIME** 10 mins
- ★ **COOK TIME** 10 mins

Ingredients

8 slices of rye bread
16 slices of Swiss or
   Emmental cheese
450g (1lb) salt beef
   or pastrami
8 tbsp sauerkraut (see
   p245), or from a jar
4 knobs of butter

For the Russian dressing

60g (2oz) mayonnaise
2 tbsp creamed
   horseradish
1 tbsp tomato ketchup
1 tsp Worcestershire sauce
salt and freshly ground
   black pepper

1 In a bowl, mix together the mayonnaise, horseradish, tomato ketchup, and Worcestershire sauce. Season well.

2 Spread the dressing over each slice of bread. Layer 4 slices of bread with 2 slices of cheese, 3–5 slices of beef, sauerkraut, and 2 more slices of cheese. Top with the remaining slices of bread.

3 Melt a knob of butter in a frying pan over a medium heat. Fry each sandwich for 1–2 minutes on each side, or until golden brown. Serve your Reuben hot with Refrigerator pickles (see p248) and kettle-cooked potato chips.

WHAT'S THE STORY?

Tales abound about who invented this sandwich, with Arnold Reuben of Reuben's Delicatessen in New York City and Reuben Kulakofsky, a grocer from Omaha, Nebraska, both strong contenders. The first Reuben was probably made in the early 20th century and, by 1956, it had won "best sandwich" in a contest sponsored by the National Restaurant Association.

NOW TRY...

PASTRAMI ON RYE

Make pastrami on rye by layering **pastrami**, **Swiss cheese**, and **brown mustard**. Melt **butter** in a pan and griddle the sandwich to melt the cheese and warm the pastrami.

TURKEY

Make this a "Rachael" instead of a Reuben by substituting the salt beef with an equal amount of **turkey**.

FRIED EGG TOPPING

Complete your Reuben by placing a **fried egg**, sunny-side up, on top of the cheese slices.

SALAMI MUFFULETTAS WITH RED PEPPERS

This classic New Orleans-style layered sandwich is given a Mediterranean twist with a layer of roasted pepper tapenade.

★ **SERVES** 4

★ **PREP TIME** 30 mins,
   plus marinating

Ingredients

1 loaf cob bread
250g (9oz) mozzarella cheese
100g (3½oz) provolone or
   Jarlsberg cheese
85g (3oz) salami, thinly sliced
100g (3½oz) mortadella,
   thinly sliced
85g (3oz) Parma ham,
   thinly sliced

For the tapenade

100g (3½oz) pitted green
   olives, chopped
2 roasted red peppers (see
   technique, right), chopped
1 shallot, sliced
2 tbsp olive oil
2 tsp red wine vinegar
1 tbsp capers
pinch each of chopped thyme,
   rosemary, and oregano
salt and freshly ground
   black pepper

1 For the tapenade, stir together the olives, peppers, shallot, oil, vinegar, capers, and the herbs in a medium bowl. Season well. Leave to marinate for 10 minutes.

2 Slice the loaf in half horizontally. Scoop out one-third of the bread from the insides of the top and bottom halves. Spread the olive mixture evenly across the top and bottom.

3 Layer the cheeses and meats onto the bottom half of the loaf. Replace the top and press down well. Wrap in cling film and marinate the sandwich for at least 1 hour, or keep chilled for up to 1 day. Cut into slices to serve.

ROASTING AND PEELING PEPPER

1 With a pair of tongs, hold the pepper over an open flame to char the skin. Rotate the pepper and char each side evenly.

2 Put the pepper into a plastic bag, seal, and allow the skin to loosen. When the pepper has cooled, peel away the charred skin.

PRETZELDOGS WITH CHEDDAR AND ALE DIP

These pretzeldogs are equally good served with the dip for adults, or simply with ketchup for children.

★ **MAKES** 8

★ **PREP TIME** 30 mins, plus rising and proving

★ **COOK TIME** 30 mins, plus cooling

Ingredients

150g (5½oz) strong white bread flour, plus extra for dusting
100g (3½oz) plain flour
½ tsp salt
1 tbsp caster sugar
1 tsp dried yeast
½ tbsp peanut or sunflower oil, plus extra for greasing
8 sausages
mustard (optional)
coarse sea salt

For the Cheddar and ale dip

300ml (10fl oz) pale ale
100g (3½oz) grated strong Cheddar cheese
2 heaped tbsp plain flour
2 tbsp double cream
1 heaped tbsp Dijon mustard
1 heaped tbsp runny honey
salt and freshly ground black pepper

1 Put the flours, salt, and sugar into a mixing bowl. In a separate bowl, sprinkle the yeast over 150ml (5fl oz) warm water. Stir once, leave for 5 minutes until dissolved, then add the oil.

2 Pour the liquid into the flour mixture, stirring it together to form a soft dough. Knead for 10 minutes on a floured work surface until pliable. Put in a lightly oiled bowl, cover loosely with cling film, and leave in a warm place for 1–2 hours until nearly doubled in size.

3 Turn out the dough onto a floured work surface and knock it back. Divide it into 8 equal pieces. Take each piece of dough and roll it under your palm to form a log shape. Using your palms, continue to roll the dough outwards towards each end, until it is about 46cm (18in) long. If the dough is difficult to stretch, hold it by either end and gently rotate it in a looping action as you would a skipping rope.

4 Take each sausage and brush with a little mustard (if using). Starting at the top, wrap the pretzel dough around the sausage in a circular twisting motion, so that it is completely sealed in, with only the top and the bottom showing. Pinch the dough together at the top and bottom to make sure it doesn't unwrap.

5 Place on baking sheets lined with baking parchment, cover with oiled cling film and a tea towel, and leave in a warm place for about 30 minutes until well puffed up. Preheat the oven to 200°C (400°F/Gas 6). Scatter the pretzeldogs with sea salt and bake for 15 minutes until golden brown and shiny. Remove from the oven and cool on a wire rack for 5 minutes before serving.

6 For the dip, bring the ale to the boil in a medium, heavy-based saucepan. Meanwhile, toss the Cheddar cheese with the flour until well combined (this will help to thicken the sauce). When the ale begins to boil, reduce the heat to low and whisk in the cheese. Cook over a low heat, whisking constantly, until the cheese melts. Add the cream, mustard, and honey to the sauce and season to taste. Cook for a further 3–5 minutes, whisking frequently, until the sauce thickens. Serve warm with the pretzeldogs.

BACON, ONION, AND CHEESE HOT DOGS

Using caramelized onion, melted cheese, and pickled cucumber takes an everyday hot dog to another level.

★ **MAKES** 4
★ **PREP TIME** 10 mins
★ **COOK TIME** 45–50 mins

Ingredients

3 tbsp olive oil
2 red onions, thinly sliced
1 tbsp caster sugar
3 tbsp balsamic vinegar
salt and freshly ground
    black pepper
4 good-quality smoked streaky
    bacon rashers, rinds removed
4 good-quality thick frankfurters,
    or other smoked sausages
4 tbsp mild sweet mustard
60g (2oz) grated Gruyère cheese
4 large hot dog buns
4 tbsp finely chopped pickled
    cucumbers (see Refrigerator
    pickles, p249), to serve

1 Heat the oil in a medium, heavy-based frying pan over a low heat. Add the onions and cook for 15 minutes, until softened but not browned. Add the sugar, vinegar, 2 tbsp water, and season well. Continue to cook for 15 minutes, or until the onions are sweet and sticky. Set aside.

2 Preheat the grill on its highest setting. Run the blade of a large knife along the surface of each rasher to stretch out the bacon if it is thickly cut; this will help it wrap easily around the sausage. Thinly cut bacon can be used as it is. Prick each sausage a couple of times with a fork, then wrap a slice of bacon around each one, in a spiral fashion, so that the meat is covered with the bacon.

3 Place the wrapped sausages, join-side down, on a baking sheet and grill for 10–15 minutes, turning only after the top is crispy and brown. When they are crispy all over, remove from the grill. Spread 1 tbsp of the mustard on top of each sausage. Arrange them together on the baking sheet, so that they are touching each other and sprinkle all over with the cheese, being sure to mound it up along each sausage. Return them to the grill and cook briefly until the cheese is melted.

4 To serve, spread a quarter of the caramelized red onions into each hot dog bun, top with a bacon and cheese sausage, and sprinkle 1 tbsp of the pickled cucumbers along the top.

COOK'S TIP These would also taste good when served with some Quick stovetop sauerkraut (see p245) instead of the caramelized red onions.

WHAT'S THE STORY?

A hot dog is simply a cooked sausage – typically either a frankfurter or wiener – in a sliced bun. There is little doubt that hot sausages were first sold on the streets of the United States by German immigrants in the mid to late 19th century, although stories differ as to the identity of their creator. Most accounts agree that hot dogs first appeared in New York City.

PULLED CHICKEN TACOS

Cooking a whole chicken like this gives a moist, flavoursome result. Use leftovers in salads or wraps.

★ **SERVES** 4
★ **PREP TIME** 30-40 mins
★ **COOK TIME** 1½ hrs

Ingredients
1 small whole chicken, about 1.35kg (3lb)
30ml (1fl oz) cider vinegar
1 tbsp chilli flakes
salt and freshly ground black pepper
1 small red onion, quartered
4 garlic cloves
8 corn tortillas

For the chicken sauce
60ml (2fl oz) cider vinegar
pinch of chilli flakes
1 tsp smoked paprika or ancho chilli powder

For the pico de gallo
3 large tomatoes, deseeded and diced
1 jalapeño or other mild green chilli, finely chopped
1 small red onion, chopped
2 garlic cloves, crushed
½ bunch of coriander, chopped
juice of 2 large limes

For the pickled onions
1 red onion, thinly sliced
250ml (9fl oz) cider vinegar

For the avocado cream
210g (7½oz) Greek yogurt
½ avocado, very ripe, peeled
juice of 1 lime
handful of coriander, chopped

1 Preheat the oven to 160°C (325°F/Gas 3). Put the chicken (breast-side down), vinegar, chilli flakes, 1 tbsp salt, onion, and garlic in a flameproof casserole or Dutch oven. Add 1 litre (1¾ pints) water and cook in the oven for 1½ hours.

2 For the pico de gallo, mix together the tomatoes, jalapeño, onion, garlic, coriander, and lime juice in a bowl. Season with salt to taste and set aside to let the flavours blend.

3 For the pickled onions, put the onion, vinegar, and 1 tbsp salt in a non-reactive saucepan (not aluminium or cast iron) over a medium heat. Simmer until the onion is translucent and light pink in colour. Remove from the heat to cool.

4 For the avocado cream, put the yogurt, avocado, lime juice, and coriander in a small bowl. Mash together with a fork until creamy. Season with a pinch of salt.

5 Remove the chicken from its cooking liquid, pull the meat from the bones, and discard the skin (reserve the bones for making stock). Using your hands, or two forks, shred the chicken. Toss with the vinegar, chilli flakes, and paprika. Season to taste.

6 Drain the pico de gallo through a fine mesh strainer. Layer the avocado cream, chicken, pico de gallo, and pickled onions on top of the tortillas and serve.

NOW TRY...

SHRIMP & TEQUILA

Toss 400g (14oz) **king prawns** with 30ml (1fl oz) **tequila**, the juice of 1 **lime**, and a pinch of **salt** and grill for 5–7 minutes, or until pink.

STEAK TACOS

Try these tacos with the **dry-rub steak** from p128, instead of the chicken.

CABBAGE SLAW

Make a quick cabbage slaw by combining ½ shredded small **red cabbage**, 1 shaved **carrot**, 1 sliced **red onion**, 3 tbsp **cider vinegar**, and a pinch of **sea salt**. Add as an extra layer to your tacos.

CURRIED LAMB SLOPPY JOES WITH NAAN BREAD

Gently spiced lamb is topped with herby yogurt and stuffed into warm bread for a new take on an old favourite.

★ **SERVES** 4
★ **PREP TIME** 20 mins
★ **COOK TIME** 50 mins

Ingredients

2 tbsp olive oil
1 small onion, finely chopped
1 carrot, finely diced
½ celery stick, finely diced
2 garlic cloves, finely chopped
5cm (2in) piece of ginger,
   finely chopped
1 jalapeño or other mild
   green chilli, deseeded and
   finely chopped
500g (1lb 2oz) minced lamb
½ tsp ground coriander
½ tsp cayenne pepper
½ tsp ground cinnamon
1 tsp ground cumin
1 tsp plain flour
500ml (16fl oz) hot
   chicken stock
salt and freshly ground
   black pepper
3 tbsp roughly chopped
   mint leaves
3 tbsp roughly chopped
   coriander
6 heaped tbsp Greek yogurt
1 spring onion, trimmed
   and finely chopped
4 warm naan breads, halved

1 Heat the oil in a large, heavy-based frying pan over a medium heat. Add the onion, carrot, and celery and cook for 10 minutes, until softened but not browned. Add the garlic, ginger, and jalapeño and cook for a further 2 minutes.

2 Increase the heat and add the lamb, breaking it down with a spoon as it goes into the pan. Cook for 5 minutes, constantly stirring to break up the meat, until well browned and separated. Sprinkle over the dried spices and the flour, and cook for a further minute or two.

3 Add the stock and stir well to combine. Bring to the boil, then reduce the heat to a low simmer and cook, uncovered, for 30–35 minutes until the liquid has evaporated and the lamb is tender. Season to taste and remove from the heat. Stir in 2 tbsp each of the chopped mint and coriander.

4 In a small bowl, mix together the Greek yogurt, the remaining herbs, and the spring onion and season to taste. To serve, spoon a portion of the meat on one half of the naan bread. Add a spoonful of the yogurt mixture and top with the other half of the naan bread.

COOK'S TIP This lamb curry is also delicious served over rice with a chopped herby cucumber and tomato salad on the side, and a squeeze of lime.

★ ★ ★
WHAT'S THE STORY?

A traditional Sloppy Joe (so-called because it's messy to eat) comprises minced beef, onions, tomatoes, and seasoning, cooked down and stuffed into a soft roll. References to the dish date back to the depression era of the 1930s, when meat was a precious commodity, and the sandwich may have been created as a way to make a little meat go a long way.

★ ★ ★

GRILLED CHEESE SANDWICH

Buttering the outside gives this sandwich a crunch that contrasts well with the melting cheese.

- ⭐ **MAKES** 1
- ⭐ **PREP TIME** 5 mins
- ⭐ **COOK TIME** 5 mins

Ingredients
2 thick slices of good-quality white bread
2 tbsp unsalted butter, softened
60g (2oz) grated good-quality strong cheese, such as Cheddar

1 Preheat a griddle pan or large, cast-iron frying pan. Spread a little butter on one side of each slice of bread and griddle for 2 minutes, buttered-side down, until the bread is lightly toasted.

2 Remove the bread from the heat. Butter the other sides lightly, being sure to spread the butter all the way to the edges.

3 Turn the bread over to the lightly griddled side and spread the grated cheese evenly over one slice, then top it with the other slice, so that the pre-griddled sides are inside and the buttered ones outside.

4 Return the sandwich to the pan and griddle for 2–3 minutes on each side, pressing down lightly with a spatula to ensure that the cheese melts. The sandwich is ready when it is golden brown and crispy, and the cheese has melted. Serve alongside Creamy tomato soup with corn and peppers (see p33).

COOK'S TIP When griddling, move the sandwich as little as possible. If you turn the sandwich more than once, it will be difficult to keep the griddle marks aligned.

Strong Cheddar, with its sharp, earthy flavour, brings a simple sandwich to life.

NOW TRY...

APPLE & MAPLE SYRUP

Before griddling the bread, peel, core, slice, and griddle 1 **sharp apple**, such as Granny Smith, until golden brown. Brush it with **maple syrup** and add it to the sandwich, along with 3 slices of **crispy bacon** for the ultimate in comfort food.

GRUYÈRE, HAM, & EGG

For a quick lunch, griddle sliced **Gruyère** and 60g (2oz) **smoked ham** in **sourdough bread**, and top with a crispy **fried egg** for an updated Croque Madame.

BRIE & CRANBERRY

Try making a grilled cheese sandwich using **walnut bread**, thickly sliced **brie** (trimmed), and 1 tbsp **cranberry sauce** from p165.

MAINS AND SIDES

GARLIC BUTTERED ROAST TURKEY

Taking the time to brine a turkey for a whole day before cooking produces a moist, flavourful result.

★ **SERVES** 6
★ **PREP TIME** 10 mins, plus brining
★ **COOK TIME** 2½ hrs, plus resting

Ingredients
2.7–5kg (6–11lb) whole turkey
2 garlic bulbs
225g (8oz) butter, softened
salt and freshly ground
  black pepper

For the brine
175g (6oz) sea salt
2 bay leaves
1 tbsp allspice
pinch of cayenne pepper
5 garlic cloves, crushed
4 lemons, sliced

1 Prepare the brine a day in advance by filling a large stock pot or flameproof casserole halfway with water and stirring in the sea salt, bay leaves, allspice, cayenne pepper, garlic, and lemons.

2 Add the turkey to the brine, making sure that it is completely submerged. Cover the pot with a lid, set aside in a cool dark place, and let it sit overnight.

3 The next day, preheat the oven to 240°C (475°F/Gas 9). Remove the bird from the brine and pat dry. Using a paring knife, cut small slits throughout the turkey, particularly in the breast and legs. Peel one bulb of garlic and stuff a garlic clove into each slit.

4 Using your hands, generously massage the butter into the skin of the turkey. If possible, lift the skin and spread it underneath. Slice the remaining bulb of garlic in half and place it in the cavity. Season well and place the turkey, breast-side up, in a large roasting tin.

5 Roast the turkey in the oven for 20 minutes, then lower the oven temperature to 190°C (375°F/Gas 5). Roast for a further 2 hours, or until a thermometer inserted into the breast reads 165°C (330°F). Check the temperature frequently to prevent the meat from burning. Remove the turkey from the oven and let it rest for at least 30 minutes before carving and serving with other Thanksgiving dishes, such as Sweet potato casserole (see p162) or Green bean casserole (see p149).

WHAT'S THE STORY?

In North America, roast turkey has become synonymous with Thanksgiving, and the foods served during the traditional celebratory dinner are meant to imitate the meals of the early settlers. However, it is likely that those 17th-century settlers actually ate more duck, goose, and venison than turkey. Thanksgiving was declared a national holiday by President Lincoln in 1863.

BOURBON AND BROWN SUGAR BBQ CHICKEN

A classic barbecue sauce is given a lift with the addition of bourbon, or whisky, for a deep, smoky flavour when grilled.

★ **SERVES** 4
★ **PREP TIME** 5 mins
★ **COOK TIME** 30 mins

Ingredients

250g (9oz) tomato ketchup
200ml (7fl oz) cider vinegar
60ml (2fl oz) bourbon
100g (3½oz) light soft
  brown sugar
1 tsp mustard powder
1 tsp cayenne pepper
  or paprika
1 tsp garlic powder
1 tsp sea salt
8 skin-on, bone-in
  chicken thighs
Boston baked beans
  (see p146), spinach, and
  4 sweetcorn cobs, to serve

1 In a medium bowl, whisk together the ketchup, vinegar, bourbon, sugar, spices, and sea salt. Set aside some of the sauce for glazing and generously baste the chicken all over with the rest.

2 Cook the chicken under a medium-hot grill for 12–15 minutes on each side, or until cooked through, basting regularly. Alternatively, preheat the oven to 180°C (350°F/Gas 4) and bake the chicken for 25–30 minutes, or until cooked through. Using a clean brush, baste the reserved sauce over the cooked chicken, and serve hot with Boston baked beans, spinach, and sweetcorn cobs.

SOUTHERN FRIED CHICKEN

The trick for keeping this dish crisp, light, and juicy is to maintain the oil at the correct temperature.

★ **SERVES** 4

★ **PREP TIME** 20 mins, plus soaking and resting

★ **COOK TIME** 15 mins

Ingredients

500ml (16fl oz) buttermilk (or to make your own, see p12)

1 tbsp hot chilli sauce

8 skin-on chicken pieces, preferably legs and small thighs

150g (5½oz) self-raising flour

25g (scant 1oz) cornflour

1 tsp salt

1 tsp garlic powder

1 tsp cayenne pepper

1 tsp paprika

1 tsp black pepper

1 litre (1¾ pints) peanut or sunflower oil, for frying

1 Whisk together the buttermilk and hot chilli sauce, and season well. Put the chicken pieces into a dish in a single layer and pour the buttermilk over them. Cover the dish in cling film and chill for at least 4 hours, or preferably overnight.

2 When you are ready to cook the chicken, put all the dry ingredients together in a large plastic bag and shake well to combine. Take the chicken pieces out of the buttermilk mixture and shake off any excess. Put the chicken pieces into the bag, one at a time, and shake until they are well covered with the coating. Lay them on a wire rack as you work, and allow them to rest for 30 minutes at room temperature (this will help the coating to stick during frying).

3 In a large, heavy-based saucepan or deep-fat fryer, heat the oil to 190°C (375°F) and carefully lower the chicken pieces into the oil, without overcrowding the pan. Cook for 5–7 minutes on each side (depending on the size of the pieces), turning them over occasionally so that they brown evenly. The temperature of the oil will dip when the chicken is added, and should be maintained at 150–160°C (300–325°F). The chicken is ready if the juices run clear when a skewer is inserted into the thickest part of the meat.

4 Remove the chicken pieces from the pan with a slotted spoon and drain well on kitchen paper. If you are cooking in more than one batch, keep the fried chicken warm in the oven at 150°C (300°F/Gas 2) while you cook the remaining pieces.

NOW TRY...

CORNFLAKE COATING

Replace the flour with 75g (2½oz) **cornflakes**. Put them in the bag with the spices, crush them with a rolling pin, then coat and fry the chicken as directed.

CHICKEN NUGGETS

For a kids' treat, dice 500g (1lb 2oz) of **chicken breast**, and coat and fry them, as directed, for 5-7 minutes. Serve with a **spicy dipping sauce**.

BAKED CHICKEN

Substitute 100g (3½oz) of the flour with an equal amount of **panko breadcrumbs**. Heat 4 tbsp of oil in a roasting pan at 180°C (350°F/Gas 4) in the oven until sizzling hot. Add the chicken, bake for 40 minutes until golden brown, and serve with **potato chips**.

BISCUIT-TOPPED CHICKEN POT PIE

Biscuits, a type of savoury scone in the US, make a quick and easy alternative to shortcrust pastry when topping a pie.

★ **SERVES** 6-8
★ **PREP TIME** 30 mins
★ **COOK TIME** 1 hr

Ingredients

3 tbsp olive oil
350g (12oz) skinless, boneless chicken breast
3 garlic cloves, crushed
1 tsp chipotle paste
1 large onion, finely chopped
3 carrots, about 100g (3½oz) each, cut into 1cm (½in) slices
2 potatoes such as Desiree, about 85g (3oz) each, cut into cubes
1 small sweet potato, about 100g (3½oz), peeled and finely diced
250g (9oz) sweetcorn kernels, or 340g can sweetcorn, drained
250g (9oz) peas
salt and freshly ground black pepper
3 tbsp plain flour
250ml (9fl oz) whole milk
250ml (9fl oz) hot chicken stock
120ml (4fl oz) double cream

For the biscuits

300g (10oz) plain flour, plus extra for dusting
2 tsp baking powder
1 tsp salt
115g (4oz) grated Cheddar cheese
4 tbsp vegetable shortening
250ml (9fl oz) whole milk
1 egg, lightly beaten, for glazing

1 In a frying pan, heat 1 tbsp of the oil and brown the chicken breast over a medium heat for 2–3 minutes on each side. Remove from the pan and set aside to cool. When cool enough to handle, cut the chicken breast into cubes.

2 Heat the remaining oil in a flameproof casserole over a medium heat and sauté the garlic. Add the chipotle paste, onion, carrots, the potatoes, sweetcorn, and peas. Season well. Cook, stirring occasionally, until the onion turns translucent.

3 Add the flour and stir, then add the chicken, milk, stock, and cream. Stir together and simmer for 15 minutes on a low heat, until the sauce has thickened.

4 Meanwhile, preheat the oven to 180°C (350°F/Gas 4). For the biscuits, mix together the flour, baking powder, salt, and cheese in a large bowl. Rub the vegetable shortening into the flour mixture with your fingertips until it resembles breadcrumbs. Make a well in the centre of the mixture, pour in the milk, and mix together until well combined.

5 Gently knead the mixture on a floured work surface to form a soft dough. Roll out the dough to a thickness of 1cm (½in). Cut rounds out of the dough with a 6cm (2½in) biscuit cutter.

6 Place the biscuits over the pie mixture in the casserole and brush each biscuit with a little beaten egg. Bake for 35–40 minutes, or until the biscuits are golden brown and the pie is bubbling. Serve hot.

CHICKEN WITH ROSEMARY DUMPLINGS

Add as many vegetables as you like to this great family favourite, and vary the herbs in the dumplings if you prefer.

★ **SERVES** 6-8
★ **PREP TIME** 30 mins
★ **COOK TIME** 3 hrs

Ingredients

1.25kg (2¾lb) skin-on, bone-in chicken thighs
1 tbsp olive oil
3 garlic cloves, crushed
300g (10oz) onion, roughly chopped
3-4 celery sticks, sliced
3 tbsp plain flour
200g (7oz) mushrooms, halved
salt and freshly ground black pepper
250ml (9fl oz) dry white wine
1 tbsp cider vinegar
200g (7oz) peas

For the dumplings

300g (10oz) plain flour
1 tsp baking powder
½ tsp salt
2 tbsp butter, cut into cubes
250ml (9fl oz) whole milk
1 tbsp chopped rosemary, plus extra to garnish

1 If you prefer, remove the skin from the chicken thighs, and in a large soup pot, brown the chicken pieces over a high heat for 1 minute on each side. Remove from the pot and set aside.

2 Add the oil to the pot and add the garlic, onion, and celery. Cook over a medium heat for 4–5 minutes, or until the onions and celery soften. Stir in the flour, mushrooms, and seasoning. Add the wine, vinegar, and 1 litre (1¾ pints) of water and bring to the boil. Return the chicken to the pot, reduce the heat, and simmer, covered, for 2½–3 hours.

3 When the chicken is falling off the bone, remove it from the pot using a slotted spoon and transfer to a plate. Discard the skin (if kept on) and shred the chicken using a fork. Discard the bones and return the chicken to the pot. Season to taste.

4 For the dumplings, mix the flour, baking powder, and salt. Rub the butter into the flour mixture with your fingertips until it resembles breadcrumbs. Make a well in the centre, stir in the milk and rosemary, and mix to form a wet batter.

5 Use a spoon to form 10–12 rough balls and gently drop them into the simmering stew, along with the peas. Cover and cook for 12–15 minutes, or until the dumplings are puffed up and cooked. Serve hot, in individual bowls, garnished with the remaining rosemary.

Rosemary is tougher than most culinary herbs, and should be chopped as finely as possible.

HOPPIN' JOHN

Spicy jalapeño and shredded kale pep up this simple dish of rice and beans, traditionally made with collard greens.

★ **SERVES** 4-6

★ **PREP TIME** 15 mins

★ **COOK TIME** 2 hrs

Ingredients

8 thick-cut smoked streaky bacon rashers

3 garlic cloves, crushed

1 onion, roughly chopped

1 green pepper, roughly chopped

3 celery sticks, roughly chopped

200g (7oz) kale, de-ribbed and roughly chopped

1 jalapeño or other mild green chilli, finely chopped

1 tsp white pepper

1 tsp chilli flakes

1 tsp dried oregano

salt

knob of butter

120ml (4fl oz) cider vinegar

450g (1lb) dried black-eyed beans

400g (14oz) long-grain white rice

1 spring onion, chopped, to garnish

1 Cook the bacon over a medium heat in a Dutch oven, heavy-based soup pot, or flameproof casserole. Stir in the garlic. Add the onion, green pepper, celery, and kale. Next, add the jalapeño, white pepper, chilli flakes, oregano, and ½ tbsp salt, or to taste.

2 Cook, stirring occasionally, for 7–10 minutes until the onions and peppers have softened. If the mixture begins to stick to the pan, add some butter, as needed.

3 Add the vinegar, beans, and 1 litre (1¾ pints) of water. Reduce the heat to a simmer, cover, and cook for 1–2 hours, until the beans are softened but not mushy.

4 About 20 minutes before the end of cooking time, bring 1 litre (1¾ pints) of water to the boil in a large, heavy-based saucepan. Add a pinch of salt and stir in the rice. Increase the heat to high and bring the water back to the boil. Cover, reduce to a low heat, and simmer until the rice has absorbed the water and softened.

5 Spoon the rice into a serving dish and top with the beans. Garnish with the spring onion and serve hot.

WHAT'S THE STORY?

Served at New Year in the South, Hoppin' John is said to bring prosperity for the coming year, with the beans resembling coins and the collard greens representing the colour of money. As for the name, some say that children hopped around waiting for it to be served; others that it was once sold on the streets of Charleston, SC, by a lame character known as "Hopping" John.

TOMATO, BASIL, AND MOZZARELLA PIZZA

This thin-crust pizza has a bright and breezy West Coast feel with the use of fresh tomatoes and herbs.

- ★ **MAKES** 2
- ★ **PREP TIME** 30 mins, plus rising
- ★ **COOK TIME** 15-20 mins

Ingredients

7g sachet active dried yeast
1 tsp caster sugar
450g (1lb) plain flour, plus extra for dusting
1 tsp salt
3 tbsp olive oil, plus extra for greasing
2 tbsp fine polenta or cornmeal, for dusting

For the topping

3 tbsp olive oil
6 ripe plum tomatoes, skinned and finely chopped
2 garlic cloves, crushed
salt and freshly ground black pepper
125g (4½oz) thinly sliced mozzarella
handful of basil leaves, roughly torn

1 Whisk the yeast and sugar in 250ml (9fl oz) of warm water until the yeast has dissolved. Cover with cling film or a clean tea towel and leave for 5 minutes until the surface is frothy.

2 Sift together the flour and salt into a large bowl. Make a well in the centre and mix in the yeast mixture, along with the oil. Bring the mixture together and add a little more water, if needed, to form a soft, pliable dough.

3 By hand or in a food processor with a dough hook, knead the dough for 5–10 minutes, until smooth and elastic. Place it in a lightly oiled bowl, cover it tightly with cling film and a clean tea towel, and leave it to rise for 30–45 minutes, or until doubled in size.

4 Meanwhile, make the tomato sauce. In a large, heavy-based frying pan, heat the oil over a medium heat and add the tomatoes and garlic. Season well and cook over a medium heat for 5 minutes, or until the tomatoes have broken down and any liquid has evaporated to leave a thick paste. (If the tomatoes are not ripe, try adding a pinch of sugar and 1 tsp of tomato purée to enhance the flavours of the sauce.) Set aside to cool.

5 Preheat the oven to 240°C (475°F/Gas 9). Scatter two 30cm (12in) square baking trays with 1 tbsp each of the polenta. Turn out the dough onto a floured surface and knock it back. Divide it into 2 equal pieces and roll out the pizzas to a diameter of 28–30cm (11–12in).

6 Place the rolled out pizzas on the prepared trays and stretch them to fit the tray. Divide the tomato sauce equally between the pizzas, then scatter the mozzarella evenly over the surface. Bake for 10–12 minutes until the surface is bubbling and crispy at the edges, and the base is crisp. Finish by scattering over the basil leaves.

NOW TRY...

PARMA HAM

Try topping each cooked pizza with 2–3 slices of **Parma ham**, roughly torn, and a handful of **baby rocket leaves**, drizzled with good-quality **olive oil**.

RICOTTA SAUCE

As an alternative to the tomato sauce, use 150g (5½oz) **ricotta cheese**, mixed with a handful of finely chopped **basil leaves** and the zest of 1 **lemon**. Season well. Spread over the base of the pizzas, top with slices of **prosciutto**, and cook as directed.

GRIDDLED CHICKEN

Cover the tomato topping with 150g (5½oz) of thinly sliced, griddled **chicken breast**, 1 tbsp finely chopped **rosemary**, and 6 tbsp of **mascarpone** mixed with 4 tbsp of grated **Parmesan cheese** before baking.

CHICKEN PARMESAN SLIDERS

Sliders are essentially mini burgers, and these chicken versions make great party food for friends and family.

★ **MAKES** 8
★ **PREP TIME** 30 mins
★ **COOK TIME** 55 mins

Ingredients

2 chicken breasts, about
   140g (5oz) each
60ml (2fl oz) olive oil, for
   dipping, plus extra for
   frying and brushing
8 mini bread rolls, 7.5-10cm
   (3-4in) in diameter
1 ball mozzarella cheese,
   drained and sliced

For the sauce

1 large onion, finely chopped
2 garlic cloves, crushed
1 tsp chopped rosemary
1 tsp chopped thyme
1 tsp chopped oregano
1 tsp chopped basil
2 tbsp tomato purée
400g can chopped tomatoes

For the breadcrumb mixture

75g (2½oz) breadcrumbs
35g (1¼oz) plain flour
85g (3oz) grated
   Parmesan cheese
salt and freshly ground
   black pepper

1 For the sauce, heat a little oil in a saucepan over a medium heat. Add the onion and fry for 3–4 minutes. Add the garlic and the herbs. Sauté for 2–3 minutes, or until the onions have softened. Add the tomato purée and continue to stir for 2–3 minutes. Add the tomatoes with their juices. Reduce the heat and simmer for 30 minutes, or until the sauce has thickened and the flavours have mellowed.

2 Meanwhile, preheat the oven to 180°C (350°F/Gas 4). In a medium bowl, mix the breadcrumbs, flour, Parmesan, and season to taste.

3 Cut each chicken breast into four pieces, so that each piece is roughly the size of the bread roll. Pour the oil into a bowl, dip the breasts in it, and then coat them in the breadcrumb mixture. Place them on a baking sheet lined with baking parchment. Bake for 15–20 minutes or until crisp, turning them halfway through to ensure they are evenly cooked.

4 Cut the rolls in half. Fill each roll with 1 tbsp of tomato sauce, one piece of the baked chicken, and a thick slice of mozzarella. Brush the insides of the top halves of the rolls with oil. Transfer the top halves, oiled-side up, and the sliders onto a baking sheet. Grill on a very low heat for 2 minutes, or until the mozzarella melts and bubbles. Assemble the sandwiches and serve hot.

CORNMEAL-CRUSTED CATFISH NUGGETS

These crispy, crunchy catfish bites are perfect with
a simple-to-prepare home-made tartare sauce.

★ **SERVES** 4
★ **PREP TIME** 10 mins,
plus chilling
★ **COOK TIME** 10 mins

Ingredients
600g (1lb 5oz) catfish nuggets
or skinless firm-fleshed white
fish fillets, such as coley
2 tbsp plain flour
1 egg, lightly beaten
100g (3½oz) fine polenta
or cornmeal
salt and freshly ground
black pepper
peanut or sunflower oil,
for frying
potato wedges, to serve

For the tartare sauce
2 cornichons, coarsely grated
6 heaped tbsp good-quality
mayonnaise
1 tbsp white wine vinegar
1 tbsp capers, very
finely chopped
finely grated zest of ½ lemon
1 heaped tbsp finely
chopped dill

1 Cut the fish into 2cm- (¾in-) thick strips. Pat it dry with kitchen paper. Put the flour, egg, and polenta in 3 shallow bowls. Season the flour well.

2 Coat the fish fingers by dusting them first with the flour, then dipping them in the egg, then rolling them in the polenta, until they are well covered. Put them on a plate, cover with cling film, and chill for 30 minutes. This helps the coating to stick.

3 Meanwhile, make the tartare sauce. First, put the cornichons on to a chopping board and chop again, finely, with a sharp knife. Mix the cornichons, mayonnaise, vinegar, capers, lemon zest, and dill, and season well. Cover and chill until needed.

4 Heat a large, deep-sided frying pan and add enough oil to cover the base. Fry the fish fingers for 2 minutes on each side, turning carefully, until golden and crisp all over. Rest them on a plate lined with kitchen paper while you cook the rest. Serve with potato wedges and the tartare sauce.

COOK'S TIP You can also add seasonings, such as ½ tsp onion powder or 1 tsp smoked paprika, to the polenta, if you like.

Dill, an aromatic herb, is best used fresh, and is frequently paired with fish dishes.

BLACKENED MAHI-MAHI WITH PINEAPPLE SALSA

This warm-water fish with a Hawaiian name is given a Caribbean twist with a sweet and spicy pineapple salsa.

- ★ **SERVES** 5
- ★ **COOK TIME** 20 mins
- ★ **PREP TIME** 4–6 mins

Ingredients

60g (2oz) butter, melted
2 tsp sea salt
2 tsp garlic powder
2 tsp freshly ground
   black pepper
1 tsp cayenne pepper
1 tsp dried oregano
1 tsp dried thyme
5 x 150g (5½oz) mahi-mahi
   (dolphinfish) fillets, skins
   removed; or a firm, white fish,
   such as snapper

For the salsa

½ pineapple, skinned and cored
   (see technique, right)
1 red pepper, halved
   and deseeded
1 red onion, finely chopped
1 jalapeño or other mild green
   chilli, deseeded (optional) and
   finely chopped
1 garlic clove, crushed
juice of 2 limes
handful of coriander,
   finely chopped

1 For the salsa, chop the pineapple and red pepper into small, similar-sized chunks and put them in a bowl. Add the onion, jalapeño, garlic, lime juice, and coriander, and stir to mix. Set aside.

2 Pour the melted butter into a wide, shallow bowl. In another wide, shallow bowl, mix the sea salt, garlic powder, black pepper, cayenne pepper, oregano, and thyme.

3 Heat a large, heavy-based frying pan over a medium-high heat. When the pan is hot, dip the fish fillets in the melted butter, coating both sides well, then dip in the seasoning.

4 Cook the fillets for 2–3 minutes on each side, or until blackened. Serve hot, topped with the pineapple salsa.

CORING A PINEAPPLE

1 With a sharp knife, cut off the top and the base. Stand it upright and cut along the contour of the flesh, removing the skin in strips from top to bottom.

2 Turn the pineapple sideways and cut it into slices of an even thickness. Use a round metal cutter to remove the hard, fibrous centre of each ring.

ZESTY PASTALAYA

Try a new twist on a classic jambalaya by replacing the customary rice with orzo, a rice-shaped pasta.

★ **SERVES** 6-8
★ **PREP TIME** 20 mins
★ **COOK TIME** 2-2½ hrs

Ingredients

1 tbsp olive oil
500g (1lb 2oz) skin-on,
    bone-in chicken thighs
3 garlic cloves, crushed
300g (10oz) onion, diced
1 green pepper, deseeded
    and roughly chopped
3 celery sticks, about
    250g (9oz) in total, sliced
2 x 400g can chopped tomatoes
2 bay leaves
juice of 1 lemon
3 tbsp Worcestershire sauce
1 tbsp hot chilli sauce
1 tsp cayenne pepper
1 tsp dried oregano
salt and freshly ground
    black pepper
500g (1lb 2oz) chorizo, sliced
200g (7oz) orzo
zest and juice of 2 lemons,
    to serve
500g (1lb 2oz) raw prawns,
    peeled and deveined

1 Heat the oil in a large soup pot over a medium heat. Cook the chicken for 2 minutes on each side until browned. Set aside. Add the garlic, onion, pepper, and celery to the pot and cook for 4–5 minutes, or until the onions are tender.

2 Return the chicken to the pot and cover with 1 litre (1¾ pints) of water. Add the tomatoes, bay leaves, lemon juice, Worcestershire sauce, hot chilli sauce, and spices. Season to taste and bring to the boil.

3 Meanwhile, in a frying pan, cook the chorizo for 3–5 minutes, or until browned. Add it to the pot. Reduce the heat to a simmer and cook, uncovered, for 1½–2 hours.

4 In a saucepan, cook the orzo in 750ml (1⅓ pints) of water with the lid slightly open for 10–12 minutes, or until tender. Drain and toss with lemon juice.

5 When the chicken is falling off the bone, remove it from the pot using a slotted spoon and transfer to a plate. Discard the skin and shred the chicken using a fork. Discard the bones and return the chicken meat to the pot. Add the prawns, cooking for 5–7 minutes, or until pink.

6 Stir in the orzo, season to taste, and remove the bay leaves. Serve hot, topped with a pinch of lemon zest and a squeeze of lemon.

BROWN ALE CIOPPINO

Traditionally made with the seafood catch of the day, cioppino can be adapted to use whatever fish or shellfish is available.

★ **SERVES** 6
★ **PREP TIME** 20 mins
★ **COOK TIME** 55 mins

Ingredients

1 tbsp butter
1 tbsp olive oil
2 garlic cloves, crushed
1 onion, roughly chopped
2 shallots, sliced
1 celery stick, including
   greens, sliced
175g (6oz) tomato purée
salt and freshly ground
   black pepper
1 tsp chilli flakes
2 x 400g can chopped tomatoes
250ml (9fl oz) dry white wine
1 litre (1¾ pints) hot fish stock
350ml (12fl oz) brown ale
6-12 top neck clams, fresh
   in shells
6-12 mussels, fresh in shells
175g (6oz) salmon fillet, cut
   into bite-sized pieces
450g (1lb) king prawns, heads
   on, peeled, and deveined
crusty bread, to serve

1 In a large, heavy-based pan, heat the butter and oil over a medium heat and add the garlic, onion, shallots, and celery. Cook, stirring occasionally, for 5–7 minutes. Stir in the tomato purée, season with salt and pepper and the chilli flakes, and cook, stirring, for 1–2 minutes.

2 Add the tomatoes with their juices, wine, stock, and ale. Stir to incorporate. Reduce the heat to a simmer and cook for 35 minutes.

3 Scrub the clams and mussels, discarding any that stay open when tapped. Add them to the pot and simmer for 5 minutes, or until they open. Discard any that do not open.

4 Stir in the salmon and prawns, and simmer for a further 5 minutes, or until the prawns are pink and the salmon is cooked through. Season to taste and serve hot with crusty bread.

SWEET AND SMOKY SHRIMP AND GRITS

This popular Southern dish of creamy cornmeal is paired with a sweet, salty, and smoky topping of shrimp and bacon.

★ **SERVES** 4
★ **PREP TIME** 15 mins
★ **COOK TIME** 1 hr

Ingredients

4 thick-cut smoked streaky
    bacon rashers
2 garlic cloves, crushed
1 onion, roughly chopped
4 large tomatoes,
    roughly chopped
85g (3oz) butter
1 tbsp light soft brown sugar
1 tsp dried chilli flakes
salt and freshly ground
    black pepper
300g (10oz) coarse polenta
500ml (16fl oz) double cream
    or whole milk
¼ tsp smoked paprika
    or ancho chilli powder
¼ tsp cayenne pepper
225g (8oz) Cheddar
    cheese, grated
juice of 1 lemon
450g (1lb) raw prawns,
    shelled and deveined
2 spring onions, chopped,
    to garnish

1 In a heavy-based frying pan, dry-fry the bacon, drain on kitchen paper, and set aside. Drain off most of the bacon grease from the pan and return to a medium-low heat. Add the garlic, onion, tomatoes, butter, sugar, chilli flakes, and season well. Cook over a low heat, stirring occasionally, for 30–45 minutes, or until the onion and tomatoes have softened.

2 After simmering the tomato mixture for 15 minutes, combine the polenta, cream, 1 litre (1¾ pints) of water, smoked paprika, and cayenne pepper in a large soup pot, and season well. Cook over a medium-low heat for 30–35 minutes, or until the polenta thickens and can hold a spoon on the surface, and about three-quarters of the liquid has been absorbed. Stir in the cheese until melted and fully incorporated, then add the lemon juice.

3 Add the prawns to the tomato mixture in the frying pan and cook for 5–7 minutes, or until the prawns turn pink. Crumble or chop the bacon.

4 Transfer the polenta to a serving dish and top with the tomato and prawn sauce, crumbled bacon, and spring onions. Serve hot.

COOK'S TIP For a lighter take on creamy grits, try almond milk instead of double cream or whole milk.

CAJUN ANDOUILLE GUMBO

Rustic Cajun-style cooking is often a one-pot affair, and this hearty gumbo is a perfect example.

★ **SERVES** 4
★ **PREP TIME** 15 mins
★ **COOK TIME** 1 hr

Ingredients

2 tbsp olive oil
1 large onion, finely chopped
1 green pepper, deseeded and cut into 2cm (¾in) cubes
2 garlic cloves, crushed
25g (scant 1oz) unsalted butter
3 tbsp plain flour
2 x 400g can chopped tomatoes
500ml (16fl oz) hot fish or chicken stock
2 dried red chillies, finely chopped
1 tsp smoked paprika or ancho chilli powder
200g (7oz) okra, trimmed and cut into 2cm (¾in) chunks
250g (9oz) American andouille smoked sausage, peeled and cut into 2cm (¾in) chunks
salt and freshly ground black pepper
1 tbsp thyme leaves
500g (1lb 2oz) raw king prawns, shelled and deveined
2 tbsp finely chopped flat-leaf parsley
boiled rice, to serve

1 Heat the oil in a large, heavy-based saucepan. Add the onion and green pepper, and fry gently for 5 minutes until soft, but not brown. Add the garlic and cook for a further 2 minutes.

2 Add the butter to the pan and allow it to melt, then add the flour and stir on a very low heat for 5 minutes, until browned. Add the tomatoes, stock, chillies, paprika, okra, and sausage, and bring to the boil. Taste and season with pepper, and salt if necessary (the stock may be salty).

3 Reduce the heat to a low simmer and add the thyme. Cook, uncovered, for 30 minutes, stirring occasionally, until the okra is soft and the gumbo well thickened.

4 Increase the heat and add the prawns. Cook the gumbo, uncovered, for a further 5 minutes, until the prawns are opaque and cooked through. Stir through the parsley and serve with rice.

COOK'S TIP If you can't get hold of American andouille sausage, you can substitute it with smoked chorizo, Merguez, or Kiełbasa zwyczajna.

NOW TRY...

CATFISH

Replace the sausage with 450g (1lb) **catfish** chunks (or other firm-fleshed white fish) and add them along with the prawns in step 4. Cook gently until the fish is opaque, stirring only occasionally.

CHICKEN & PANCETTA

Replace the prawns with 600g (1lb 5oz) skinless and boneless **chicken thighs**, cut into 3cm (1¼in) chunks, and replace the sausage with the same amount of **diced pancetta**. Add the chicken at the end of step 1, and brown it with the vegetables before continuing as usual.

VEGETARIAN

Remove the sausage and the prawns. Add 1 **aubergine**, cut into 1cm (½in) chunks, along with the green peppers in step 1. Add 2 large **sweet potatoes**, peeled and cut into 1cm (½in) chunks, 10 minutes before the end of cooking time in step 3, or until the potato is just soft, before serving over rice.

SPICY CHORIZO-STYLE DIRTY RICE

This Cajun dish traditionally uses chicken gizzards to give the rice a "dirty" appearance. Here, chicken livers do the job just as well.

★ **SERVES** 4–6
★ **PREP TIME** 15 mins
★ **COOK TIME** 1 hr, plus resting

Ingredients

4 tbsp olive oil
1 onion, finely chopped
1 celery stick, trimmed
and finely sliced
1 red pepper, deseeded and
cut into 1cm (½in) cubes
1 green pepper, deseeded and
cut into 1cm (½in) cubes
400g (14oz) spicy chorizo-style
sausage, skinned
200g (7oz) chicken livers,
cleaned, trimmed, and
finely chopped
1 red chilli, deseeded and
finely chopped
2 garlic cloves, finely chopped
1 tsp smoked paprika or ancho
chilli powder
1 tsp coriander seeds, crushed
300g (10oz) long-grain rice
salt and freshly ground
black pepper
750ml (1⅓ pints) hot
chicken stock
leaves from 1 large sprig
of thyme
handful of flat-leaf parsley,
finely chopped
1 tbsp finely chopped oregano
mixed leaf salad, to serve
crusty bread, to serve

1 Preheat the oven to 160°C (325°F/Gas 3). Heat 3 tbsp of oil in a large, cast-iron, flameproof casserole, and add the onion, celery, and peppers. Cook over a low heat for 5–7 minutes, until softened. Remove the vegetables and set aside.

2 Add the remaining oil to the casserole, then crumble the sausagemeat into the pan, along with the chicken livers. Increase the heat and cook for 5 minutes, until the sausagemeat is broken up, seared, and no longer pink.

3 Add the chilli, garlic, paprika, and coriander seeds, and cook for a further 2–3 minutes. Return the vegetables to the casserole, then stir in the rice. Season well, and add the stock.

4 Bring to the boil, cover, and transfer to the oven. Cook for up to 40 minutes, stirring once or twice, until the rice is cooked and the stock has been absorbed. Remove from the oven and rest for 5 minutes. Stir in the herbs, check the seasoning, and serve with a mixed leaf salad and crusty bread.

Chorizo can be bought fresh, cured, or dried. Softer chorizo is better for cooking.

SEARED TUNA AND CREAMY BUTTER BEAN PASTA

Fresh tuna and creamy butter beans give that classic dish, tuna casserole, a sophisticated twist.

★ **SERVES** 4
★ **PREP TIME** 10 mins
★ **COOK TIME** 30 mins

Ingredients

1 tbsp olive oil
4 tuna steaks, about
    350g (12oz) in total
salt and freshly ground
    black pepper
450g (1lb) thin spaghetti,
    such as angel hair

For the sauce

250ml (9fl oz) double cream
1 tbsp plain flour
2 tbsp butter
juice of 1 lemon
salt and freshly ground
    black pepper
400g can butter beans

1 First, make the sauce. In a saucepan, combine the cream, flour, butter, lemon juice, and seasoning over a medium heat. Bring to the boil, then reduce the heat to a simmer and cook for 10–15 minutes. Stir in the beans and simmer for a further 5 minutes.

2 Meanwhile, heat the oil in a heavy-based frying pan over a high heat. Sprinkle both sides of the tuna steaks with salt and pepper. Cook each steak for 2–3 minutes on each side – the tuna should remain pink in the middle.

3 Boil the spaghetti in a saucepan of salted water until tender, or according to the packet instructions. Drain well and toss the pasta in the bean sauce and divide between 4 plates. Cut the tuna into thick slices and serve hot on a bed of spaghetti.

A taste of the
SOUTHWEST

Southwestern cooking, with its fresh, vibrant flavours and strong, bold colours, evolved out of a happy marriage of Spanish, Native American, and Mexican cuisines.

FOODS AND FLAVOURS

★ **Corn**, in all its incarnations, is considered a sacred food by the Native Americans; before the arrival of European settlers, more than 40 varieties were cultivated.

★ **Dried beans**, usually black or pinto beans, are a major feature of the cuisine, and are typically slow-cooked, baked, or refried (see below).

★ **Chillies**, whether red or green, hot or mild, are the primary source of heat in the region's best-known dish – chilli (or chilli con carne) – which can be red, green, or white.

★ **Tortillas**, now available made of either corn or wheat, were originally made only of ground corn – using yellow, white, or the unusual blue corn of the area.

★ **Navajo fry bread**, a simple flat bread prepared on an iron skillet, is similar in style to the ubiquitous Mexican tortilla.

The mainstays of the Southwestern diet are rice and tomatoes – both of which were introduced by Spanish settlers – corn, a variety of dried beans, fresh coriander, and the ever-present chilli peppers that appear in many of the region's dishes. Beef and pork are the main meats eaten here.

Southwestern cuisine combines a mixture of cooking styles belonging to the various groups of people who came to live in the region, which was settled early by Spanish colonists travelling north from Mexico, and who learned to cook alongside their Native American neighbours. Today, both quick, fierce heat and long, slow cooking methods are used to prepare a variety of dishes, from stews rich with tomatoes and spices, to grilled marinated beef ("carne asada"), which is sliced paper thin for topping tacos laden with herbs. Unusual vegetables, such as jícama, tomatillos (see above), and nopales – the peeled pads of the prickly pear cactus – all grow well in the dry heat, and feature in many local dishes.

When preserving chillies for the coming year, tradition dictates that strings equal to the height of each family member should be made to ensure a good supply until the next harvest.

Chipotle chillies are smoked, dried jalepeño chillies, and are used widely in the cuisine of the southwest.

A new take on a classic Mexican dish, the breakfast burrito can be as varied as you like.

Some purists insist that chilli be made with meat only, but for many, beans are an essential addition.

HISTORIC
NEW MEXICO
U.S.
66
ROUTE

Enchiladas, a type of stuffed and baked tortilla wrap, lend themselves well to a variety of fillings.

The southwest boasts some of the most dramatic landscapes in the country.

Strings of chillies, known as "ristras", are a decorative way of preserving chillies for several months.

COUNTRY FRIED STEAK WITH PEPPER GRAVY

Also known as "chicken fried steak" for its similarity to fried chicken, this Southern dish is home cooking at its best.

★ **SERVES** 4
★ **PREP TIME** 15 mins, plus soaking
★ **COOK TIME** 35 mins

Ingredients

4 x 150g (5½oz) tenderized rump or sirloin steaks, whole
250ml (9fl oz) whole milk
salt and freshly ground black pepper
1 tsp cayenne pepper
1 egg
200g (7oz) plain flour
150ml (5fl oz) peanut or sunflower oil, for frying

For the gravy

30g (1oz) plain flour
500ml (16fl oz) whole milk

For the home fries

1kg (2¼lb) waxy potatoes, such as Desiree
4 smoked streaky bacon rashers
1 onion, chopped
2 garlic cloves, crushed
pinch of chilli flakes

1 Soak the steaks overnight in milk with salt and black pepper, and a pinch of cayenne pepper. The following day, take out the steaks and set aside. Beat the egg into the milk in a small bowl. In a separate bowl, combine the flour with salt and black pepper, and the remaining cayenne pepper.

2 In a frying pan, heat the oil until hot. Toss each steak in the flour, then dip into the milk mixture, and again in the flour. Fry for 3–5 minutes on each side, or until golden brown and cooked through. Watch the meat carefully so that it does not burn.

3 Once the meat is cooked, remove from the pan and set aside. Drain two-thirds of the oil. For the gravy, add the flour to the remaining oil in the pan and whisk to a thick paste. Slowly add the milk, 250ml (9fl oz) at a time, stirring constantly. Once a thick gravy has formed, remove from the heat and season generously with black pepper.

4 For the home fries, cook the potatoes in a pan of boiling water for 20 minutes. Drain the potatoes and set aside to cool. When cool enough to handle, leaving the skins on, cut the potatoes into 2cm (¾in) strips.

5 In a large, non-stick frying pan, dry-fry the bacon until crisp. Crumble the bacon and add the potatoes along with the onion, garlic, and chilli flakes. Season to taste. Cook over a medium heat until crisp. Serve the steaks with a generous portion of the gravy and home fries on the side.

SPAGHETTI AND HERBED TURKEY MEATBALLS

Minced turkey makes a healthy, low-fat alternative to minced beef in this popular family dish.

★ **SERVES** 4
★ **PREP TIME** 20 mins
★ **COOK TIME** 1 hr 10 mins

Ingredients

olive oil, for frying and drizzling
450g (1lb) dried spaghetti

For the sauce

3 garlic cloves, crushed
1 onion, chopped
1 tsp dried rosemary
1 tsp dried oregano
1 tsp dried thyme
2 tbsp tomato purée
2 x 400g can chopped tomatoes

For the meatballs

450g (1lb) turkey, minced
60g (2oz) breadcrumbs
1 shallot, sliced
bunch of basil, chopped
1 egg, beaten
salt and freshly ground
  black pepper

1 First, make the sauce. Heat a little oil in a saucepan over a medium heat. Sauté the garlic and onion briefly, then add the rosemary, oregano, and thyme. Cook for 2–3 minutes, or until the onion has softened slightly. Stir in the tomato purée, then add the chopped tomatoes with their juices. Reduce the heat and simmer to thicken for 1 hour.

2 Meanwhile, preheat the oven to 180°C (350°F/Gas 4). For the meatballs, mix the turkey, breadcrumbs, shallot, basil, egg, and seasoning in a bowl. Using your hands, form the mixture into twelve 5cm (2in) balls and place them on a baking sheet lined with baking parchment.

3 Bake for 35–40 minutes, or until browned, sizzling, and cooked through. Remove from the oven and put them into the simmering sauce, stirring to incorporate.

4 Cook the pasta in a large pan of boiling salted water for 8–10 minutes, or according to packet instructions. Drain, drizzle over a little oil, and toss well. Serve the spaghetti hot, topped with a generous portion of the sauce and meatballs.

THREE BEAN CHILLI

A big pot of chilli is an easy way to make a little meat go a long way.

★ **SERVES** 4–6
★ **PREP TIME** 10 mins
★ **COOK TIME** 2 hrs

Ingredients

1 green pepper, deseeded
   and roughly chopped
1 red pepper, deseeded
   and roughly chopped
1 onion, roughly chopped
1 jalapeño or other mild
   green chilli, roughly
   chopped
2 tbsp olive oil
2 x 400g can chopped
   tomatoes
340g can sweetcorn,
   drained
400g can each of
   red kidney beans,
   black beans, and
   cannellini beans
3 garlic cloves,
   finely chopped
450g (1lb) minced beef
½ tbsp salt and ½ tsp
   freshly ground
   black pepper
1 tsp chilli flakes
1 tbsp chilli powder
1 tbsp ground cumin

To serve

Southern-style cornbread
   (see p228)
grated Cheddar cheese
soured cream

1 Combine the peppers, onion, and jalapeño in a Dutch oven or large flameproof casserole with a drizzle of oil. Add the tomatoes, sweetcorn, and beans. Stir well to incorporate.

2 In a heavy-based frying pan, heat the remaining oil over a medium heat. Add the garlic and fry for 1 minute, then add the beef and cook, stirring occasionally, for 3–4 minutes, or until browned all over. Transfer to the casserole, season with the salt and pepper, and add the spices.

3 Place the uncovered casserole over a low heat and simmer for 2 hours, stirring occasionally, or until the vegetables are tender. Alternatively, place the dish in an oven preheated at 180°C (350°F/Gas 4). Season to taste. Serve hot with cornbread, Cheddar cheese, and soured cream.

WHAT'S THE STORY?

The official state dish of Texas, chilli (also known as chilli con carne) was popular with the American frontier settlers of the 19th century. Today, there is much debate about whether it should be made with or without beans. Some purists insist on a simple combination of onions, tomatoes, chillies, spices, and meat, but more often canned or dried beans are added too.

NOW TRY...

WHITE CHILLI

Brown 2 diced **chicken breasts** and add 400g can each of **cannellini beans** and **chickpeas**, drained; 2 sliced **shallots**; 3 **garlic cloves**; 750ml (1⅓ pints) **hot chicken stock**; and the spices and seasoning from the main recipe. Simmer, uncovered, for 2–3 hours until the liquid reduces to a thick sauce.

VEGGIE OPTION

Substitute the meat with 125g (4½oz) **bulghur wheat** for a hearty vegetarian chilli. Add to step 1 along with the garlic, seasoning, and spices and skip step 2.

FIVE ALARM CHILLI

In step 1, add 2 **red peppers**, another **jalapeño** or other mild green chilli, and stir in ½ tbsp **cayenne pepper**, ½ tbsp **chipotle paste**, and ½ tbsp **smoked paprika** or ancho chilli powder. Cook as per the main recipe and serve with chopped **coriander** and diced **avocado**.

SWEET AND SPICY MEATLOAF

Sweet pepper jelly makes a tasty alternative to the traditional ketchup topping for this classic family dish.

★ **SERVES** 6
★ **PREP TIME** 15 mins
★ **COOK TIME** 1 hr

Ingredients

450g (1lb) minced beef
1 onion, chopped
70g (2¼oz) panko breadcrumbs
    or day-old breadcrumbs
3 garlic cloves, crushed
1 tsp chilli flakes
1 tsp chipotle paste
salt and freshly ground
    black pepper
1 egg, beaten
4 tbsp Hot pepper jelly
    (see p248)
mashed potatoes (see p156),
    to serve

1 Preheat the oven to 180°C (350°F/Gas 4). In a large bowl, combine the meat, onion, breadcrumbs, garlic, chilli flakes, and chipotle paste, and season well. Add the egg and, using your hands or a large spoon, mix all the ingredients together until well combined. Shape the meat mixture into a loosely formed ball.

2 Line a baking sheet with baking parchment and transfer the meatball to the baking sheet. Using your hands, mould the meatball into a rectangular loaf. Top generously with hot pepper jelly and bake for 1 hour, or until a thermometer inserted into the meat reads 77°C (170°F).

3 Slice the loaf with a sharp, serrated knife and serve hot with mashed potatoes and additional pepper jelly on the side.

Chilli flakes often include the spicy seeds, so use sparingly if you don't like your food too hot.

SPICY GRILLED BRISKET

Cooking the brisket long and slow, wrapped in foil to preserve the juices, means the meat will be tender and falling apart.

★ **SERVES** 6-8

★ **PREP TIME** 5 mins,
   plus chilling

★ **COOK TIME** 4-5 hrs,
   plus resting

Ingredients

1 tsp cayenne pepper
1 tsp garlic powder
1 tsp oregano
1 tsp black pepper
2 tbsp ground coffee
1 tsp chipotle paste
1 tsp peanut or sunflower oil
1 tbsp sea salt
beef brisket, about 2.25kg (5lb)
barbecued corn (see p153) or
   potato salad (see p50),
   to serve

1 The night before you plan to cook the brisket, mix together the cayenne pepper, garlic, oregano, black pepper, coffee, chipotle paste, oil, and sea salt. Rub this mixture evenly across all sides of the brisket. Wrap the beef with foil and let it chill overnight.

2 On the top rack of a gas barbecue, cook the brisket in the foil for 4–5 hours at 130–150°C (250–300°F), with the lid closed. Alternatively, cook in the oven at 150°C (300°F/Gas 2) for 4–5 hours, or until a thermometer inserted into the meat reads 90°C (194°F). Remove from the heat and let it rest, covered in foil and its juices, for 1 hour. Slice and serve warm with barbecued corn and potato salad.

COOK'S TIP For a smoky flavour, add a pan of hickory chips tossed in 250ml (9fl oz) of water to the barbecue.

SLOW-COOKED POT ROAST

This rich dish is cooked long and slow, until the meat almost falls apart, and is served with buttery egg noodles.

★ **SERVES** 4

★ **PREP TIME** 20 mins

★ **COOK TIME** 4 hrs

Ingredients

90g (3¼oz) butter, softened
3 garlic cloves, finely chopped
900g (2lb) topside or silverside beef cut
1 onion, roughly chopped
12 cremini or button mushrooms, halved
2 beetroots, roughly chopped
2 carrots, roughly chopped
2 waxy potatoes, such as Desiree, cut into cubes
1 sweet potato, peeled and roughly chopped
1 bay leaf, finely chopped
1 tbsp chopped rosemary
1 tbsp chopped oregano
1 tbsp chopped thyme
250ml (9fl oz) hot chicken stock
250ml (9fl oz) red wine
salt and freshly ground black pepper
250g (9oz) dried egg noodles

1 In a Dutch oven or flameproof casserole, melt 2 tbsp of the butter and sauté the garlic over a medium heat for 1–2 minutes. Add the meat and cook for 1 minute on each side to brown. Remove the meat and set aside.

2 Add the onion and mushrooms to the casserole and fry for 2–3 minutes. Then add another 2 tbsp butter, the beetroot, carrots, potatoes, and sweet potato, and stir in the herbs. Add the stock and wine, and season well.

3 Return the meat to the casserole, nestling it on top of the root vegetables. Cover and simmer, checking and stirring occasionally, for 3½–4 hours, or until the meat is tender. Remove the meat and cut it into thick slices; it should fall apart easily. Strain the gravy into a jug.

4 Cook the noodles in a saucepan of salted boiling water until soft, or according to the instructions on the packet. Drain and toss with the remaining butter. Lay out the vegetables on a serving plate and top with the sliced meat. Serve hot with the noodles and the gravy.

Beetroot has an earthy, sweet taste, perfect for this warming, wintry dish.

CLASSIC BURGERS

Using very lean meat can make the burger dry. A little fat keeps the meat juicy, basting it from within.

- ★ **SERVES** 4
- ★ **PREP TIME** 20 mins, plus chilling
- ★ **COOK TIME** 10 mins

Ingredients

400g (14oz) good-quality minced beef
50g (1¾oz) fresh white breadcrumbs
1 egg yolk
½ red onion, finely chopped
½ tsp dried mustard powder
½ tsp celery salt
1 tsp Worcestershire sauce
freshly ground black pepper

To serve

4 burger buns, halved
1 round lettuce, shredded
2 tomatoes, thickly sliced
1 small red onion, finely sliced
1 gherkin, finely sliced
4 tbsp No-cook spicy summer relish (see p244)

1 Prepare a barbecue for cooking. In a large bowl, mix together all the burger ingredients until well combined.

2 With damp hands (to help stop the mixture sticking to your fingers), divide the mixture into 4 balls and roll each between your palms until smooth. Flatten each ball out into a large, fat disk to a thickness of 3cm (1¼in), and pat the edges in to tidy them up.

3 Place the burgers on a plate, cover with cling film, and chill for 30 minutes (this will help them to keep their shape during cooking).

4 Cook over a hot barbecue for 6–8 minutes, turning as needed, until the meat is springy to the touch and the edges charred. While the hamburgers are grilling, grill the buns for 1–2 minutes on the insides only, until lightly charred. Serve the burgers and buns with a selection of accompaniments, and let everyone assemble their own burgers as they prefer.

NOW TRY...

MOROCCAN STYLE

Replace the beef with **minced lamb**, and the spices with 4 tbsp finely chopped **mint leaves**, ½ tsp **ground cinnamon**, and ½ tsp **ground cumin**. Serve inside warm **pitta bread** with a spoonful of **minted Greek yogurt**.

ASIAN TWIST

For a leaner burger, replace the beef with **minced chicken** or **turkey**, and the spices with 1 **red chilli**, finely chopped, 3cm (1¼in) of fresh grated **ginger**, finely chopped, and 4 tbsp finely chopped **coriander**. Serve with **soured cream** and Thai **sweet chilli sauce**.

PATTY MELT

Follow the recipe for the Grilled cheese sandwich on p90 but use a **rustic loaf** and add some shop-bought **caramelized onions** and a **grilled burger** to the cheesy filling (making sure the sandwich starts and finishes with a layer of grated cheese).

DRY-RUB STEAK WITH CHIMICHURRI SAUCE

Crusty on the outside and juicy on the inside, this sweet, spicy steak pairs beautifully with the fresh and piquant sauce.

★ **SERVES** 4

★ **PREP TIME** 15 mins, plus minimum 1 hr resting

★ **COOK TIME** 8-20 mins, plus resting

Ingredients

1 flank, skirt, or feather steak, about 675g (1½ lb)

For the dry rub

1 tbsp light soft brown sugar

1 tbsp thyme leaves

½ tsp dried mustard powder

¼ tsp garlic salt

¼ tsp smoked paprika or ancho chilli powder

freshly ground black pepper

For the chimichurri sauce

6 tbsp olive oil, plus extra for brushing

1½ tbsp red wine vinegar

1 tbsp lemon juice

handful of flat-leaf parsley leaves, about 15g (½oz)

2 tbsp chopped coriander

1 tbsp chopped oregano leaves

2 garlic cloves, chopped

1 tsp dried red chilli flakes

salt and freshly ground black pepper

1 In the small bowl of a food processor, grind all the ingredients for the dry rub together to form a fine powder.

2 Place the steak on a large piece of cling film and rub the mixture all over. Wrap it tightly in the cling film and chill for at least 1 hour.

3 Place all the ingredients for the chimichurri sauce in a blender, or the small bowl of a food processor, and process to a thick, emulsified green sauce. Place in a serving bowl, cover in cling film, and chill for at least 1 hour, to allow the flavours to develop.

4 When you are ready to cook, take the steak and the sauce out of the fridge and allow them to come to room temperature. Brush the steak with a little oil, and barbecue or grill for 4–10 minutes on each side, depending on how you like your meat. For rare, allow 4–6 minutes on each side; for medium, 6–8 minutes; and for well done, 8–10 minutes.

5 Remove from the heat and allow the meat to rest, covered lightly in foil, for at least 10 minutes before slicing and serving with the chimichurri sauce.

SLOW-COOKED PULLED PORK WRAPS

Here, the pork is cooked until it is juicy and falls apart easily, then it is shredded and smothered in delicious sauce.

★ **SERVES** 6-8

★ **PREP TIME** 30 mins, plus marinating

★ **COOK TIME** 3 hrs, plus resting

Ingredients

2kg (4½lb) bone-in pork shoulder
salt, for rubbing

For the marinade

2 tbsp peanut or sunflower oil, plus extra for rubbing
1 onion, finely chopped
2 garlic cloves, crushed
100g (3½ oz) tomato ketchup
4 tbsp cider vinegar
1 tsp Tabasco or other hot chilli sauce
1 tsp Worcestershire sauce
1 tsp dried mustard powder
2 tbsp runny honey

To serve

selection of tortilla wraps
soured cream
peach salsa (see p10) or salsa verde (see p79)
guacamole (see p11)
lettuce
finely sliced red onions

1 To make the marinade, heat the oil in a small, heavy-based pan. Fry the onion over a medium heat for 5 minutes until softened. Add the garlic and cook for 1 minute. Add the remaining ingredients along with 100ml (3½fl oz) of water, and whisk well.

2 Bring to the boil, reduce the heat to a simmer, and cook, uncovered, for 20 minutes until reduced to a thick sauce. Use a hand-held blender or food processor to blend it until smooth. Leave to cool. Rub the pork with the marinade, then place in a large, shallow dish. Cover and marinate in the fridge for at least 4 hours, but preferably overnight.

3 Preheat the oven to 180°C (350°F/Gas 4). Put the pork and marinade in an oven tray just big enough to fit it. Put a piece of greaseproof paper over the top (to stop the skin sticking to the foil) and seal with a double layer of foil. Cook the pork for 2½ hours.

4 Prepare a barbecue for grilling. Remove the meat from the oven. Pat the skin dry with kitchen paper and rub in a little oil, then some salt. Grill it over the hot barbecue for 10–15 minutes on each side, skin-side down first; carefully turn with tongs, but do not turn it until the crackling is crispy and charred in places.

5 Meanwhile, pour the juices from the oven tray into a saucepan and first pour, then skim off all the fat. Reduce the sauce over a medium heat to a thick pouring consistency.

6 Cut the crackling off the meat and leave it uncovered (or it will go soft) while you rest the meat, wrapped in foil, for 10 minutes. When ready to serve, cut the crackling into shards. Shred the pork into a juicy pile, pour over the sauce, and serve with the wraps and accompaniments.

STOVETOP BRUNSWICK STEW

The county of Brunswick, Virginia, and Brunswick, Georgia, both claim this thick, tomato-based stew as their own.

★ **SERVES** 6-8
★ **PREP TIME** 15 mins
★ **COOK TIME** 3 hrs

Ingredients

1 tbsp butter
800g (1¾lb) skin-on, bone-in
   chicken thighs
350g (12oz) bone-in pork loin
2 garlic cloves, crushed
300g (10oz) onion, diced
100g (3½oz) celery sticks, sliced
250g (9oz) white potatoes,
   skin on, chopped
340g can sweetcorn, with
   its juices
400g can butter beans, with
   their juices
2 x 400g can chopped tomatoes,
   with their juices
1 tsp chilli flakes
2 tbsp Worcestershire sauce
salt and freshly ground
   black pepper

1 In a large soup pot, heat the butter and brown the chicken and pork over a medium heat for 1–2 minutes on each side. Remove from the pot and set aside.

2 Add the garlic, onion, celery, and potatoes to the pot and sauté for 4–5 minutes, or until the onions soften. Stir in the sweetcorn, beans, tomatoes, chilli flakes, and Worcestershire sauce. Return the meat to the pot and stir well.

3 Add 250ml (9fl oz) of water. Bring to the boil, reduce the heat, and simmer, uncovered, for 3 hours. Remove the meat from the pot with a slotted spoon and transfer to a plate. Discard the chicken skin and shred the meat using a fork. Discard the bones and return the meat to the stew. Season to taste and serve hot.

MOLE SHREDDED PORK ENCHILADAS

Mole is a traditional Mexican sauce flavoured with chilli and a little dark chocolate for a deep, rich flavour.

- ⭐ **SERVES** 4
- ⭐ **PREP TIME** 20 mins
- ⭐ **COOK TIME** 1½ hrs

Ingredients

900g (2lb) pork tenderloin
   or fillet
225g (8oz) grated Cheddar or
   Monterey Jack cheese
4 large tortillas

For the mole sauce

1 tsp olive oil
1 onion, finely chopped
3 garlic cloves, crushed
30g (1oz) plain or
   dark chocolate
2 x 400g can chopped tomatoes
1 tsp chipotle paste
pinch of cayenne pepper
pinch of ground cinnamon
pinch of sugar
salt and freshly ground
   black pepper

1 For the mole sauce, heat the oil in a large saucepan over a medium heat. Add the onion and sauté for 4 minutes until soft, then add the garlic and sauté for a further minute. Stir in the chocolate, tomatoes, chipotle, cayenne pepper, cinnamon, and sugar. Season well. Reduce the heat to a simmer.

2 In a frying pan, seal the pork for about 30 seconds on each side over a high heat. Transfer the pork to the saucepan containing the mole sauce, turning once to coat. Simmer the meat in the sauce for 1 hour, stirring occasionally. Remove the pork from the sauce and pull the meat apart with a fork.

3 Preheat the oven to 180°C (350°F/Gas 4). Divide the meat and half the cheese between the 4 tortillas. Roll up the tortillas tightly.

4 Spoon half the mole sauce into a large flameproof casserole or baking dish. Lay the stuffed tortillas, seam-side down, in a row over the sauce. Top them with the remaining sauce and cheese and bake for 25 minutes. Serve hot alongside the Refried black beans with pico de gallo from p166.

Dark chocolate can be used to enhance savoury dishes, as it's not too sweet. Use good-quality chocolate (at least 70 per cent cocoa solid).

TWICE-COOKED BABY BACK RIBS

Slow-cooking these ribs in foil in a low oven effectively steams them, so they become melt-in-the-mouth tender.

★ **SERVES** 4

★ **PREP TIME** 30 mins, plus marinating

★ **COOK TIME** 2½ hrs

Ingredients
1 rack of baby back ribs, about 1kg (2¼lb)

For the dry rub
2 tbsp light soft brown sugar
2 tsp smoked paprika or ancho chilli powder
1 tsp dried mustard powder
½ tsp ground cumin
½ tsp celery salt
½ tsp garlic salt
½ tsp freshly ground black pepper

For the barbecue sauce
4 tbsp peanut or sunflower oil
1 small onion, finely diced
2 garlic cloves, crushed
4 tbsp apple juice
3 tbsp ketchup
2 tbsp cider vinegar
1 heaped tbsp dark soft brown sugar
1 tbsp honey
2 tsp hot chilli sauce
1 tsp Worcestershire sauce
1 heaped tsp mild mustard
1 tsp smoked paprika or ancho chilli powder
¼ tsp celery salt
¼ tsp allspice
salt and freshly ground black pepper

1 Mix all the ingredients for the dry rub together in a small bowl. Rinse the ribs and then pat them dry with kitchen paper. Place the ribs on a large piece of strong foil and rub one-third of the dry rub mixture on the bony side, and the remaining two-thirds on the more fleshy side of the ribs. Rub the spices in really well, then wrap the ribs tightly in the foil, making sure that they are completely sealed in. Chill for 1 hour.

2 Preheat the oven to 150°C (300°F/Gas 2). Place the wrapped ribs on a large oven tray and cook, fleshy-side up (so that they arch slightly away from the tray) for 2 hours.

3 For the barbecue sauce, heat the oil in a small, heavy-based saucepan and fry the onion over a medium heat for about 5 minutes, until softened but not browned. Add the garlic and cook for a further 2 minutes. Add the remaining ingredients, along with 4 tbsp of water, whisk them together, and bring to the boil. Reduce the heat to a low simmer and cook, uncovered, for 15 minutes, until thickened and reduced. Blend the sauce until smooth, either in a blender or in the pan using a hand-held blender. Pour half into a bowl to use for brushing the ribs and reserve the other side for serving.

4 Preheat the barbecue or grill. When the ribs are cooked, remove them from the oven and unwrap them, being careful of any steam and hot liquid that may escape. Place them, fleshy-side down, on a board and brush the top liberally with the barbecue sauce. Cook them, bony-side down, over the hot coals, while brushing the fleshy side with more of the sauce.

5 Turn them carefully once the underside is dark brown and crispy (about 5 minutes, depending on the heat of the barbecue), and cook the other side for a further 5 minutes. Serve on a board, chopped into individual ribs, with the extra barbecue sauce on the side.

COOK'S TIP Prepare the meat up to 2 days in advance, then finish off on the barbecue or grill when ready to eat, so long as it is cooked through.

PINEAPPLE-GLAZED BAKED HAM

A whole ham is a good choice for feeding a crowd, and the sweet and sour glaze adds flavour and colour to the finished dish.

★ **SERVES** 8-10
★ **PREP TIME** 20 mins
★ **COOK TIME** 2½ hrs

Ingredients

2kg (4½lb) piece of smoked
   ham or gammon

For the glaze

3 heaped tbsp pineapple jam
2 tbsp pineapple juice
1 tbsp clear honey
1 heaped tbsp light soft
   brown sugar
2 tbsp wholegrain mustard
salt and freshly ground
   black pepper

1 Preheat the oven to 160°C (325°F/Gas 3). Put the ham, skin-side up, on a rack inside a large roasting tin, and pour water to a depth of 2.5cm (1in) into the tin. Cover tightly with foil, making sure it is well sealed so that no steam escapes. Cook for 2 hours.

2 Meanwhile, mix all the glaze ingredients together in a saucepan and bring to the boil. Reduce to a simmer and cook for 5–7 minutes, until thick.

3 Remove the ham from the oven and increase the temperature to 200°C (400°F/Gas 6). Remove the skin (leaving a thin layer of the fat), cut a criss-cross pattern in the fat, and baste with some of the glaze, as shown below.

4 Pour away the water in the tin and return the ham to the oven for 30 minutes, brushing with glaze every 10 minutes until browned and crispy. Serve hot with Rainbow potato gratin (see p158) and Green bean casserole (see p149).

SCORING AND GLAZING HAM

1 Using a sharp knife, score the fat down to the meat in a criss-cross pattern. This will allow the glaze to penetrate and flavour the meat.

2 Using a palette knife, spread some of the glaze mixture evenly over the scored fat.

PORK CHOPS WITH APPLE AND BACON COMPOTE

Transform a simple midweek supper dish with a sweet, salty apple compote, made using the meaty pan juices.

★ **SERVES** 4
★ **PREP TIME** 10 mins
★ **COOK TIME** 25 mins

Ingredients

4 x 2.5cm (1in) thick boneless pork loin chops (about 175g/6oz each), butterflied, all fat removed
2 tbsp olive oil
2 tbsp unsalted butter
salt and freshly ground black pepper

For the compote

1 small red onion, finely chopped
2 thick-cut smoked streaky bacon rashers, finely chopped
1 dessert apple, peeled, cored, and finely chopped
1 tbsp finely chopped sage leaves
125ml (4½fl oz) hot chicken stock
60ml (2fl oz) single cream
1 tsp good-quality maple syrup

1 To butterfly a pork chop, place it on a cutting board. Using a sharp knife, make a horizontal incision, about 2.5cm (1in) deep, down the length of the chop. Make sure that the top and bottom layers are of uniform thickness. Once you've cut the entire length, cut deeper into the loin, pulling back the top layer as you go, until you are about 2.5cm (1in) from the edge. Open up the flaps, as you would a book, and lay them flat on the board. Remove any fat. Repeat for the remaining chops.

2 In a large, heavy-based frying pan, heat 1 tbsp each of the oil and butter. Season the pork chops well and pan-fry for 3–4 minutes on each side, until well browned and cooked through. If you only have room to fry 2 at a time, keep the cooked ones warm in an oven at a low temperature, loosely covered with foil, while you fry the rest, adding a little extra oil and butter, if necessary.

3 While the pork is resting, heat the remaining oil and butter in the pan. Add the onion and fry over a medium heat for 5 minutes, until softened but not browned. Add the bacon and cook for a further 2 minutes until crisp. Finally, add the apple and sage, and cook for a further 2 minutes, or until the apple begins to soften.

4 Increase the heat and add the chicken stock. Allow the mixture to bubble up, then add the cream and maple syrup. Reduce the heat to a low simmer and cook the compote for about 5 minutes, or until the liquid has reduced, leaving a thick, rich sauce. Adjust the seasoning, if necessary, and serve alongside the pork chops, with the mashed potatoes from p156 and the collard greens from p148.

COOK'S TIP When you are ready to serve the pork chops, carefully drain any cooking liquid that has gathered in the warming dish into the compote, for added flavour. If it makes the compote too thin, cook for a further 1–2 minutes to reduce the liquid.

MAC 'N' CHEESE

A thick, creamy mac 'n' cheese is everybody's idea of a tasty supper – the ultimate family favourite.

★ **SERVES** 4
★ **PREP TIME** 10 mins
★ **COOK TIME** 15 mins

Ingredients
300g (10oz) dried
   macaroni
salt and freshly ground
   black pepper
50g (1¾oz) butter
50g (1¾oz) plain flour
450ml (15fl oz) whole milk
150g (5½oz) grated strong
   Cheddar cheese
50g (1¾oz) finely grated
   Parmesan cheese
steamed broccoli, to serve

1 Cook the macaroni in boiling salted water according to the packet instructions. Drain and transfer to a shallow ovenproof dish.

2 Meanwhile, melt the butter in a saucepan. Whisk in the flour over a low heat and cook for 2 minutes, whisking constantly, until the mixture begins to bubble and separate.

3 Take the pan off the heat and whisk in the milk, a little at a time, whisking well between each addition, until it has all been added and the sauce is smooth. Return to the heat and cook, stirring until the sauce thickens. Reduce the heat to low and cook, stirring occasionally, for 5 minutes. Be sure to whisk right into the edges of the saucepan, as this is where the sauce can burn if left undisturbed. Add 100g (3½oz) of the Cheddar cheese and stir until it has melted.

4 Preheat the grill on its highest setting. Pour the sauce over the macaroni, season with pepper, and stir well to coat. Sprinkle over the remaining Cheddar cheese and the Parmesan. Place on a baking tray and grill for 5 minutes, or until bubbling. Serve with steamed broccoli.

Dried pasta is a storecupboard essential. Try to keep a few different shapes to hand.

NOW TRY...

TOMATO & RICOTTA

For a lighter version, heat 225g (8oz) of **soft cheese** over a low heat with 250g (9oz) **ricotta** and 2 heaped tbsp of plain flour. Bring to the boil, stirring until it melts. Add 60g (2oz) of grated Parmesan and season well. Pour over the cooked pasta, add some chopped **basil** and 12 halved **cherry tomatoes**, and grill as usual.

TUNA & PETIT POIS

Add 1 can **tuna**, drained and mashed, and 150g (5^1/$_2$oz) frozen **petit pois** to the sauce at the end of step 3 and cook as directed.

MAC 'N' CHEESE BALLS

Turn leftover mac 'n' cheese into delicious appetizers. Roll tablespoons of the mixture between damp palms to form small balls. Coat in flour, then a little **beaten egg**, then some **Parmesan-flavoured breadcrumbs**. Deep-fry in batches of 4 for 2–3 minutes in hot oil (about 180ºC/350ºF), turning occasionally, until golden brown and crispy.

RED BEANS AND QUINOA

Red beans and rice is a classic Creole dish. Using quinoa instead of rice gives it a healthy, modern twist.

★ **SERVES** 4-6

★ **PREP TIME** 15 mins

★ **COOK TIME** 1 hr

Ingredients

1 tbsp olive oil

3 garlic cloves, crushed

1 onion, chopped

1 green pepper, deseeded and chopped

1 red pepper, deseeded and chopped

2 x 400g can red kidney beans, drained

400g can chopped tomatoes

450g (1lb) spicy turkey sausages

salt and freshly ground black pepper

1 tsp chilli flakes

1 tsp finely chopped thyme

1 tsp finely chopped sage

400g (14oz) brown or red quinoa

1 In a large saucepan, heat the oil over a medium heat. Sauté the garlic, then stir in the onion and cook until browned. Add the peppers, beans, and tomatoes, then reduce the heat to a simmer.

2 Cook the sausages in a frying pan for 10 minutes. Remove from the pan, cut into 1cm (½in) slices, and stir into the vegetable mixture, along with the seasoning, chilli flakes, thyme, and sage. Simmer, uncovered, for 45 minutes.

3 Meanwhile, add the quinoa to a large, heavy-based saucepan filled with 1 litre (1¾ pints) of water. Bring to the boil, then reduce to a simmer, cover, and cook for 30 minutes, or until all the water has been absorbed. Fluff the quinoa with a fork and serve, topped with the sausage and vegetable mixture.

COOK'S TIP For a vegetarian version, simply omit the turkey sausage and cook as usual.

Quinoa, a newly fashionable but ancient superfood, is a great source of plant-based protein.

VEGETABLE FAJITAS WITH CORIANDER CREAM

Prepare all the vegetables beforehand, as fajitas require cooking the ingredients fast and serving them hot.

★ **SERVES** 4
★ **PREP TIME** 15 mins
★ **COOK TIME** 15 mins

Ingredients
4 large Portobello
   mushrooms, sliced
2 sweetcorn cobs
2 tbsp olive oil, for frying
2 garlic cloves, crushed
1 jalapeño or other mild green
   chilli, finely chopped
3 medium onions,
   roughly chopped
1 large green pepper, deseeded
   and roughly chopped
8 small tortillas

For the marinade
1 tbsp olive oil
juice of 3 limes
1 tsp chipotle paste
salt and freshly ground
   black pepper

For the coriander cream
210g (7½oz) Greek yogurt
juice of 1 lime
bunch of coriander, chopped

1 To make the marinade, mix together the oil, lime juice, and chipotle paste in a bowl and season to taste. Stir in the mushroom slices, cover, and marinate for 10 minutes. For the coriander cream, mix together the yogurt, lime juice, and coriander in a small bowl.

2 Hold the corn upright on a board and, with a sharp knife, cut downwards to shear off the kernels (see technique, p152). Heat the oil in a deep, straight-sided frying pan. Add the garlic, jalapeño, onions, pepper, and sweetcorn kernels. Cook, stirring frequently, for 3–5 minutes, or until golden brown and cooked through. Remove the vegetables from the pan.

3 Add the mushrooms, along with the marinade, to the pan and cook over a medium to high heat for 1–2 minutes on each side until brown.

4 Layer the tortillas with the fajita vegetables, mushrooms, and coriander cream. Serve hot.

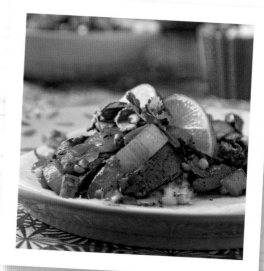

JALAPEÑO, ONION, AND CHEDDAR HUSHPUPPIES

These bite-sized treats are made with deep-fried cornbread batter, enhanced with spicy jalapeños and salty cheese.

★ **MAKES** 20

★ **PREP TIME** 15 mins, plus resting

★ **COOK TIME** 15 mins

Ingredients

150g (5½oz) fine polenta or cornmeal

75g (2½oz) self-raising flour

1 tsp baking powder

1 tsp caster sugar

½ tsp cayenne pepper

½ tsp salt

freshly ground black pepper

60g (2oz) finely grated strong Cheddar cheese

1 large jalapeño or other mild green chilli, finely chopped

4 large spring onions, trimmed and finely chopped

250ml (9fl oz) buttermilk (or to make your own, see p12)

1 egg

1 litre (1¾ pints) peanut or sunflower oil, for frying

1 Sift the polenta, flour, baking powder, sugar, cayenne pepper, and salt into a large bowl and season well with black pepper. Add the cheese, jalapeño, and spring onions and mix well to combine.

2 Whisk together the buttermilk and egg in a jug. Make a well in the centre of the dry ingredients and whisk in the buttermilk to form a thick batter. Leave to rest for 10 minutes.

3 In a large, heavy-based saucepan or deep-fat fryer, heat the oil to 190°C (375°F), as shown in the technique on p144. Using a lightly greased tablespoon measurer, form small, rounded spoonfuls of the batter and drop them quickly into the hot oil.

4 Cook for 2–3 minutes, turning occasionally, until they are puffed up and golden brown all over. Remove the cooked hushpuppies from the oil with a metal slotted spoon and drain them on kitchen paper. Serve immediately.

COOK'S TIP When deep-frying, do not overcrowd the pan as the hushpuppies will not brown well. It is better to cook in batches. Never fill a pan more than half full with oil, as its level will rise when you add the hushpuppies, and could cause the hot oil to bubble over.

ONION RINGS WITH CHIPOTLE AÏOLI

This tasty side dish is an excellent accompaniment to dry-rub steak (see p128) and also works as a stand-alone appetizer.

★ **MAKES** 20
★ **PREP TIME** 15 mins
★ **COOK TIME** 15 mins

Ingredients
1 litre (1¾ pints) peanut or
   sunflower oil, for frying
130g (4¾oz) plain flour
1 tsp smoked paprika or
   ancho chilli powder
½ tsp cayenne pepper
½ tsp salt
1 large onion
250ml (9fl oz) milk
2 eggs
150g (5½oz) fresh white
   breadcrumbs
1 tbsp hot chilli sauce

For the aïoli
220g (7¾oz) mayonnaise
1 tbsp chipotle paste
4 garlic cloves, diced
juice of 1 lemon

1 In a large, heavy-based saucepan or deep-fat fryer, heat the oil to 190°C (375°F) for deep-frying (see technique, below). In a medium bowl, combine the flour, paprika, cayenne pepper, and salt.

2 Peel and cut the onion into 1cm (½in) slices and pull apart the rings. Toss the onion rings in the flour mixture, remove, and set aside.

3 Add the milk, eggs, breadcrumbs, and hot chilli sauce to the flour mixture. Dip the onion rings in the batter, coating evenly on both sides, and fry them in the oil for 3–4 minutes, or until golden brown. Remove with a slotted spoon and let them cool slightly on a wire rack.

4 While the rings are frying, mix together all the ingredients for the aïoli in a small bowl. Serve the onion rings hot with the aïoli.

HEATING OIL FOR DEEP-FRYING

1 Add the oil to the saucepan or deep-fat fryer, filling it no more than half full. Heat to 190°C (375°F) and add a cube of bread to test if the oil is ready.

2 Leave the bread to sizzle in the oil for 1 minute. If the oil is hot enough, the bread should turn golden brown. Remove with a slotted spoon.

WARM EDAMAME SUCCOTASH

Although lima beans are more traditionally used in succotash, edamame give this salad a pleasing bite and modern twist.

★ **SERVES** 4
★ **PREP TIME** 10 mins
★ **COOK TIME** 10-12 mins

Ingredients

2 sweetcorn cobs

200g (7oz) frozen, shelled edamame (soy beans)

2 tbsp olive oil

1 small red onion, finely chopped

2 garlic cloves, finely chopped

60g (2oz) pancetta, finely diced

2 tbsp balsamic vinegar

1 tsp soy sauce

½ tsp caster sugar

salt and freshly ground black pepper

150g (5½oz) cherry tomatoes, halved

2 spring onions, trimmed and finely chopped

2 heaped tbsp mint, finely chopped, plus extra to serve

1 Hold the corn cob upright on a cutting board and, using a sharp knife, cut down the sides to release the kernels (see technique, p152). Put the kernels and edamame in a large pan of boiling water and cook for 2–3 minutes until just cooked, but still al dente. Drain the vegetables and put them in a bowl of iced water – this will help to stop the cooking process and preserve their colour. Drain well and set aside.

2 Heat the oil in a large, heavy-based frying pan over a medium heat. Cook the onion for 5 minutes, until softened but not browned. Add the garlic and pancetta, and cook for a further 3–4 minutes until the pancetta is crispy.

3 Remove from the heat and stir in the vinegar, soy sauce, and sugar, and season well. Add the corn and edamame mix, tomatoes, spring onions, and mint to the pan and stir well to combine. Tip the salad out into a serving bowl and scatter with more mint, if desired. Serve warm or at room temperature.

COOK'S TIP If edamame are not available, try using small broad beans instead. For best results, briefly blanch the beans and peel to reveal their bright green flesh.

Cherry tomatoes are sweet, sharp, and acidic, and add colour and flavour to any dish.

BOSTON BAKED BEANS

These beans are cooked to a traditional recipe that dates back to the time of the first settlers to America.

- ★ **SERVES** 4-6
- ★ **PREP TIME** 15 mins
- ★ **COOK TIME** 2½ hrs

Ingredients

300g (10oz) thick-cut smoked bacon, chopped, or diced pancetta

3 x 400g can Great Northern beans or cannellini beans

300g (10oz) onion, diced

3 garlic cloves, chopped

300ml (10fl oz) molasses

1 tsp garlic powder

60ml (2fl oz) cider vinegar

2 tsp mustard powder

1 tsp paprika

2 tsp salt and pinch of freshly ground black pepper

20g (¾oz) chopped parsley, to garnish

1 Preheat the oven to 160°C (325°F/Gas 3). In a heavy-based soup pot or flameproof casserole, brown the bacon over a high heat for 5 minutes on each side. Remove from the pot and set aside.

2 Add 1 can of beans with their juices and one-third of the onion to the pot, then add one-third of the garlic over it and top with one-third of the bacon. Repeat to make two more layers.

3 In a medium bowl, whisk together the molasses, garlic powder, vinegar, mustard powder, paprika, and salt and pepper. Pour over the bean mixture, then bake, uncovered, in the oven for 2½ hours. Season to taste, and serve hot, garnished with the parsley.

Molasses has a rich, dark, toffee-like flavour, similar to dark treacle.

NOW TRY...

TEX-MEX TWIST

Substitute the Great Northern beans with the same quantity of **black beans**, and replace the molasses with 400g can **chopped tomatoes** (with their juices) and 1 tbsp **chipotle paste**.

VEGAN OPTION

Replace the bacon with 125g (4½oz) **slivered almonds** and substitute 1 can of Great Northern beans with 1 can of **chickpeas**.

HONEY & KETCHUP

Try a brown sugar variation by substituting the molasses with the same amount of **runny honey** and adding 60g (2oz) **brown sugar** and 100g (3½oz) **tomato ketchup**.

COLLARD GREENS AGRODOLCE

Agrodolce, a traditional Italian sweet-and-sour sauce, is given an American twist here with the use of maple syrup.

★ **SERVES** 4
★ **PREP TIME** 15 mins
★ **COOK TIME** 15–20 mins

Ingredients

3 tbsp olive oil
1 large onion, finely diced
125g (4½oz) pancetta,
    finely chopped
2 garlic cloves, crushed
300g (10oz) collard greens
    or spring greens, de-ribbed
    and finely shredded,
    prepared weight
200ml (7fl oz) hot chicken stock
salt and freshly ground
    black pepper
2 tbsp balsamic vinegar
1 tbsp maple syrup

1 Heat the oil in a large, heavy-based saucepan over a medium heat. Fry the onion over a medium heat for 5 minutes, until softened but not browned. Add the pancetta and cook for 2 minutes, until it begins to crisp up. Then add the garlic and cook for a further minute.

2 Add the shredded greens to the pan, in 2 batches if necessary, to allow them to wilt. Toss them in the onion and pancetta. Add the stock and season well. Bring the pan to the boil, reduce to a simmer, and cook, covered, for 5 minutes, until the greens have wilted.

3 Remove the lid and increase the heat to high. Cook the greens for a further 5 minutes, stirring frequently, until the liquid has evaporated and the greens are soft.

4 Add the vinegar and maple syrup, and cook for a minute until the remaining liquid has reduced to a syrupy glaze. Check the seasoning and serve.

Collard greens are a favourite green of the South, but any dark leafy greens can be used as substitutes.

GREEN BEAN CASSEROLE

This modern twist on a classic Thanksgiving side has the green beans smothered in a rich, garlicky sauce before baking.

★ **SERVES** 6-8
★ **PREP TIME** 15 mins
★ **COOK TIME** 40 mins

Ingredients

500ml (16fl oz) double cream
2 tbsp plain flour
115g (4oz) butter, diced
3 garlic cloves, crushed
salt and freshly ground
   black pepper
225g (8oz) button mushrooms,
   quartered
450g (1lb) green beans, trimmed
1 tbsp olive oil
100g (3½oz) shallots, sliced
   into thin rings

1 Preheat the oven to 180°C (350°F/Gas 4). In a saucepan, whisk together the cream, flour, butter, garlic, and seasoning over a medium heat. Simmer for 5 minutes, or until thickened. Stir in the mushrooms and simmer for a further 15 minutes.

2 Meanwhile, bring a large saucepan of salted water to the boil and blanch the beans for 45–60 seconds, or until they turn bright green. Drain, and rinse them in cold water to stop the cooking process.

3 In a frying pan, heat the oil and quickly sauté the shallots over a medium-high heat until they brown. Spread the beans evenly in a flameproof casserole and pour over the mushroom cream sauce. Sprinkle the shallots over the sauce and bake, uncovered, for 30–35 minutes, or until the beans are tender but still retain some bite. Serve hot with Garlic buttered roast turkey (see p94).

COLESLAW

Light on the mayo and with a mild heat of mustard and chilli, this coleslaw makes a perfect side dish.

★ **SERVES** 6

★ **PREP TIME** 20 mins

Ingredients

110g (3¾oz) mayonnaise
60ml (2fl oz) cider vinegar
1 tsp mustard powder
1 tbsp Dijon mustard
1 tsp garlic powder
1 tsp chilli flakes
salt and freshly ground
    black pepper
½ green cabbage
1 red onion, thinly sliced
4 small carrots, grated
3 celery sticks,
    thinly sliced

1 In a medium bowl, mix together the mayonnaise, vinegar, powdered and Dijon mustards, garlic powder, and chilli flakes. Season well.

2 Hold the cabbage, cut-side down, on a chopping board and cut in half lengthways, straight through the stalk. Slice out the core from each wedge and cut across the cabbage, creating broad or fine shreds. Transfer to a large bowl.

3 Add the other vegetables and mix well until the vegetables are well coated in the mayonnaise. Served chilled.

SERVE WITH

DELI-STYLE
REUBEN
SEE PAGE 80

SOUTHERN FRIED
CHICKEN
SEE PAGE 96

NOW TRY...

ASIAN SLAW

Combine 1 shredded **cabbage**, 2 grated **carrots**, 1 sliced **red pepper**, a handful of chopped **coriander leaves**, 4 tbsp **rice vinegar**, 2 tbsp **sesame oil**, 2 tbsp **tahini**, 1 tbsp crushed **ginger**, and 1 tbsp crushed **garlic**. Season to taste.

BROCCOLI & BACON

Toss 1 chopped **raw broccoli head** with 225g (8oz) smoked **bacon bits**, 100g (3½oz) **mayonnaise**, 1 tbsp **Dijon mustard**, and 60ml (2fl oz) **cider vinegar**. Season to taste.

APPLE & CARROT

Grate 3 **red apples** and 3 **carrots**, and toss with 60ml (2fl oz) **cider vinegar**, 100g (3½oz) **mayonnaise**, and 160g (5¾oz) **dried cherries**. Season well.

CREAMED CORN WITH BASIL AND PARMESAN

Here, fresh corn is cooked in the style of a risotto, with Parmesan and basil added to complete the Italian feel.

★ **SERVES** 4-6
★ **PREP TIME** 10 mins
★ **COOK TIME** 30 mins

Ingredients

4 sweetcorn cobs, about 500g (1lb 2oz), kernel weight
50g (1¾oz) unsalted butter
2 tsp olive oil
1 onion, finely chopped
250ml (9fl oz) good-quality hot chicken or vegetable stock
100ml (3½fl oz) double cream
1 tsp plain flour
50g (1¾oz) finely grated Parmesan cheese
2 tbsp finely chopped basil
salt and freshly ground black pepper

1 Remove the kernels and "milk" from the sweetcorn cobs, as shown in the technique below. Try using really young, fresh corn for this recipe, as the skins will be softer and easier to break down on cooking.

2 Melt the butter and oil in a medium, heavy-based saucepan. Add the onion and cook over a low heat for 5 minutes, until softened but not browned. Add the corn and its juices along with the stock to the pan; the corn should be barely covered by the liquid. Bring to the boil, reduce to a simmer, and cook, covered, for 15 minutes, until the corn starts to soften. If you prefer a smoother, creamed corn, use a hand-held blender to partially liquidize the corn while it is still in the pan.

3 Remove the lid, add the cream, sprinkle over the flour, and increase the heat. Cook over a high heat, stirring frequently, for 7–10 minutes, until the cream has reduced and thickened and the corn is soft. Remove from the heat, then stir in the Parmesan and basil. Season to taste at the end of the cooking time. Salting at the beginning may cause the skin of the kernels to toughen and result in a less creamy texture.

REMOVING CORN KERNELS

1 **Hold the corn cob upright** on a chopping board and use a sharp knife to cut down the sides to release the kernels. Rotate the cob and repeat.

2 **To extract the "milk"**, hold the cob upright in a bowl and scrape down the sides with the knife's blunt edge. This starchy juice will thicken the dish.

BARBECUED CORN WITH LIME AND CHILLI BUTTER

This butter is an easy way to flavour grilled vegetables, meat, or fish. It freezes well for up to 6 months.

★ **SERVES** 4
★ **PREP TIME** 10 mins
★ **COOK TIME** 10 mins, plus freezing

Ingredients
100g (3½oz) unsalted butter, softened
finely grated zest of 1 lime
½ tsp chilli powder or cayenne pepper
½ tsp salt
freshly ground black pepper
4 sweetcorn cobs
a little olive oil

1 Prepare a barbecue for cooking. In a small bowl, mash the butter with the lime zest, chilli powder, and salt and pepper.

2 Cut a piece of greaseproof paper, about 15cm (6in) square. Put the butter in the middle of one edge of the paper and shape it like a sausage. Roll the butter sausage up in the paper, then twist the ends so the butter forms a tight shape. Leave in the freezer for at least 30 minutes before use (or freeze until needed).

3 Cook the sweetcorn cobs in a large pan of boiling water for up to 5 minutes until the corn is tender (this will depend on the size and age of the cobs). Drain well, rub them in a little oil, and grill for 6 minutes over a hot barbecue, turning them frequently, until they are lightly charred on all sides.

4 Serve the sweetcorn with a 1cm- (½in-) thick disk of the chilled butter on top to melt.

A taste of the
MIDWEST

FOODS AND FLAVOURS

★ **Pierogi**, a type of stuffed dumpling, was popularized by Polish immigrants to the region.

★ **Chilli** is known as a classic from the Southwest, but the Midwest has its own version, too, which is mildly spiced with cinnamon and cloves.

★ Scandinavian immigrants introduced **lefse** – thin tortilla-like pancakes made from flour and mashed potatoes.

★ As well as the **wheat**, **corn**, and **potatoes** grown on the Great Plains, the rich grasslands are a centre for **beef** production.

★ **Iowa** is an important centre of pork production for the US.

★ Chicago is home to **"deep-dish" pizza**, which is famously thick – and heavy with sauce and cheese.

Pot-roasting is an easy way to get the maximum flavour and tenderness out of cheaper cuts of meat.

The landlocked states of the Midwest, known as both the "heartland" and "breadbasket" of America, are home to vast plains of wheat, corn, and soya beans.

The German immigrants that first settled here in the 1700s were soon followed by settlers from Britain, and Northern and Eastern Europe – notably Scandinavia and Poland. The food they brought with them was homespun, comforting, and ideal for the long, cold winters of the region.

When people gathered to eat as families or in large community groups, stews, casseroles, and one-pot dishes were the main staples. Usually full of meat, potatoes, and vegetables, they were easy to prepare, satisfying, and nutritious – and a great way to feed large numbers of people.

The settlers soon found that the rivers of the Midwest were teeming with freshwater trout – making up for a lack of seafood. The land to the north thronged with elk and venison, and, during the summer, fresh huckleberries – a wild crop similar to blueberries that still resists cultivation – abounded.

The fertile flatlands of the Great Plains are home to huge arable farms.

The pasty, a hand pie stuffed with meat, potatoes, and turnips, arrived with the Cornish tin miners, who came to the area around Michigan in the mid-19th century to work in the mines of the Upper Peninsula.

A sloppy Joe sandwich is full of flavour, but something of a challenge to eat without making a mess!

Potato salad can be made in many ways, but a classic mayonnaise-based one is always popular.

Chicago – the home of deep-dish pizza, hot dogs, and Italian beef sandwiches.

Mac 'n' cheese may be the ultimate comfort food, and everyone has their own spin on this classic dish.

GARLIC AND SHALLOT MASHED POTATOES

For an indulgent treat, nothing beats these creamy mashed potatoes with caramelized shallots and garlic.

★ **SERVES** 4

★ **PREP TIME** 15 mins

★ **COOK TIME** 25 mins

Ingredients

5 large potatoes, such as
    Desiree, cut into quarters

115g (4oz) butter, diced, plus
    extra for frying

2 shallots, sliced into rings

2 garlic cloves, crushed

100ml (3½fl oz) soured cream

juice of 1 lemon

salt and freshly ground
    black pepper

1 Leaving the skins on, cook the potatoes in a saucepan of boiling water for about 20 minutes, or until tender.

2 Meanwhile, in a frying pan, heat a knob of butter over a medium heat and sauté the shallots and garlic until softened and browned.

3 When the potatoes have softened, drain well and transfer them to a large bowl. With the skin still on, use a potato masher or fork to mash the potatoes.

4 Stir in the soured cream, butter, lemon juice, and the sautéed shallots and garlic. Season to taste and serve hot.

PEELING GARLIC

1 Place each garlic clove on a cutting board. Cover with the flat side of a large knife and pound with the palm of your hand.

2 Peel away the papery skin and discard it. Then cut off the ends of each clove, and finely chop or crush the garlic.

SWEET POTATO PARMESAN TOTS

Sweet, salty, and slightly spicy, these bite-sized treats make a great accompaniment to any meal.

★ **MAKES** 30
★ **PREP TIME** 20 mins
★ **COOK TIME** 40 mins, plus cooling

Ingredients
4 large sweet potatoes
60g (2oz) grated
    Parmesan cheese
30g (1oz) plain flour
1 tsp garlic powder
1 tsp mustard seeds
1 tsp cayenne pepper
1 litre (1¾ pints) peanut or
    sunflower oil, for frying

For the honey mustard dip
60g (2oz) Dijon mustard
60g (2oz) mayonnaise
85g (3oz) honey

1 Boil the sweet potatoes for 10–15 minutes, or until cooked but firm. The potatoes should be soft enough to be easily pierced with a fork, but firm enough to be grated.

2 Allow the potatoes to cool until you can comfortably handle them. Once cool enough, peel off the skin and grate the potatoes. Combine the grated potatoes with the Parmesan cheese, flour, garlic powder, mustard seeds, and cayenne pepper.

3 In a large, heavy-based saucepan or deep-fat fryer, heat the oil to 190°C (375°F), as shown in the technique on p144. Take about 1 tbsp of the potato mixture and roll it between your palms to form a ball. Repeat to make the remaining balls.

4 Fry the balls in batches of 6 for 2–3 minutes each, or until brown. Remove them with a slotted spoon and let them rest on a wire rack while you fry the remaining balls.

5 For the honey mustard dip, combine the mustard, mayonnaise, and honey in a small bowl. Stir well to incorporate all the ingredients. Serve the potato tots hot with the dip.

Sweet potatoes are a healthy, vitamin-packed alternative to white potatoes.

RAINBOW POTATO GRATIN

Try layering as many different-coloured potatoes as you can find for this eye-catching dish.

★ **SERVES** 4
★ **PREP TIME** 20 mins
★ **COOK TIME** 45 mins

Ingredients

900g (2lb) sweet potatoes;
   purple potatoes, such as
   salad blue; and yellow, waxy
   potatoes such as Charlottes
   (total weight)
500ml (16fl oz) double cream
4 garlic cloves, crushed
225g (8oz) grated
   Cheddar cheese
salt and freshly ground
   black pepper
pinch of chilli flakes

1 Preheat the oven to 180°C (350°F/Gas 4). Leaving the skin on, scrub the potatoes well and cut them into thin slices (see the technique below). In a small saucepan, add the cream and garlic, and bring to the boil over a medium heat. Remove from the heat and set aside.

2 In a medium flameproof casserole, layer the potatoes and cheese, sprinkling a little salt and pepper between each layer. Finish with a generous layer of cheese.

3 Pour the cream around the edge of the potatoes, so as not to disturb the layers. Season well and add a pinch of chilli flakes. Bake for 45 minutes, or until the potatoes are golden brown and the cheese starts to bubble.

COOK'S TIP If salad blue potatoes are not available, try using fresh beetroot instead.

SLICING A POTATO

To cut with a knife, hold the potato firmly on a chopping board and cut it into slices of uniform thickness, as desired.

If using a mandolin, hold the potato in the carrier to protect your fingers as you slide it up and down the sharp blade, which can be adjusted.

SLOW-COOKED BLACK BEANS

It's a good idea to make more than you'll need, as these versatile beans keep well and the flavour improves overnight.

★ **SERVES** 4-6

★ **PREP TIME** 20 mins, plus soaking

★ **COOK TIME** 1½ hrs

Ingredients

200g (7oz) dried black beans
2 tbsp olive oil
1 red onion, finely chopped
1 large garlic clove, finely chopped
1 large jalapeño or other mild green chilli, finely chopped
60g (2oz) pancetta, finely diced
700ml (1 pint 3½fl oz) hot chicken stock
freshly ground black pepper
chopped coriander leaves, to garnish (optional)
soured cream, to serve (optional)

1 Put the dried beans in a large bowl, cover well with cold water, and allow them to soak overnight. The beans will swell as they soak, so leave enough room for them to expand. Drain the beans and rinse them well under cold running water.

2 Heat the oil in a medium, heavy-based saucepan. Fry the onion over a medium heat for 5 minutes, until softened but not browned. Add the garlic and jalapeño and cook for another minute. Finally, add the pancetta and cook for 3–4 minutes, until crispy and golden brown.

3 Add the beans and chicken stock to the pan. Season to taste with pepper (the stock and pancetta are salty). Bring to the boil, reduce to a low simmer, and cook, uncovered, for 1 hour, or until the cooking liquid is reduced.

4 Cover and cook on a very low heat for 30–45 minutes, until the beans are tender and the liquid has reduced and thickened. Serve on its own, or with a sprinkling of coriander and a bowl of soured cream on the side.

Dried black beans, a mainstay of Mexican cuisine, have a rich smoky flavour.

CORNMEAL-CRUSTED FRIED OKRA

Cornmeal (you can also use fine polenta) gives a crunchy coating to deep-fried food. Use young okra for the best result.

★ **SERVES** 6-8
★ **PREP TIME** 15 mins
★ **COOK TIME** 15-20 mins

Ingredients
130g (4¾oz) plain flour
2 tsp smoked paprika or
  ancho chilli powder
1 tsp cayenne pepper
2 tsp salt
2 large eggs
150g (5½oz) fine polenta
  or cornmeal
24 okra, cut into 1cm (½in) slices
1 litre (1¾ pints) peanut or
  sunflower oil, for frying
cider vinegar, to serve

1 In a bowl, combine the flour with 1 tsp smoked paprika, ½ tsp cayenne pepper, and 1 tsp salt, and set aside. Whisk the eggs in a second bowl. In a third bowl, mix the polenta with the remaining smoked paprika, cayenne pepper, and salt.

2 Toss the okra in the flour mixture, dip each briefly in the eggs, then coat well in the polenta mixture.

3 Heat the oil to 190°C (375°F) in a large, heavy-based saucepan or deep-fat fryer, as shown in the technique on p144. Fry the okra, in batches, in the hot oil for 3–5 minutes, or until golden brown.

4 Remove them with a slotted spoon and let them cool on a wire rack while you fry the remaining batches. Serve with cider vinegar as a dip for a tangy twist.

SWEET POTATO CASSEROLE WITH BACON

Traditionally served with turkey at Thanksgiving, the smooth, sweet potato contrasts well with the crunchy, salty topping.

★ **SERVES** 8
★ **PREP TIME** 20 mins
★ **COOK TIME** 1 hr

Ingredients

1.8kg (4lb) sweet potatoes, peeled and chopped
4 eggs
300g (10oz) caster sugar
350g (12oz) unsalted butter, melted and cooled
250ml (9fl oz) milk
1 tsp vanilla extract

For the topping

450g (1lb) thick-cut smoked streaky bacon
1 tbsp ground cinnamon
25g (scant 1oz) caster sugar
60g (2oz) butter
150g (5½oz) light soft brown sugar
125g (4½oz) chopped pecans

1 Preheat the oven to 180°C (350°F/Gas 4). Cook the potatoes in a saucepan of boiling water for 10–15 minutes, or until tender. Drain well, mash until smooth, and set aside.

2 In a frying pan, dry-fry the bacon over a medium-high heat for 10–15 minutes, turning occasionally, until evenly browned and crisp. Remove from the pan and drain on paper towels. Sprinkle with the cinnamon and caster sugar. Set aside. When it is cool enough to handle, crumble the bacon.

3 Place the eggs, sugar, and melted butter in a large bowl and, using a balloon whisk or an electric hand whisk, whisk until well combined; the mixture should be golden and silky. Add the milk and vanilla extract, then mix in the potatoes until well blended. Spoon the mixture into a large ovenproof casserole with a capacity of about 4 litres (7 pints).

4 Melt the butter and combine with the brown sugar, crumbled bacon pieces, and pecans. Sprinkle over the potato mixture in the casserole. Bake in the oven for 45 minutes. If the topping starts to brown, cover the dish with foil. Serve hot.

COOK'S TIP For a much-loved take on this festive casserole, mix 45g (1½oz) mini marshmallows into the topping mixture.

Pecan nuts, a Southern crop, are used there in both savoury and sweet dishes.

FRIED GREEN TOMATOES WITH BASIL CREAM

A crispy coating and herbed cream dip turn these firm tomatoes into an irresistibly tasty side dish.

★ **SERVES** 4

★ **PREP TIME** 15–20 mins, plus soaking and resting

★ **COOK TIME** 15 mins

Ingredients

8 green tomatoes

200ml (7fl oz) buttermilk (or to make your own, see p12)

½ tsp smoked paprika or ancho chilli powder

salt and freshly ground black pepper

50g (1¾oz) fine polenta or cornmeal

25g (scant 1oz) panko or day-old breadcrumbs

25g (scant 1oz) finely grated Parmesan cheese

3 tbsp finely chopped basil

1 litre (1¾ pints) peanut or sunflower oil, for frying

150g (5½oz) crème fraîche

finely grated zest of ½ lemon

1 Slice the tops and bottoms off the tomatoes and, depending on the size of the tomatoes, cut them into 2 or 3 equal slices, about 5mm (¼in) thick. Lay them in a single layer in a large, shallow dish. Whisk the buttermilk with the smoked paprika and season well. Pour the buttermilk over the tomatoes. Cover with cling film and chill for at least 2 hours before cooking.

2 Place the polenta, breadcrumbs, and Parmesan in a food processor and pulse until well combined. Mix in 1 tbsp of the chopped basil and season well.

3 When the tomatoes have soaked, drain them well. Toss them in the polenta crust, making sure that they are evenly coated on all sides, then leave them to rest for at least 30 minutes on a wire rack to allow the coating to set a little – this will help it to stick during frying.

4 Pour the oil into a large, heavy-based frying pan to a depth of at least 1cm (½in). When the oil is hot, add the tomatoes, being careful not to overcrowd the pan. Cook them for 2–3 minutes, turning them once, until they are golden brown on both sides. Remove them with a slotted spoon and let them rest on a wire rack.

5 To make the basil cream, whisk together the crème fraîche, the remaining basil and lemon zest, and season well.

Green tomatoes are simply underripe red tomatoes, and have a fresh, delicate taste.

SPICED CRANBERRY AND ORANGE SAUCE

Fresh cranberries need a fair amount of sugar to counter their acidity. This sauce is perfect served with roast turkey (see p94).

★ **SERVES** 8

★ **PREP TIME** 5 mins

★ **COOK TIME** 10 mins

Ingredients

350g (12oz) cranberries

250ml (9fl oz) fresh
    orange juice

finely grated zest of 1 large
    orange (see technique, below)

1 cinnamon stick

100g (3½oz) caster sugar

60g (2oz) light soft brown sugar

1 tbsp maple syrup

1 Put the cranberries in a small, heavy-based saucepan and cover them with the orange juice. Add the orange zest, cinnamon stick, and sugars.

2 Bring the liquid to the boil, then reduce to a simmer and cook over a low heat for 10 minutes, stirring occasionally, until the cranberries have softened and burst, and the mixture has thickened and reduced.

3 Take the sauce off the heat, remove the cinnamon stick, and stir in the maple syrup. Serve the sauce either warm or at room temperature. You can also use it cold in a leftover turkey sandwich, mixed with good-quality mayonnaise and watercress, or in the Grilled cheese sandwich from p90.

ZESTING AN ORANGE

For grated zest, hold the orange firmly in one hand and rub it diagonally, rather than vertically, across the fine holes of a grater.

For thread-like strips, hold the orange firmly in one hand and scrape its surface with a zester to create thread-like strips.

REFRIED BLACK BEANS WITH PICO DE GALLO

Enjoy this Mexican-style side dish of mashed beans with a tomato salsa over rice for a satisfying meat-free meal.

★ **SERVES** 6
★ **PREP TIME** 15 mins
★ **COOK TIME** 2 hrs

Ingredients
450g (1lb) dried black beans
1 onion, roughly chopped
3 garlic cloves, roughly chopped
salt and freshly ground
   black pepper
1 tsp olive oil

For the pico de gallo
2 tomatoes, diced
1 red onion, finely chopped
handful of coriander, chopped
juice of 2 limes

To serve
1 avocado, halved, stoned,
   and thinly sliced (see
   technique, p11)
30g (1oz) grated Cheddar
   cheese (optional)
soured cream (optional)

1 Put the dried beans, onion, and garlic into a medium soup pot. Cover with water, season, and bring to the boil over a high heat. Reduce the heat and simmer, covered, for 2 hours, or until the beans turn soft. Drain the beans but reserve 250ml (9fl oz) of the liquid.

2 Put the bean mixture and reserved liquid in a food processor, or use a hand-held blender, and blend until smooth.

3 In a heavy-based saucepan, heat the oil over a medium heat. Spoon the blended beans into the pan and cook, stirring frequently, for 5–6 minutes, or until thickened.

4 To make the pico de gallo, mix the tomatoes and onion with the coriander and lime juice. Serve the beans hot, topped with the pico de gallo, sliced avocado, and, if desired, cheese or soured cream.

SERVE WITH

PULLED CHICKEN TACOS
SEE PAGE 86

MOLE PORK ENCHILADAS
SEE PAGE 132

SAUSAGE AND CHESTNUT STUFFING

Fresh rosemary and chunky chestnuts add flavour and texture to this hearty bread and sausage stuffing.

★ **SERVES** 6
★ **PREP TIME** 15 mins
★ **COOK TIME** 45–50 mins

Ingredients

200g (7oz) spicy pork sausages
vegetable oil, for frying
2 garlic cloves, crushed
3 shallots, sliced
450g (1lb) chestnuts, peeled
   and halved
1 loaf day-old French or
   crusty bread
1 tbsp chopped rosemary
450ml (15fl oz) hot
   chicken stock
salt and freshly ground
   black pepper

1 Preheat the oven to 180°C (350°F/Gas 4). Remove the skin from the sausages and crumble the sausagemeat. Heat a little oil in a frying pan and cook the sausagemeat over a medium heat for 5 minutes, or until browned. Remove from the pan and set aside, then fry the garlic and shallots for 5 minutes.

2 If using raw chestnuts, rather than pre-cooked and peeled, carve an x-shaped mark on each chestnut and boil for 10–15 minutes, or until soft. When cool enough to handle, peel back the shells to reveal the meat.

3 Cut the bread into 1cm (½in) slices, then tear them into quarters. Put the sausages and bread into a large flameproof casserole. Mix in the garlic, shallots, chestnuts, and rosemary. Pour the stock over the bread mixture and season to taste.

4 Bake for 35–40 minutes, or until crisp and browned. Serve hot with the Garlic buttered roast turkey from p94.

Chestnuts, with their sweet, meaty flesh, pair perfectly with sausagemeat and all types of pork.

FESTIVE CORNBREAD STUFFING

Clementines and cranberries give a seasonal flair to this colourful stuffing, traditionally served with roast turkey.

★ **SERVES** 6-8
★ **PREP TIME** 15 mins
★ **COOK TIME** 35-40 mins

Ingredients

500g (1lb 2oz) crumbled
  cornbread (see p228)
3 garlic cloves, crushed
1 onion, finely chopped
3 clementines, peeled
  and segmented
  (see technique, below)
85g (3oz) dried cranberries
115g (4oz) butter, diced
1 litre (1¾ pints)
  vegetable stock

1 Preheat the oven to 180°C (350°F/Gas 4). Put the cornbread into a large mixing bowl. Add the garlic and onion, then stir in the clementines, cranberries, and butter.

2 Add the stock and stir, making sure that the stuffing is fully incorporated. Scoop the stuffing generously into a lightly greased 23 x 23cm (9 x 9in) baking tray.

3 Bake in the preheated oven for 35–40 minutes, or until golden brown. Remove from the oven and leave to cool for 5 minutes before turning out onto a wire rack. Serve hot.

SEGMENTING CITRUS FRUIT

1 With a sharp knife, slice away the top and bottom of the fruit, then work all the way around it, slicing away the skin and pith.

2 Slice between each segment, leaving the thin layer of membrane behind until you have cut out all the segments.

DESSERTS

PECAN AND ORANGE BANANAS FOSTER

This decadent dessert, with its rich, buttery sauce drizzled on toasted brioche, takes only minutes to prepare.

★ **SERVES** 4
★ **PREP TIME** 15 mins
★ **COOK TIME** 10 mins

Ingredients

50g (1¾oz) pecan nuts, roughly chopped
60g (2oz) unsalted butter
4 heaped tbsp dark soft brown sugar
juice and grated zest of 1 orange
2 large underripe (not green) bananas, peeled and cut into 1cm (½in) cubes
4 thickly cut slices of brioche bread
60ml (2fl oz) dark rum
4 large scoops of good-quality vanilla ice cream (see p194)

1 In a large, heavy-based frying pan, dry-fry the pecans over a medium heat for 3–4 minutes, stirring occasionally, until they begin to brown in places. Remove from the heat and set aside. Wipe the pan clean.

2 Heat the butter, sugar, and the orange juice and zest (reserving a little zest for garnishing) over a medium heat, stirring until the sugar dissolves. Increase the heat and cook for 2–3 minutes, until the sauce reduces slightly and begins to look glossy.

3 Add the bananas to the pan and cook for a further 2–3 minutes over a high heat, until the sauce reduces further. Meanwhile, toast the brioche. If desired, cut the bread into 7cm (2¾in) rounds.

4 When the bananas are just tender, add the pecans and the rum and cook for 1 minute to heat it up, then use a match to carefully light the alcohol. The pan will flare up, so be careful, but the flames should die away within 1 minute.

5 Top each brioche round with a scoop of ice cream, pour over a quarter of the caramelized bananas, and garnish with the reserved orange zest. Serve immediately.

★★★
WHAT'S THE STORY?
Bananas Foster – a dessert flambéed with rum and served with ice cream and caramel sauce – was first made at Brennan's restaurant in New Orleans in 1951. At the time, the city was the main port of entry for imported bananas, and the dish was created in honour of regular diner and good friend of the restaurant's owner, Richard Foster.
★★★

CHOCOLATE BREAD PUDDING

A few storecupboard essentials can turn stale bread into this simple yet delicious dessert.

★ **SERVES** 8

★ **PREP TIME** 15 mins

★ **COOK TIME** 35 mins, plus soaking

Ingredients

1 day-old baguette

250g (9oz) plain or dark chocolate chips

4 eggs

1 tsp vanilla extract

500ml (16fl oz) whole milk

110g (3¾oz) light soft brown sugar

vanilla ice cream or whipped cream, to serve

1 Preheat the oven to 180°C (350°F/Gas 4). Remove the ends of the baguette and cut the bread into 1cm (½in) thick slices. Put one layer of bread in a flameproof casserole and sprinkle over some chocolate chips. Add more layers of bread, sprinkling chocolate chips between the layers as you go. Top with the remaining chips.

2 In a bowl, mix the eggs, vanilla extract, milk, and sugar. Pour the mixture over the bread and leave to soak for 10–15 minutes.

3 Put the casserole in the oven and bake for about 35 minutes, or until the liquid is absorbed and the bread is crisp. Slice and serve with vanilla ice cream or whipped cream.

Baguette, when fresh, is delicious just as it is, but leave it for a day before using in this dish.

POUND CAKE BANANA PUDDING

This Southern version of an English trifle often uses cookies or wafers. Here, home-made pound cake makes a far tastier version.

★ **SERVES** 8-10

★ **PREP TIME** 30 mins

★ **COOK TIME** 10 mins, plus chilling

Ingredients

1 pound cake (see p219)
6 ripe bananas, cut into
   5mm (¼in) slices

For the pudding

500ml (16fl oz) whole milk
4 tbsp cornflour
100g (3½oz) caster sugar
1 tbsp butter
1 tsp vanilla extract

For the whipped cream

500ml (16fl oz) double cream
2 tbsp caster sugar
1 tsp vanilla extract

1 Preheat the oven to 190°C (375°F/Gas 5). First, make the pudding. In a saucepan, bring the milk almost to the boil over a high heat, then reduce the heat to a simmer. Stir in the cornflour and sugar, and whisk continuously until thickened. Remove from the heat and add the butter and vanilla. Chill.

2 Cut the pound cake into 1cm (½in) thick slices and toast them on a baking tray in the oven for 10 minutes, or until both sides are well toasted. Place half the cake slices in a single layer at the bottom of a 23 x 33cm (9 x 13in) cake pan. Top with half the banana slices.

3 Pour the pudding over the first layer evenly. Add the second layer of cake and top with the remaining bananas.

4 In a large bowl, whisk the cream, sugar, and vanilla extract with an electric hand whisk until stiff. Using a spatula, spread it over the bananas. Chill for 45 minutes to 1 hour before serving.

STRAWBERRY SHORTCAKE

This classic summer dessert is best served with freshly baked shortcake and ripe, juicy strawberries.

★ **MAKES** 12
★ **PREP TIME** 20 mins
★ **COOK TIME** 35 mins

Ingredients

225g (8oz) plain flour
75g (2½oz) fine polenta
    or cornmeal
1 tbsp baking powder
¼ tsp salt
50g (1¾oz) caster sugar
115g (4oz) butter, chilled
    and diced, plus extra
    for greasing
125ml (4½fl oz) whole milk
125ml (4½fl oz) buttermilk
    (or to make your own,
    see p12)
2 tsp vanilla extract

For the filling

15–20 large strawberries,
    hulled and halved
1 tbsp runny honey
250ml (9fl oz)
    whipping cream
30g (1oz) caster sugar

1 Preheat the oven to 180°C (350°F/Gas 4). In a medium bowl, mix together the flour, polenta, baking powder, salt, and sugar. Add the butter to the flour mixture and work it into the dry ingredients with your hands, incorporating well, until the mixture resembles coarse breadcrumbs. Stir the milk, buttermilk, and 1 tsp vanilla extract into the dry ingredients and mix well.

2 Grease the base and sides of a 12-hole muffin tin. Pour in the batter and bake in the oven for 35 minutes, or until golden brown. Remove and leave to cool slightly on a wire rack.

3 For the filling, put the strawberries into a bowl, add the honey, and toss until well coated. Using an electric hand whisk or mixer, whisk the cream, sugar, and the remaining vanilla extract until stiff.

4 Slice the shortcakes in half and fill each with whipped cream and strawberries. Serve warm.

NOW TRY...

FRESH BASIL

For a refreshing twist, toss the
strawberries with honey and
a handful of torn fresh **basil**.

MANGO & LIME

Make a tropical shortcake by substituting
the strawberries with 1 large diced
mango, tossed in the juice of 1 **lime**.

BERRIES & CREAM

Bake the shortcake batter in a greased
23cm (9in) round cake tin. Turn out the
shortcake onto a large plate and top with
300g (10oz) **mixed berries**, 1 tbsp runny
honey, and 200ml (7fl oz) **whipping cream**.

CHOCOLATE-CRUSTED KEY LIME PIE

This pie takes its name from the small limes that grow in the Florida Keys, where the recipe originated.

- ★ **SERVES** 6-8
- ★ **PREP TIME** 20 mins
- ★ **COOK TIME** 15-20 mins, plus cooling

Ingredients

250g (9oz) chocolate digestive biscuits

60g (2oz) caster sugar

125g (4½oz) unsalted butter, melted and cooled

5 limes

3 large egg yolks

400g can condensed milk

cream, to serve

1 Preheat the oven to 180°C (350°F/Gas 4). Crush the digestive biscuits in a plastic food bag with a rolling pin, or use a food processor. Mix the biscuit crumbs and sugar with the butter in a large bowl until it resembles wet sand.

2 Pour the biscuit mixture into a 23cm (9in) loose-bottomed tart tin and press it firmly into the bottom and sides of the tin. Make sure the filling is packed as firmly as possible, and that there is a good side to the case so that the filling can be contained, unlike a cheesecake base. Place the tart case on a baking tray and bake for 10 minutes. Set aside to cool.

3 Meanwhile, finely grate the zest of 3 limes into a bowl and, if you like, use a zester to pare long strands of zest from a fourth lime to decorate. Juice all 5 limes and set aside.

4 Place the egg yolks into the bowl with the lime zest, and whisk with an electric whisk until the egg has thickened. Pour in the condensed milk and continue whisking for another 5 minutes. Add the lime juice and whisk again until it is incorporated. Pour the mixture into the tin and bake for 15–20 minutes, or until set but still wobbly in the centre.

5 Remove the pie from the oven and leave it to cool completely. Serve the pie decorated with the fine strands of lime zest, if using, and accompanied by cream.

COOK'S TIP A common baking mistake with deep-filled sweet tarts is to overcook them. Remove them from the oven when they still have a slight wobble to them at the centre. They will cool and set to an unctuous, creamy texture. Overcooking will result in a tart with an unpleasantly "rubbery" texture.

Key limes have a distinct fragrance that sets them apart from their larger cousins, Persian limes.

PECAN, MAPLE, AND BOURBON PIE

This sweet, crunchy pie originated in the South, where pecan nuts are widely grown.

★ **SERVES** 6-8

★ **PREP TIME** 20 mins, plus chilling

★ **COOK TIME** 1 hr 20 mins, plus cooling

Ingredients

150g (5½oz) plain flour, plus extra for dusting

100g (3½oz) unsalted butter, chilled and diced

50g (1¾oz) caster sugar

1 egg yolk

½ tsp vanilla extract

crème fraîche or whipped cream, to serve (optional)

For the filling

150ml (5fl oz) maple syrup

60g (2oz) butter

175g (6oz) light soft brown sugar

few drops of vanilla extract

pinch of salt

3 eggs

2 tbsp bourbon

200g (7oz) pecan nuts

1 Using your fingertips, rub together the flour and butter, or pulse in a food processor until the mixture forms fine crumbs. Stir in the sugar. Beat the egg yolk with the vanilla and mix them into the dry ingredients, bringing the mixture together to form a soft dough. Add a little water to bring the dough together, if needed. Wrap in cling film and chill for 1 hour. Preheat the oven to 180°C (350°F/Gas 4).

2 Roll out the pastry on a well-floured surface to 3mm (⅛in) thick. It will be fragile, so if it begins to crumble, bring it together again with your hands and gently knead to get rid of any joins. Use it to line a 23cm (9in) loose-bottomed tart tin, leaving an overlapping edge of at least 2cm (¾in). Prick the base all over with a fork.

3 Line the pastry case with baking parchment and weigh it down with baking beans. Place the case on a baking sheet and blind bake for 20 minutes. Remove the beans and paper, and bake for a further 5 minutes if the centre still looks a little uncooked.

4 For the filling, pour the maple syrup into a saucepan, and add the butter, sugar, vanilla extract, and salt. Place the pan over a low heat, and stir constantly until the butter has melted and the sugar dissolved. Remove the pan from the heat and leave the mixture to cool until it feels just tepid, then beat in the eggs, one at a time, along with the bourbon. Stir in the pecan nuts, reserving enough for the top, then pour the mixture into the pastry case. Arrange the reserved pecan nuts evenly across the top, pushing them in slightly.

5 Bake for 40–50 minutes, or until just set. Cover with a sheet of foil if it is browning too quickly. Remove the pie from the oven, transfer to a wire rack, and leave to cool for 15–20 minutes. Remove from the tin and either serve it warm or leave it on the wire rack to cool completely. Serve with crème fraîche or whipped cream, if desired.

BOSTON CREAM TRIFLE

This rich trifle draws inspiration from the traditional Boston cream pie, with its luscious layers of sponge and creamy custard.

- ★ **SERVES** 10
- ★ **PREP TIME** 45 mins, plus cooling and chilling
- ★ **COOK TIME** 45 mins, plus cooling

Ingredients

225g (8oz) plain flour
2 tsp baking powder
pinch of salt
115g (4oz) butter, softened, plus extra for greasing
175g (6oz) caster sugar
2 eggs, at room temperature
1 tsp vanilla extract
120ml (4fl oz) milk
600g (1lb 5oz) berries, such as blackberries, strawberries (hulled and halved), raspberries, and blueberries

For the custard

250ml (9fl oz) milk
250ml (9fl oz) double cream
1 vanilla pod, split and seeds scraped
3 egg yolks
2 tbsp cornflour
75g (2½oz) caster sugar
pinch of salt
1 tbsp unsalted butter, softened
1 tsp vanilla extract

For the ganache

350g (12oz) plain or dark chocolate, broken into small pieces
250ml (9fl oz) double cream

1 For the custard, heat the milk, cream, and vanilla pod in a saucepan over a medium heat. Bring it to a simmer and remove from the heat immediately.

2 In a medium bowl, whisk together the yolks, cornflour, caster sugar, and salt. Gradually add the hot milk mixture, whisking constantly. Transfer to a clean saucepan and cook over a low heat, stirring constantly, until the custard is thick enough to coat the back of a spoon. Sieve the custard into a bowl to remove the vanilla pod and any lumps. Stir in the butter and vanilla extract. Place a sheet of cling film over the bowl, making sure it touches the top of the custard, and chill.

3 Preheat the oven to 180°C (350°F/Gas 4). Double sift the flour, baking powder, and salt into a bowl and set aside. Using an electric hand whisk, cream together the butter and sugar in a separate bowl until light and fluffy. Add the eggs, one at a time, whisking between additions, then add the vanilla extract. Fold in the flour mixture using a large metal spoon, one-third at a time, alternating with the milk. Continue to fold until the batter is smooth and everything is well incorporated.

4 Grease and line a 23cm (9in) square cake tin and pour the batter into the pan, making sure it spreads evenly. Bake for 25 minutes, or until golden brown and springy to the touch. Remove from the oven and let it cool.

5 For the ganache, heat the chocolate and cream in a small heatproof bowl over a saucepan of simmering water (see technique for melting chocolate on p238). The bowl should not touch the water. Stir occasionally until the chocolate melts. Remove from the heat and set aside.

6 Slice the cake into 12 x 12cm (5 x 5in) squares and place a layer of cake at the bottom of a tall glass bowl. Spread the berries evenly on top of the cake, reserving a handful for garnishing. Pour the custard evenly over the berries, then top with the remaining cake slices. Pour the ganache over the top and smooth it out. Top with the reserved berries and place in the fridge to chill. Serve chilled.

LEMON AND GRAPEFRUIT MERINGUE PIE

An all-time classic dessert, the addition of grapefruit to the more usual lemon juice enhances the sweet and sour flavour.

★ **SERVES** 12

★ **PREP TIME** 25 mins, plus chilling

★ **COOK TIME** 1 hr

For the pastry
150g (5½oz) plain flour
2 tbsp caster sugar
pinch of salt
6 tbsp butter, chilled and cut into cubes
1 tbsp vegetable shortening

For the filling
juice of 2 large lemons
juice of 1 small grapefruit
175g (6oz) caster sugar
60g (2oz) cornflour
5 egg yolks
1 tsp vanilla extract

For the meringue
6 egg whites
3 tbsp caster sugar
¼ tsp vanilla extract
1 tsp cream of tartar

1 For the pastry, sift the flour, sugar, and salt into a medium bowl and mix well to combine. Rub the butter and shortening into the flour mixture with your fingertips until it resembles breadcrumbs. Stir in 60ml (2fl oz) of cold water and mix until a rough ball forms. Wrap in cling film and chill for 1 hour.

2 Preheat the oven to 180°C (350°F/Gas 4). Roll the pastry out on a floured work surface to fit the base of a lined 23cm (9in) square baking tin, gently pushing it into the edges to form a flat square. Bake for 30 minutes, or until golden brown. Remove from the oven and increase the temperature to 190°C (375°F/Gas 5).

3 To make the filling, combine 450ml (15fl oz) of water, the lemon and grapefruit juice, sugar, and cornflour in a saucepan over a medium heat. Whisk for 2–3 minutes, until thickened. Put the egg yolks in a large bowl.

4 Spoon the lemon and grapefruit mixture into the egg yolks, a little at a time, stirring well to incorporate. Return the filling to the pan and cook over a medium heat for a further 5 minutes. Remove from the heat and add the vanilla extract. Stir in more lemon juice to taste, if necessary. Spread the filling evenly over the pie crust.

5 For the meringue, whisk the egg whites, sugar, vanilla extract, and cream of tartar with an electric hand whisk on high speed until stiff peaks form.

6 Use a pastry knife or large spoon to spread the meringue over the filling. Bake for 20 minutes, or until golden brown. Allow to cool completely before serving.

Grapefruit, an often overlooked citrus fruit, adds a complexity of flavour to lemon and lime dishes.

MERINGUE-TOPPED SWEET POTATO PIE

Another classic and a close relative of the pumpkin pie, here a rich, sweet shortcrust is used for a truly crisp crust.

★ **SERVES** 6
★ **PREP TIME** 15 mins, plus chilling
★ **COOK TIME** 1½ hours

Ingredients

150g (5½oz) plain flour, plus extra for dusting
100g (3½oz) unsalted butter
50g (1¾oz) caster sugar
1 egg yolk
½ tsp vanilla extract

For the filling

400g (14oz) sweet potato, peeled and chopped into small chunks
85g (3oz) unsalted butter
100g (3½oz) muscovado sugar
3 tbsp single cream
1 egg
½ tsp ground nutmeg
½ tsp ground cinnamon
icing sugar, for dusting

For the meringue

3 egg whites, at room temperature
85g (3oz) caster sugar
1 tsp cornflour

1 For the pastry, rub the flour and butter together in a bowl with your fingertips until the mixture resembles fine breadcrumbs. Stir in the sugar. Add the egg yolk and vanilla extract to the flour mixture and bring together to form a smooth dough, adding 1–2 teaspoons cold water, if needed. Wrap in cling film and chill in the refrigerator for 30 minutes.

2 For the filling, cook the sweet potato chunks in a saucepan of boiling water for 10–15 minutes, or until tender. Drain, return to the pan, and mash. Stir in the butter, sugar, cream, egg, and spices. Beat well to combine, then set aside.

3 Preheat the oven to 180°C (350°F/Gas 4). Roll out the pastry on a floured surface to a round large enough to line a 20cm (8in) loose-bottomed tart tin. Place the pastry in the tin, pressing down well into the bottom and around the edges. Trim off any excess pastry, prick the bottom with a fork, and line with baking parchment. Place the tin on a baking tray and fill with baking beans. Bake for 20 minutes. Remove the beans and paper and bake for a further 5 minutes if the centre is uncooked.

4 Spoon the filling into the pastry case and level with the back of a spoon. Bake for 35–45 minutes, or until the filling is set. Just before the filling is set, whisk the egg whites to stiff peaks. Whisk in the sugar and cornflour.

5 Remove the pie from the oven and spread the meringue over the top, making sure it is attached to the pastry on all sides (this will keep it from shrinking). Return the pie to the oven and cook for a further 10–15 minutes until the meringue is golden. Sprinkle with icing sugar before serving.

APPLE PIE

Thinly slicing the apples in this classic American pie gives the filling a soft, melting texture.

★ **SERVES** 6-8

★ **PREP TIME** 25 mins, plus chilling

★ **COOK TIME** 1 hr

Ingredients

350g (12oz) plain flour
50g (1¾oz) caster sugar
200g (7oz) unsalted butter, chilled

For the filling

400g (14oz) Granny Smith (or other tart apples), peeled and cored weight
400g (14oz) Royal Gala (or other sweet apples), peeled and cored weight
2 tbsp lemon juice
3 tbsp plain flour
4 tbsp caster sugar
4 tbsp light soft brown sugar
1 tsp ground cinnamon
1 egg, beaten with 1 tbsp cold water, for glazing

Granny Smiths are great for baking as they keep their texture once cooked.

1 In a food processor or by hand, mix together the flour, sugar, and butter until the mixture resembles fine breadcrumbs. Add 5–6 tbsp of iced water and bring it together to form a soft dough. Wrap the pastry in cling film and chill for 1 hour before using.

2 Preheat the oven to 190°C (375°F/Gas 5). Remove the pastry from the fridge, cut off one-third, then rewrap the smaller piece and return it to the fridge.

3 On a floured work surface, roll out the larger piece of pastry into a disk large enough to line a 24cm (9½in) pie dish. Lightly press the pastry into the dish and trim off any excess with a pair of scissors, allowing a 1cm (½in) overhang all around. Place in the fridge.

4 Cut the apples into 5mm (¼in) slices and mix with the lemon juice in a large bowl until well combined. Sprinkle the flour, 3 tbsp of caster sugar, the brown sugar, and the cinnamon over the apples and toss them together so that all the pieces are coated in the mixture.

5 Pack the apples into the pie case, mounding the fruit slightly higher in the middle and ensuring it is well pressed down. Roll the reserved pastry into a disk large enough to cover the pie. Brush the edges of the pastry with a little egg wash, place the pastry lid on top, and use your fingers to crimp the pastry together. Trim off any excess pastry with a small, sharp knife. Brush the top with egg wash, sprinkle with the remaining caster sugar, and cut 2 small slits in the top.

6 Bake in the oven for 1 hour. (If using a ceramic or glass pie dish, place on a metal baking tray to ensure the pastry bottom cooks thoroughly, extending the cooking time if necessary.) If the crust browns too early, cover it with foil, but remove it 5 minutes before the end of the cooking time to allow the top to remain crisp. Remove from the oven and leave to cool. Serve with vanilla ice cream or whipped cream.

NOW TRY...

GRUYÈRE & PEAR

Finely grate 50g (1¾oz) **Gruyère cheese** into the pastry at step 1 and use 800g (1¾lb) **Conference pears** instead of the apples.

STREUSEL TOPPING

Replace the pastry lid with a mixture of 25g (scant 1oz) each of **light soft brown sugar**, **plain flour**, and **butter**, mixed to fine breadcrumbs with 60g (2oz) finely chopped **pecans** and 1 tsp **cinnamon**.

SALTED CARAMEL

This sauce complements the pie perfectly. Gently heat a small jar of shop-bought **caramel sauce** (to make your own, see p194) in a small, heavy-based saucepan, then whisk in 3-4 tbsp **double cream** and a pinch of **sea salt flakes**.

PECAN AND MAPLE PUMPKIN PIE

This version of the classic dessert produces a delicate, just-set pie, gently flavoured with cinnamon and mixed spice.

★ **SERVES** 6-8

★ **PREP TIME** 30 mins, plus chilling

★ **COOK TIME** 1–1¼ hrs, plus cooling

Ingredients

150g (5½oz) plain flour, plus extra for dusting

100g (3½oz) unsalted butter, chilled and diced

50g (1¾oz) caster sugar

1 egg yolk

½ tsp vanilla extract

For the filling

75g (2½oz) pecan nuts, roughly chopped

3 eggs

100g (3½oz) light soft brown sugar

2 tsp ground cinnamon

1 tsp mixed spice

4 tbsp maple syrup

400ml (14fl oz) double cream

400g can processed pumpkin, or 400g (14oz) roasted and puréed pumpkin

1 To make the pastry, rub the flour and butter together in a large bowl with your fingertips until the mixture resembles breadcrumbs. Stir in the sugar. In a separate bowl, beat together the egg yolk and vanilla extract, then add to the flour mixture and bring the mixture together to form a soft dough, adding a little water if needed. Wrap in cling film and chill for 30 minutes.

2 Preheat the oven to 180°C (350°F/Gas 4). On a lightly floured surface, roll out the pastry to a thickness of 3mm (⅛in) and use it to line a 23cm (9in) loose-bottomed tart tin, leaving an overlapping edge of at least 2cm (¾in). Prick the bottom with a fork, line with baking parchment, and fill with baking beans.

3 Place the tin on a baking tray and bake for 20 minutes. Remove the beans and parchment, and bake for a further 5 minutes if the centre is uncooked. Sprinkle the pecan nuts over the bottom of the pastry case.

4 For the filling, whisk the eggs, brown sugar, half the cinnamon, the mixed spice, half the maple syrup, and half the cream together in a large bowl. When they are well blended, beat in the pumpkin to make a smooth filling. Partially pull out an oven rack from the oven and place the tin on it. Pour the filling into the case and slide the rack back into the oven.

5 Bake for 45–50 minutes until the filling is quite set, but before it begins to bubble up at the edges. Trim off the pastry edge while still warm, then set the pie aside to cool in its tin for 15 minutes before turning out.

6 Lightly whip the remaining cream until soft peaks start to form, stir in the remaining ground cinnamon and maple syrup, and serve with the pie.

COOK'S TIP The pie will keep for up to 2 days, chilled in an airtight container.

LATTICE-TOPPED CHERRY PIE

The juice from the fruit is thickened with flour to help bring the filling together in this hugely popular pie.

★ **SERVES** 8

★ **PREP TIME** 40-45 mins, plus chilling

★ **COOK TIME** 20-25 mins

Ingredients

250g (9oz) plain flour, plus extra for dusting

½ tsp salt

125g (4½oz) lard or white vegetable fat, chilled and diced

75g (2½oz) unsalted butter, chilled and diced

For the filling and glaze

500g (1lb 2oz) cherries, stoned (see technique, p242)

200g (7oz) caster sugar, plus 1 tbsp for sprinkling

45g (1½oz) plain flour

¼ tsp almond extract (optional)

1 egg, beaten

1 Sift together the flour and salt into a bowl. Rub the lard and butter into the flour with your fingertips until crumbs begin to form. Sprinkle with 3 tbsp of water and blend until the dough turns into a ball. Wrap in cling film and chill for 30 minutes.

2 Preheat the oven to 200°C (400°F/Gas 6) and put in a baking sheet. On a floured surface, roll out two-thirds of the dough to a thickness of 3mm (⅛in) and use it to line a 23cm (9in) pie dish, leaving an overhang of at least 2cm (¾in). Press the dough into the dish and chill for 15 minutes.

3 For the filling, put the cherries in a bowl and add the sugar, flour, and almond extract (if using). Mix well, then spoon into the case.

4 Roll out the remaining dough into a rectangle. Cut out 12 strips, each 1cm (½in) wide, and arrange them in a lattice-like pattern on top of the pie; trim the pastry. Use the beaten egg to glaze the lattice and secure the strips to the edge of the pie. Sprinkle the sugar over the top, place on the baking sheet, and bake for 20–25 minutes until the pastry is golden brown. Serve at room temperature or chilled.

PEACH COBBLER

Gently poaching firmer peaches helps to break them down so that they cook more evenly.

- ★ **SERVES** 6-8
- ★ **PREP TIME** 25 mins
- ★ **COOK TIME** 30-35 mins

Ingredients

50g (1¾oz) caster sugar
8 ripe peaches, peeled,
   stoned, and quartered
1 tsp cornflour
juice of ½ lemon

For the topping

225g (8oz) self-raising flour
2 tsp baking powder
75g (2½oz) caster sugar
pinch of salt
½-¾ tsp ground cinnamon,
   to taste
75g (2½oz) unsalted butter
1 egg
100ml (3½fl oz) buttermilk
   (or to make your own,
   see p12)
1 tbsp light soft
   brown sugar
ice cream, custard,
   or cream, to serve

1 Preheat the oven to 190°C (375°F/Gas 5). For the filling, heat the sugar and 3–4 tbsp of water in a large, wide, heavy-based saucepan. Once the sugar has dissolved, add the quartered peaches, cover, and cook over a medium heat for 2–3 minutes.

2 In a small bowl, mix the cornflour with the lemon juice to make a paste, then add it to the peaches. Continue to cook uncovered over a low heat until the liquid thickens around the peaches. Transfer the peaches and syrup to a shallow ovenproof dish.

3 To make the topping, sift the flour, baking powder, sugar, salt, and cinnamon into a large bowl. Rub in the butter with your fingertips until the mixture resembles fine breadcrumbs. Whisk together the egg and buttermilk in a separate bowl. Add the liquid to the dry ingredients and bring together to form a soft, sticky dough.

4 Drop heaped tablespoons of the dough over the surface of the fruit, leaving a little space between them. Sprinkle with the sugar. Bake for 25–30 minutes until golden and bubbling. It is ready when a skewer inserted into the centre of the topping comes out clean. Set aside to cool for 5 minutes before serving with ice cream, custard, or cream.

Peaches, cooked when just ripe, make their own thick, sweet sauce in this cobbler.

NOW TRY...

APPLE & BLACKBERRY

For an autumnal twist, replace the peaches with 1kg (2¼lb) **apples**, peeled, cored, and roughly chopped, along with 250g (9oz) **blackberries** to step 1 and cook as per the main recipe but bake for 40–45 minutes.

QUICK SPICED PLUM

Toss 1kg (2¼lb) **plums**, stoned and halved, in 60g (2oz) light soft brown sugar along with 1 tsp cinnamon, ¼ tsp **nutmeg** and ¼ tsp **allspice**. Place straight in the ovenproof dish and skip to step 3.

PEACH & BLUEBERRY

For a Southern twist, add 150g (5½oz) **blueberries** to 6 prepared **peaches**. For the topping, replace 75g (2½oz) of the self-raising flour with an equal quantity of **fine polenta or cornmeal** and cook as usual.

PINEAPPLE UPSIDE-DOWN CAKES WITH BASIL CREAM

This classic dessert gets a gourmet makeover with the addition of a light, creamy sauce laced with basil.

★ **MAKES** 4
★ **PREP TIME** 20 mins
★ **COOK TIME** 40 mins

Ingredients
50g (1¾oz) unsalted butter,
    plus extra for greasing
100g (3½oz) light soft
    brown sugar

For the cakes
432g can pineapple chunks
    in natural juice
75g (2½oz) unsalted butter,
    softened
100g (3½oz) caster sugar
2 eggs
½ tsp vanilla extract
150g (5½oz) self-raising flour

**For the pineapple and
basil cream**
200ml (7fl oz) juice from
    the canned pineapple
100ml (3½fl oz) double cream
1 tsp finely chopped basil
1 tsp lime juice

1 Melt the butter in a small, heavy-based saucepan over a medium heat. Add the brown sugar and cook for 2–3 minutes, stirring constantly, until dissolved. Divide the mixture between 4 large greased ramekins.

2 Drain the pineapple and reserve the liquid. Take 125g (4½oz) of the pineapple and reserve the rest for another time. If the chunks are large, dice them first and then divide between the ramekins.

3 Preheat the oven to 180°C (350°F/Gas 4). Using an electric hand whisk, cream the butter and caster sugar together in a bowl until light and fluffy. Beat in the eggs and vanilla extract until well combined. Sift in the flour and gently fold it in. Distribute the mixture evenly between the ramekins.

4 Place the ramekins on a baking tray and bake in the centre of the oven for 25–30 minutes, until well risen and golden brown, and a cocktail stick inserted into the centre comes out clean.

5 Meanwhile, pour the reserved pineapple juice into a small, heavy-based saucepan and bring to the boil. Cook for about 5 minutes, until it has reduced to 100ml (3½fl oz). Add half the cream and continue to reduce for a further 5–7 minutes, until you have only 50ml (1¾fl oz) left. Remove from the heat and chill until needed.

6 Remove the cakes from the oven and allow them to cool in the ramekins before turning them out onto serving plates. Leave the ramekins over the cakes for 2–3 minutes to ensure that all the syrup drips down into the cake.

7 When you are ready to serve (they should be warm, but not too hot), mix the remaining cream into the chilled pineapple cream. Add the chopped basil and lime juice, and whisk together until thick. Serve alongside the warm cakes.

COOK'S TIP If the cakes have risen to a peak, cut off a little from the top to give a flatter finish to the cakes. This will enable them to stand up properly when turned out.

BLUEBERRY RIPPLE CHEESECAKE

The marbled effect on this cheesecake is simple to achieve and always looks impressive.

- ★ **SERVES** 8
- ★ **PREP TIME** 20 mins
- ★ **COOK TIME** 40 mins, plus cooling

Ingredients

50g (1¾oz) unsalted butter, plus extra for greasing
125g (4½oz) digestive biscuits
150g (5½oz) blueberries
150g (5½oz) caster sugar, plus 3 tbsp
400g (14oz) cream cheese
250g (9oz) mascarpone
2 large eggs, plus 1 large egg yolk
½ tsp vanilla extract
2 tbsp plain flour, sifted

For the compote

100g (3½oz) blueberries
1 tbsp caster sugar
squeeze of lemon

1 Preheat the oven to 180°C (350°F/Gas 4). Grease the base and sides of a 20cm (8in) round deep springform cake tin. Put the biscuits into a plastic food bag and crush with a rolling pin until they turn into fine crumbs.

2 Melt the butter in a saucepan set over a low heat; it should not begin to turn brown. Add the crumbs to the pan and stir until they are coated in butter. Remove from the heat. Press the crumbs into the base of the tin, pushing them down with the back of a spoon.

3 Put the blueberries and 3 tbsp sugar in a food processor, and process until smooth. Push the mixture through a nylon sieve (metal will taint it) into a small saucepan. Bring to the boil, then simmer for 3–5 minutes, or until thickened and jammy. Set aside.

4 Place the remaining sugar and the next 5 ingredients for the cheese mix in the processor. Process the cream cheese mixture until smooth and very well combined. Pour the mixture onto the biscuit base and smooth the top with a palette knife. Drizzle over the berry jam and make swirls by drawing a metal skewer through the mix.

5 Boil a kettle of water. Wrap the sides of the cake tin with tin foil and place in a deep roasting tray. Pour hot water into the tray, to come halfway up the cake tin; this prevents the mixture from cracking.

6 Bake for 40 minutes until set but still a bit wobbly. Turn off the oven and wedge open the door. After 1 hour, remove the cake from the oven and place on a wire rack. Remove the sides of the tin. Slide 1 or 2 fish slices between the biscuit base and the base of the tin. Transfer the cheesecake to a serving plate or cake stand, and leave to cool completely.

7 Meanwhile, put all the ingredients for the compote in a small pan. Heat gently, stirring occasionally, until all the sugar dissolves. Transfer the compote to a jug to serve.

COOK'S TIP The compote can be made 3 days in advance and chilled until needed.

PEANUT BUTTER ICE CREAM SANDWICHES

Soft, rich chocolate cookies, salty peanut butter, and creamy vanilla ice cream – the perfect trio for the ultimate treat.

★ **MAKES** 4

★ **PREP TIME** 20 mins

★ **COOK TIME** 10 mins, plus cooling and freezing

Ingredients

50g (1¾oz) solid plain or dark chocolate (70 per cent cocoa)

50g (1¾oz) unsalted butter

75g (2½oz) caster sugar

75g (2½oz) light soft brown sugar

1 egg

1 tbsp whole milk

1 tsp vanilla extract

125g (4½oz) plain flour

4 tbsp crunchy peanut butter

4 scoops of good-quality vanilla ice cream (see p194)

1 Preheat the oven to 180°C (350°F/Gas 4). Place the chocolate and butter in a heatproof bowl over a saucepan of simmering water, making sure the bowl does not touch the water (see technique for melting chocolate on p238). Stir constantly and remove the bowl from the heat as soon as the chocolate has melted. Set aside to cool.

2 When the chocolate mixture has cooled, beat in the sugars, egg, milk, and vanilla extract. Sift in the flour and fold to combine. Place large tablespoons of the batter, spaced well apart, on 2 baking trays lined with baking parchment to make 8 large cookies. Bake in the centre of the oven for 10 minutes, until just crispy at the edges but still soft in the middle. The cookies will firm up further as they cool.

3 Leave the cookies to cool on the baking trays for 5 minutes before transferring them to a wire rack to cool completely, then put them in the freezer for 10 minutes before serving.

4 To serve, spread the flat half of a cookie with a tablespoonful of the peanut butter. Spread the flat half of another (try to match up the sizes of the pairs of cookies) with a scoop of the vanilla ice cream, sandwich together, and serve immediately.

COOK'S TIP For an even richer cookie, add a handful of white or dark chocolate chips to the mixture before baking. You can even experiment with different ice cream flavours for the filling.

Vanilla ice cream is delicious served alone or as a cold, creamy contrast to a warm dessert.

CARAMEL AND CHOCOLATE CRUNCH SUNDAE

A topping of salted caramel sauce and crunchy chocolate pretzels take this home-made vanilla ice cream to another level.

★ **SERVES** 4

★ **PREP TIME** 15 mins, plus chilling and churning

★ **COOK TIME** 20 mins

Ingredients

250ml (9fl oz) whipping cream
450ml (15fl oz) whole milk
6 egg yolks
125g (4½oz) caster sugar
1 tsp vanilla extract
chocolate-covered pretzels
(see p238)

For the salted caramel sauce

200g (7oz) caster sugar
115g (4oz) butter, diced
120ml (4fl oz) double cream
1 tsp vanilla extract
1 tsp sea salt

1 Heat the cream and milk in a heavy-based saucepan over a medium heat, until hot but not boiling. In a separate bowl, whisk together the egg yolks, sugar, and vanilla extract. Very gradually whisk the hot cream and milk into the egg mixture in a thin stream, whisking constantly.

2 Return the custard to the rinsed-out pan and heat over a medium heat, whisking constantly, until it thickens and just coats the back of a spoon. Do not heat it too fast or for too long, or the eggs will "scramble". Remove the custard from the heat and transfer to a clean, cold bowl immediately, whisking for a couple of minutes to cool it down.

3 Cool the custard completely, then cover the surface with a layer of cling film (placing it directly on the custard) to prevent a skin forming. Transfer to the fridge and chill for a minimum of 4 hours, or overnight.

4 Pour the chilled custard into an ice-cream maker and churn it until it is a thick, scoopable ice cream. Transfer it to a plastic container and freeze until needed.

5 To prepare the salted caramel sauce, melt the sugar in a heavy-based frying pan over a medium heat. As it melts, whisk frequently for 7–10 minutes, until it becomes amber brown. Add the butter and whisk to combine.

6 Remove from the heat and add the cream. Continue whisking as the caramel bubbles, until it settles into a smooth mixture. Whisk in the vanilla extract and sea salt. Set aside to cool completely.

7 To serve, roughly crush some chocolate-covered pretzels from p238 in a plastic food bag and scatter over the ice cream. Finish with a drizzle of the salted caramel sauce.

COOK'S TIP For a healthier version, try using a spoonful of the Fresh berry compote with vanilla and thyme from p242 or the dried fruit compote from p60, and top with a handful of fresh blueberries, for some added texture.

APPLE DUMPLINGS WITH VANILLA ICE CREAM

Simple to make, these individual apple dumplings look amazing on a plate. Serve with shop-bought ice cream if time is short.

★ **MAKES** 4

★ **PREP TIME** 25 mins, plus chilling

★ **COOK TIME** 45 mins

Ingredients

4 Golden Delicious apples, peeled and cored

4 tbsp butter

1 tsp ground cinnamon, plus extra for coating

1 egg, beaten

2 tbsp light soft brown sugar

For the pastry

375g (13oz) plain flour, plus extra for dusting

1 tsp salt

3 tbsp caster sugar

175g (6oz) butter, chilled and cut into cubes

60g (2oz) vegetable shortening

For the ice cream

250ml (9fl oz) whole milk

250ml (9fl oz) double cream

1 vanilla pod, split

4 egg yolks

100g (3½oz) light soft brown sugar

1 tsp ground cinnamon

1 First, make the ice cream. In a saucepan, whisk together the milk and cream, and add the vanilla pod. Let it simmer for 20 minutes on a low heat. Remove from the heat and discard the vanilla pod.

2 In a separate saucepan, whisk together the egg yolks, sugar, and cinnamon. Spoon the cream mixture into the eggs, a little at a time, and whisk until well combined. Simmer on a low heat for 10–12 minutes, or until thickened. Transfer to a bowl, cover, and chill for 1 hour, or until thoroughly chilled.

3 To make the pastry, combine the flour, salt, and sugar in a bowl. Rub the butter and shortening into the flour mixture with your fingertips until it resembles breadcrumbs. Stir in 60ml (2fl oz) of cold water to form a soft dough. Wrap in cling film and chill for 1 hour.

4 Pour the cream mixture into an ice-cream maker and churn it for 20–30 minutes, depending on the machine, or until creamy and firm. Transfer it to an airtight container and freeze for at least 30 minutes.

5 Preheat the oven to 160°C (325°F/Gas 3). Divide the dough into 4 equal pieces. Roll them out on a floured work surface to form 15cm (6in) rounds. Wrap each disk around an apple. Fill each apple core with a tbsp of butter and ¼ tsp of cinnamon, and pinch the dough closed around the apple. Transfer the apples to a 23cm (9in) square baking tray.

6 Brush each apple with the egg and sprinkle over the brown sugar and a little cinnamon. Bake for 45 minutes, or until the pastry is golden and the apple has softened. Serve each apple hot with a scoop of ice cream and a drizzle of Salted caramel sauce (see p194).

SPICED APPLE AND PEAR CRISP

Give a simple apple crisp an autumnal twist with juicy pears and gentle spicing.

★ **SERVES** 4-6
★ **PREP TIME** 20 mins
★ **COOK TIME** 35 mins

Ingredients
2 tbsp butter
3 apples, peeled and
   thickly sliced
3 pears, peeled and
   thickly sliced
2 tbsp light soft brown sugar
pinch of ground cinnamon
pinch of ground ginger
juice of 1 lemon
vanilla ice cream, to serve

For the topping
150g (5½oz) rolled oats
150g (5½oz) plain flour
225g (8oz) light soft
   brown sugar
115g (4oz) butter, melted
1 tsp ground cinnamon
pinch of salt

1 Preheat the oven to 180°C (350°F/Gas 4). Melt the butter in a large saucepan over a low heat. Add the apples, pears, sugar, cinnamon, ginger, and lemon juice. Simmer over a medium-low heat, stirring occasionally, for 6–8 minutes, or until the apples and pears have browned and softened slightly.

2 Meanwhile, mix together the oats, flour, sugar, butter, cinnamon, and salt in a bowl. Spoon the fruit mixture into the bottom of a 20cm (8in) round flameproof casserole. Top with the oat mixture, spreading it evenly.

3 Bake in the oven for 30–35 minutes, or until golden brown and bubbling. Serve hot with vanilla ice cream on the side.

Apples and pears, the quintessential fruits of autumn, will keep for months when stored at a low, constant temperature.

COCONUT FUNNEL CAKES

Often served at fairs and amusement parks, these coconut-infused funnel cakes make a delicious home-made treat.

★ **MAKES** 4-6

★ **PREP TIME** 10 mins

★ **COOK TIME** 25 mins

Ingredients

2 eggs

250ml (9fl oz) whole milk

250ml (9fl oz) coconut milk

300g (10oz) plain flour

1 tsp vanilla extract

4 tbsp sugar

2 tbsp baking powder

pinch of salt

500ml (16fl oz) coconut
   or vegetable oil

icing sugar, to decorate

shaved coconut, to decorate

1 Whisk together the eggs, milk, and coconut milk. Add the flour, vanilla extract, sugar, baking powder, and salt. Stir well to combine and transfer to a plastic food bag.

2 In a large, heavy-based saucepan or deep-fat fryer, heat the oil to 190°C (375°F) as shown in the technique on p144. When the oil is hot enough, snip a hole in one corner of the bag and squeeze a portion of the batter into the pan, making a swirling shape in a circular motion. Fry for 2–3 minutes on each side, or until both sides are golden brown.

3 Remove from the oil with tongs and drain on a wire rack. Repeat with the remaining batter to make the rest of the cakes. Decorate with sifted icing sugar and shaved coconut. Serve hot.

Coconut products, such as milk, oil, and dried coconut itself, each have their own distinctive taste and uses in the kitchen.

BAKING, CANDY, AND PRESERVES

PECAN CARAMEL CINNAMON BUNS

Sweet, sticky, and oozing with home-made caramel, these cinnamon buns are perfect for a sumptuous weekend brunch.

★ **MAKES** 9
★ **PREP TIME** 40 mins, plus rising
★ **COOK TIME** 30 mins

Ingredients
7g sachet active dried yeast
100g (3½oz) caster sugar
125ml (4½fl oz) whole milk
115g (4oz) butter
pinch of salt
1 egg
550g (1¼lb) plain flour, plus extra for dusting
vegetable oil, for greasing

For the caramel sauce
200g (7oz) light soft brown sugar
115g (4oz) butter, cut into cubes
1 tsp vanilla extract
125ml (4½fl oz) double cream

For the filling
90g (3¼oz) butter
85g (3oz) light soft brown sugar
1 tbsp ground cinnamon
125g (4½oz) chopped pecans

For the icing
125g (4½oz) icing sugar
1 tbsp whole milk

1 Dissolve the yeast in 60ml (2fl oz) warm water with a pinch of sugar. Set aside for 5–7 minutes, or until it begins to bubble. In a saucepan, heat the milk and butter over a low heat until the butter has melted. Remove immediately from the heat. In a medium bowl, mix the yeast mixture, the remaining sugar, salt, egg, the melted butter mixture, and half the flour. Stir to incorporate, then add the remaining flour, until the mixture comes together to form a dough.

2 Knead the dough for 5 minutes, adding flour as necessary so that the dough is not tacky. Put it in an oiled bowl, cover with cling film, and keep in a warm place for 1 hour until well risen.

3 Meanwhile, make the caramel sauce. In a heavy-based frying pan, melt the sugar, stirring constantly with a whisk. The sugar will clump, but continue to stir. Once the sugar has melted and reached a dark brown colour, add the butter. Continue to stir as the butter melts and incorporates. Add the vanilla extract and cream, and continue stirring until the boiling has stopped. Remove from the heat and let it cool.

4 Preheat the oven to 180°C (350°F/Gas 4). Turn out the dough onto a floured surface and roll it out to a thickness of 1cm (½in). To make the filling, melt the butter and mix with the sugar, cinnamon, and pecans. Spread the filling evenly over the dough. Roll the dough up to form a tight spiral.

5 Pour the caramel sauce into a 23 x 23cm (9 x 9in) baking tin. Cut the dough roll into 9 equal slices and press into the caramel sauce. Bake for 25–30 minutes, or until the buns are golden brown and the caramel is bubbling. The centre of the buns should remain slightly gooey and undercooked. Whisk together the icing sugar and milk and pour the icing over the hot buns. Serve hot.

CHOCOLATE AND CHERRY DEVIL'S FOOD CAKE

This classic uses kirsch to enhance the richness of the chocolate, adding a wonderful depth of flavour to the cake.

★ **SERVES** 8-10

★ **PREP TIME** 30 mins

★ **COOK TIME** 30-35 mins, plus cooling

Ingredients

100g (3½oz) unsalted butter, softened, plus extra for greasing

275g (9½oz) caster sugar

2 large eggs

200g (7oz) self-raising flour

75g (2½oz) cocoa powder

1 tsp baking powder

4 tbsp kirsch

175ml (6fl oz) whole milk

1 tsp vanilla extract

For the icing

160g (5¾oz) unsalted butter, cut into cubes

30g (1oz) cocoa powder

160g (5¾oz) icing sugar

3-4 tbsp whole milk

1 small can cherries, drained and roughly chopped

25g (scant 1oz) dark chocolate, to garnish

1 Preheat the oven to 180°C (350°F/Gas 4). Grease two 20cm (8in) round cake tins and line the bases with baking parchment. In a medium bowl, use an electric whisk to cream together the butter and sugar until light and fluffy.

2 Beat in the eggs one at a time, whisking well after each addition. In a separate bowl, sift together the flour, cocoa powder, and baking powder. In another bowl, mix together the kirsch, milk, and vanilla extract.

3 Beat alternate spoonfuls of the dry and liquid ingredients into the cake batter. Once the mixture is well blended, divide it evenly between the two tins.

4 Bake for 30–35 minutes until the cakes are springy to the touch and a skewer inserted into the centre comes out clean. Leave to cool in the tins for a few minutes, then turn out onto a wire rack to cool completely. Remove the baking parchment.

5 For the icing, melt the butter in a frying pan over a low heat. Add the cocoa powder and continue to cook for a minute or two, stirring frequently. Allow to cool completely.

6 Sift in the icing sugar, beating thoroughly to combine. Blend in the milk, 1 tbsp at a time, until smooth and glossy. Allow to cool (it will thicken) and then mix half the icing with the cherries and use to sandwich the cakes together. Decorate the top and sides of the cake with the remaining half of the icing. Finally, use a vegetable peeler to create chocolate shavings and scatter them evenly over the top of the cake.

COOK'S TIP This cake will keep in an airtight container in a cool place for up to 5 days.

ANGEL FOOD CAKE WITH BLACKBERRY SAUCE

This show-stopping sponge cake, made without the addition of butter or oil, is as light as air.

★ **SERVES** 8

★ **PREP TIME** 20 mins

★ **COOK TIME** 35 mins, plus cooling

Ingredients

250g (9oz) caster sugar

1 tsp salt

100g (3½oz) super-fine flour or twice-sifted plain flour (see Cook's tip, right)

12 large eggs, at room temperature, separated

2 tsp vanilla extract

whipped cream, to serve

For the blackberry sauce

350g (12oz) blackberries

350g (12oz) runny honey

juice of 1 lemon

1 Heat the oven to 180°C (350°F/Gas 4). In a food processor, process the sugar and salt until very fine. Sift the flour and half the sugar mixture into a bowl and set aside.

2 Put the egg whites in another bowl and add the vanilla extract. Using an electric hand whisk or mixer, whisk for 5 minutes, or until the egg whites are stiff. Add the remaining sugar mixture, a little at a time, and keep beating so that the mixture remains stiff.

3 Add the flour and sugar mix into the egg mixture and fold it in with a rubber spatula. When well incorporated, spoon the batter into a non-greased 25cm (10in) bundt pan, or a ring mould with a capacity of 2.5 litres (5 pints), and bake for 35 minutes. Allow the cake to cool for 1 hour in the pan.

4 Meanwhile, put the blackberries, honey, and lemon juice in a non-reactive saucepan (not aluminium or cast-iron) and cook over a low heat. Simmer, stirring continuously, until the blackberries break down. Set aside to cool.

5 To serve, turn the cake out onto a plate. Slice, spoon over the blackberry sauce, and serve with freshly whipped cream.

COOK'S TIP If using plain flour, sift it twice to produce a very light cake. For the best result, lift the sieve high above the bowl, allowing the flour to come into contact with as much air as possible, as it floats down.

Blackberries are soft fruits that freeze well. Frozen ones can be used as a substitute when cooking.

DOUBLE CHOCOLATE BROWNIES

Brownies are better when slightly undercooked, as they retain their moist interior and store better, too.

- ★ **MAKES** 16-20
- ★ **PREP TIME** 15 mins
- ★ **COOK TIME** 40 mins, plus cooling

Ingredients

115g (4oz) butter, melted, plus extra for greasing
100g (3½oz) caster sugar
110g (3¾oz) light soft brown sugar
4 eggs
1 tsp vanilla extract
100g (3½oz) plain flour
175g (6oz) cocoa powder
¼ tsp bicarbonate of soda
225g (8oz) plain or dark chocolate chips

1 Preheat the oven to 150°C (300°F/Gas 2). Using an electric hand whisk or mixer, combine the butter, sugars, eggs, and vanilla extract in a large bowl until well mixed.

2 In a separate bowl, combine the flour, cocoa powder, and bicarbonate of soda. Stir the flour mixture into the butter mixture, one-third at a time, making sure that it is well incorporated before each addition. Mix in the chocolate chips.

3 Grease and line a 23 x 23cm (9 x 9in) baking tray or brownie tin and spoon the batter into it. Use a spatula to spread the batter evenly, ensuring the corners are filled.

4 Bake for 35–40 minutes, or until cooked through and firm. Remove from the oven and leave the brownie to cool in the tin, then turn out and cut into 16–20 squares.

Plain chocolate chips are a must in any cook's cupboard for those last-minute baking projects.

NOW TRY...

CHERRY & WALNUT

For nutty brownies, substitute the chocolate chips with 80g (2¾oz) **dried cherries** and 120g (4¼oz) **crushed walnuts**. Add to the batter and distribute evenly.

PEANUT BUTTER

Spoon 250g (9oz) **smooth peanut butter** over half the batter and top with the rest of the batter to create a rich middle layer. Then bake as directed in step 4.

BUTTERSCOTCH

Try replacing the chocolate chips with the same quantity of **butterscotch pieces**.

PUMPKIN PIE SPICE BEIGNETS

Popular in New Orleans, these fritters are believed to have been brought to Louisiana by French settlers in the 18th century.

★ **MAKES** 40

★ **PREP TIME** 20 mins, plus rising and chilling

★ **COOK TIME** 20 mins

Ingredients

7g sachet active dried yeast
250ml (9fl oz) double cream
60g (2oz) butter
100g (3½oz) caster sugar
2 eggs
750g (1lb 10oz) plain flour, plus extra for dusting
1 litre (1¾ pints) peanut or sunflower oil, for frying

For the pumpkin pie spice

1 tbsp ground cinnamon
½ tbsp ground ginger
½ tbsp ground nutmeg
½ tbsp ground cloves
75g (2½oz) icing sugar

1 Dissolve the yeast in 125ml (4½fl oz) warm water with a pinch of sugar. Leave to stand for 5–7 minutes, or until it begins to bubble.

2 In a saucepan, heat the cream and butter over a low heat until the butter has melted. Remove immediately from the heat. In a large bowl, mix the sugar, eggs, yeast mixture, and the melted butter and cream. Add half the flour and stir to incorporate. Gradually add the remaining flour, one-third at a time, until the mixture comes together to form a large ball of dough.

3 Knead the dough for 5–7 minutes, adding flour as needed so that the dough is not tacky. Form the dough into a ball and place in a covered bowl or freezer bag. Chill for 4–6 hours until doubled in size. Turn out the dough onto a floured surface and roll it out to a thickness of 1cm (½in). Cut into 4cm (1½in) squares.

4 To make the pumpkin pie spice, mix together the cinnamon, ginger, nutmeg, cloves, and icing sugar in a small bowl.

5 In a large, heavy-based saucepan or deep-fat fryer, heat the oil to 190°C (375°F), as shown in the technique on p144. Fry the squares, 5 or 6 at a time, for 1–2 minutes on each side, or until golden brown and puffed. Remove with a slotted spoon and transfer to a wire rack to cool.

6 Using a sieve or fine mesh strainer, sprinkle over the spice mixture and serve hot. For a true New Orleans experience, try these delicious desserts with a cup of café au lait, with equal parts coffee and cream.

Nutmeg gives a sweet spiciness and delicate warmth to sweet and savoury dishes.

RED VELVET CUPCAKES

These fashionable cupcakes taste great and, with red-toned cake against a pale, buttery cream cheese icing, look beautiful, too.

★ **MAKES** 18-20
★ **PREP TIME** 25 mins
★ **COOK TIME** 22-25 mins, plus cooling

Ingredients

125g (4½oz) unsalted butter, softened
250g (9oz) caster sugar
2 eggs, lightly beaten
2 tsp red food colouring
1 tsp vanilla extract
250g (9oz) self-raising flour
4 tbsp cocoa powder
200ml (7fl oz) buttermilk (or to make your own, see p12)
1 tsp cider vinegar
1 tsp bicarbonate of soda

For the icing

50g (1¾oz) cream cheese
50g (1¾oz) unsalted butter, softened
200g (7oz) icing sugar
1 tsp vanilla extract

1 Preheat the oven to 180°C (350°F/Gas 4). Place the butter and sugar in a large bowl. Using an electric hand whisk, cream them together until the mixture is very light and fluffy. Whisk in the eggs, food colouring, and vanilla extract until they are well combined.

2 Sift together the flour and cocoa powder. Add one-third of the flour to the cake batter and whisk it in well. Add half of the buttermilk and whisk it again, then another one-third of the flour, the rest of the buttermilk, and the final one-third of the flour, making sure to whisk well between additions. Mix together the cider vinegar and bicarbonate of soda in a separate bowl and quickly fold into the batter.

3 Place 18–20 cupcake cases in two deep 12-hole muffin tins (they will help the cupcakes keep their shape). Spoon the batter into the cases, filling each two-thirds full. Bake for 22–25 minutes, until springy to the touch. Do not open the oven until at least 20 minutes baking time has passed. Transfer to a wire rack to cool completely.

4 To make the icing, beat the cream cheese, butter, icing sugar, and vanilla extract until light and creamy, and transfer to a piping bag fitted with a star-shaped nozzle (if using).

5 Pipe the icing onto the cupcakes, or if icing by hand, use the back of a spoon dipped in warm water to smooth the surface of each cake.

COOK'S TIP The cupcakes can be made up to 1 day ahead and stored, un-iced, in an airtight container. They are best iced on the day they are to be eaten.

STRAWBERRIES AND CREAM WHOOPIE PIES

Best served immediately, these strawberry-layered whoopie pies make a lovely addition to a summer party.

★ **MAKES** 10
★ **PREP TIME** 40 mins
★ **COOK TIME** 12 mins

Ingredients

175g (6oz) unsalted butter, softened
150g (5½oz) light soft brown sugar
1 large egg
1 tsp vanilla extract
225g (8oz) self-raising flour
75g (2½oz) cocoa powder
1 tsp baking powder
150ml (5fl oz) whole milk
2 tbsp Greek yogurt or thick plain yogurt
150ml (5fl oz) double cream, whipped
250g (9oz) strawberries, hulled and thinly sliced
icing sugar, for dusting

1 Preheat the oven to 180°C (350°F/Gas 4). Line several baking sheets with baking parchment. Using an electric hand whisk, cream the butter and sugar until fluffy. Beat in the egg and vanilla extract. In a bowl, sift together the flour, cocoa, and baking powder. Mix the dry ingredients and the milk into the batter alternately, a spoonful at a time. Fold in the yogurt.

2 Put heaped tablespoons of the batter onto the baking sheets, leaving space for the mixture to spread. Dip a tablespoon in warm water and use the back to smooth over the surface of the cakes.

3 Bake for 12 minutes, until well risen. Leave the cakes for a few minutes, then turn out onto a wire rack to cool.

4 Spread the cream onto the flat side of half the cakes. Top with a layer of strawberries and a second cake. Dust with icing sugar and serve. These pies do not store and should be eaten on the day.

TRIPLE-LAYERED COCONUT CAKE

There is something very indulgent about a triple-layered cake, and this one, stuffed with whipped cream, is no exception!

- ★ **SERVES** 8-10
- ★ **PREP TIME** 30 mins
- ★ **COOK TIME** 35 mins, plus cooling

Ingredients

225g (8oz) butter, softened, plus extra for greasing
400g (14oz) caster sugar
115g (4oz) coconut oil
2 tsp vanilla extract
4 eggs, at room temperature
4 egg whites, at room temperature
550g (1¼lb) plain flour, plus extra for dusting
½ tsp salt
1 tbsp baking powder
375ml (13fl oz) coconut milk
45g (1½oz) shredded coconut, to decorate

For the whipped cream

500ml (16fl oz) double cream
50g (1¾oz) caster sugar
1 tsp vanilla extract

1 Preheat the oven to 180°C (350°F/Gas 4). Using an electric hand whisk or a mixer, cream together the butter, sugar, and oil. Beat in the vanilla extract, and then the eggs, one at a time. Once the eggs are fully incorporated, beat in the egg whites until light and fluffy.

2 Sift together the flour, salt, and baking powder into a bowl. Add to the egg mixture, one-third at a time, alternating with the coconut milk. Beat together until fully incorporated and the mixture is light and fluffy.

3 Grease three 23cm (9in) round cake tins and lightly dust them with flour. Divide the batter evenly between the tins. Bake for 30–35 minutes, or until a toothpick inserted into the centre comes out clean. Allow the cakes to cool for 10 minutes in the tin before transferring to a wire rack to cool completely.

4 Toss the shredded coconut in a frying pan over a medium heat until toasted. For the whipped cream, whip the cream, sugar, and vanilla extract until stiff.

5 Place one cake on a plate and spread one-third of the whipped cream over it. Place the second cake over the cream and spread another one-third of the cream. Then top with the third cake and spread over the remaining cream. Sprinkle with the toasted coconut and serve.

CHOCOLATE FUDGE CUPCAKES

These decidedly grown up cupcakes are truly decadent topped with a rich, dark chocolate ganache and fresh raspberries.

★ **MAKES** 12
★ **PREP TIME** 30 mins
★ **COOK TIME** 20 mins, plus cooling

Ingredients

60g (2oz) cocoa powder
85g (3oz) plain or dark chocolate
115g (4oz) butter, softened
200g (7oz) caster sugar
3 eggs, at room temperature
150g (5½oz) plain flour
1 tsp bicarbonate of soda
2 tsp baking powder
pinch of salt
120ml (4fl oz) whole milk
raspberries, to garnish

For the ganache

350g (12oz) plain or dark chocolate
350ml (12fl oz) double cream

1 Preheat the oven to 180°C (350°F/Gas 4). In a small saucepan, heat the cocoa, chocolate, and 200ml (7fl oz) of water over a low heat. Whisk together until fully incorporated.

2 Using an electric hand whisk, cream together the butter and sugar in a large bowl until light and fluffy. Add the eggs, one at a time, beating thoroughly between each addition. Whisk this into the chocolate mixture. In another bowl, sift the flour, bicarbonate of soda, baking powder, and salt.

3 Add the dry ingredients to the chocolate mixture in thirds, alternating with the milk. Beat until the mixture is light and well blended. Place 12 cupcake cases into a 12-hole muffin tin. Spoon the batter into the cases, filling each two-thirds full.

4 Bake for 17–20 minutes, or until a toothpick inserted into the centre of a cupcake comes out clean. Transfer the cupcakes to a wire rack to cool.

5 To make the ganache, melt the chocolate and cream in a small heatproof bowl over a saucepan of simmering water, making sure the bowl does not touch the water (see technique for melting chocolate on p238). When the chocolate has melted, take it off the heat and whisk until smooth and completely combined. Set aside.

6 When the ganache returns to room temperature, whip until fluffy. Let it chill, then spoon onto the cupcakes. Garnish with raspberries and serve.

Raspberries, with their sweet yet tart flavour, pair well with rich, dark chocolate.

BLUEBERRY CRUMB CAKE

Here, the sweet, crumbly streusel topping is enhanced with little nuggets of pecan nuts for extra crunch.

★ **SERVES** 16
★ **PREP TIME** 20 mins
★ **COOK TIME** 50 mins

Ingredients

115g (4oz) butter, plus extra for greasing
160g (5¾oz) light soft brown sugar
1 tsp vanilla extract
2 eggs
225g (8oz) plain flour, plus 2 tbsp for tossing
pinch of salt
½ tsp baking powder
½ tsp bicarbonate of soda
250ml (9fl oz) milk
250g (9oz) blueberries

For the topping

60g (2oz) butter, melted
75g (2½oz) plain flour
160g (5¾oz) light soft brown sugar
125g (4½oz) chopped pecans
1 tsp ground ginger
1 tsp ground cinnamon

1 Preheat the oven to 180°C (350°F/Gas 4). Using an electric hand whisk, cream together the butter and sugar until light and fluffy. Add the vanilla extract and eggs, one at a time, whisking well between each addition.

2 Sift the flour, salt, baking powder, and bicarbonate of soda into a bowl. Fold into the butter mixture, a little at a time, alternating with the milk. Stir to combine.

3 In a separate bowl, toss the blueberries with 2 tbsp of flour, then fold them into the mixture. Scoop the batter into a greased 23 x 35cm (9 x 14in) baking tin and spread evenly.

4 For the topping, mix together the butter, flour, sugar, pecans, and spices. Sprinkle over the batter. Bake for 45–50 minutes, or until the cake has risen, and a skewer inserted into the centre comes out clean. Serve hot with a cup of coffee.

A taste of the
PACIFIC NORTHWEST

ALASKA

With some of the longest coastlines in the country and a cool, wet climate, the states of the Pacific Northwest are renowned for their seafood and for the rich bounty of the land.

FOODS AND FLAVOURS

★ The **geoduck**, a giant clam that can live for up to 150 years and weighs more than 4.5kg (10lb), is a local delicacy, as well as being popular in Japanese cuisine.

★ The many **berries** of the area, including huckleberries, yellow raspberries, and boysenberries, are used in a variety of pies, preserves, and compotes (see below).

★ **Salmon**, pulled from the cold, deep waters of the Pacific, is often smoked on cedar planks to enhance its rich, full flavour.

★ **Apples** are just one of the fruits widely produced here, and many varieties can be found in local farmers' markets.

★ Seattle's **Pike Place Market** is rightly famous for its fresh local produce, and as the best place to buy fish straight from the sea.

The Pacific Northwest was one of the last regions of the US to be colonized, with the first sizeable group of immigrants not settling the region until the 1840s. They arrived to find high mountains, fertile valleys, an abundance of wild game and berries, and the shorelines and rivers full of salmon and trout. In fact, some of the best fishing in the country is found in far-flung Alaska, where the Pacific salmon is highly prized.

As a more recently established cuisine, the food here is less clearly defined than it is, say, in the Southeast, with the character of a dish often coming from the quality of the local ingredients rather than any one style. However, the influence of centuries-old Native American cuisine can still be seen and, in recent years, the local Asian community has introduced its own distinctive flavours.

Pike Place Market is one of the longest-running farmers' markets in the country, dating back to 1907.

Alaskan King crabs are a classic local catch. Some of these giant crustaceans can grow legs measuring an incredible 1.8m (6ft) in length.

Salmon is perhaps the best-known Alaskan export, and one of which it can be justly proud.

ALASKA
EWC 630
THE LAST FRONTIER

All around the San Francisco Bay area, local versions of cioppino, the seafood stew, can be found.

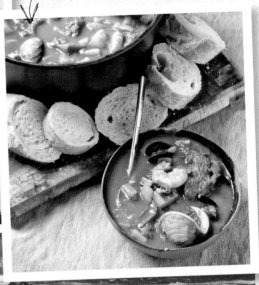

The coastlines of the Pacific Northwest, especially those around Big Sur, are known for their rugged, natural beauty.

Seattle has a good claim for being the birthplace of the modern coffee culture.

Fresh, seared tuna steaks give a classic tuna spaghetti casserole a modern makeover.

CHOCOLATE COURGETTE BUNDT CAKE

Courgettes can be used in the same way as carrots in carrot cake. The grated vegetables keep the cake moist for days.

- ★ **SERVES** 6-8
- ★ **PREP TIME** 20 mins
- ★ **COOK TIME** 55 mins

Ingredients

115g (4oz) butter, softened, plus extra for greasing
60ml (2fl oz) coconut oil
200g (7oz) caster sugar
225g (8oz) light soft brown sugar
½ tsp vanilla extract
2 eggs, at room temperature
300g (10oz) plain flour
2 tsp baking powder
60g (2oz) cocoa powder
pinch of salt
400g (14oz) courgette, grated
icing sugar, for dusting

1 Preheat the oven to 160°C (325°F/Gas 3). Using an electric hand whisk, beat together the butter, oil, sugars, and vanilla extract in a large bowl. Add the eggs, one at a time, whisking well between each addition.

2 Sift together the flour, baking powder, cocoa, and salt into a bowl. Add to the butter mixture, a little at a time, beating in until well combined.

3 Using a rubber spatula, fold the grated courgette into the batter, stirring well so that it is fully incorporated and well coated.

4 Scoop the batter into a greased 23cm (9in) bundt tin and bake for 45–55 minutes, or until a toothpick inserted into the centre comes out clean. Using a sieve or fine mesh strainer, lightly dust the cake with icing sugar. Serve warm.

COOK'S TIP If you don't have a bundt tin, you can easily make your own with a 25cm (10in) round cake tin and a small dariole mould or ramekin. Grease as usual and fill the mould with baking beans to hold it in place in the middle of the tin. Then pour the batter around it.

Courgettes have a subtle flavour, so will not overwhelm this sweet treat.

LEMON SOURED CREAM POUND CAKE

Replacing some of the butter with soured cream keeps the pound cake moist, and the lemons add a nice, tart flavour.

★ **SERVES** 8-10
★ **PREP TIME** 20 mins
★ **COOK TIME** 45 mins, plus cooling

Ingredients

225g (8oz) butter, softened, plus extra for greasing
400g (14oz) caster sugar
6 eggs
1 tsp vanilla extract
450g (1lb) plain flour
¼ tsp bicarbonate of soda
200g (7oz) soured cream

For the glaze
1 tbsp whole milk
juice of 1 lemon
125g (4½oz) icing sugar

1 Preheat the oven to 180°C (350°F/Gas 4). Using an electric hand whisk, beat the butter in a large bowl and gradually add the sugar, beating until light and fluffy. Add the eggs, one at a time, whisking well between each addition. Beat in the vanilla extract.

2 Sift together the flour and bicarbonate of soda into a bowl. Add to the egg mixture, one-third at a time, alternating with the soured cream.

3 Spoon the batter into a greased fluted 25cm (10in) round cake tin or bundt tin (or see Cook's Tip, opposite). Bake for 40–45 minutes, or until golden brown and firm. Allow the cake to cool for 10 minutes before turning it out onto a serving plate.

4 For the glaze, whisk together the milk, lemon juice, and sugar. Slowly pour the glaze evenly over the cake. Serve warm.

CHOCOLATE CHIP COOKIES

These easy-to-make cookies are soft and chewy, and incredibly moreish.

★ **MAKES** 15

★ **PREP TIME** 10 mins

★ **COOK TIME** 15 mins, plus cooling

Ingredients

100g (3½oz) unsalted butter, softened

100g (3½oz) caster sugar

100g (3½oz) light soft brown sugar

1 large egg

1 tsp vanilla extract

175g (6oz) plain flour

½ tsp baking powder

½ tsp salt

100g (3½oz) milk chocolate chips

1 Preheat the oven to 180°C (350°F/Gas 4). In a large bowl, cream together the butter and sugars with an electric hand whisk until light and fluffy. Beat in the egg and vanilla extract.

2 Sift together the flour, baking powder, and salt and mix into the wet mixture, until well combined.

3 Finally fold through the chocolate chips. Place tablespoons of the cookie mixture onto several baking sheets, making sure that they are spaced well apart as they will spread while cooking.

4 Bake the cookies in the middle of the oven for 13–15 mins, until they are lightly coloured and just cooked. Leave the cookies to cool on the baking sheets for 5 minutes before transferring to a wire rack to cool completely. Serve with a glass of milk.

★★★ WHAT'S THE STORY?

The creator of the chocolate chip cookie is said to be a Mrs Ruth Wakefield, owner of the Toll House restaurant in Massachusetts. She devised them by accident in 1930, while trying to make regular chocolate cookies. By 1936, she had published her recipe for "chocolate crunch cookies". Soon after, manufacturers were making chocolate chips specifically for baking.

NOW TRY...

WHITE CHOC CHIPS

Replace the milk chocolate chips with 75g (2½oz) each of **white chocolate chips** and roughly chopped **macadamia nuts**. Bake as usual.

FESTIVE TWIST

For a seasonal treat, replace the chocolate chips with 75g (2½oz) each of roughly chopped **pistachios** and **dried cranberries**. Bake as usual.

TRIPLE CHOCOLATE

For the ultimate chocolate treat, replace 25g (scant 1oz) of the flour with an equal amount of **unsweetened cocoa powder**. Add 75g (2½oz) each of **dark** and **white chocolate chips**, and bake as usual.

CRANBERRY OATMEAL COOKIES

These chewy cookies are packed with fibre-filled oats
and dried fruit for a healthy treat.

★ **MAKES** 16
★ **PREP TIME** 15 mins
★ **COOK TIME** 15 mins

Ingredients

100g (3½oz) unsalted butter,
   softened
50g (1¾oz) dark soft
   brown sugar
150g (5½oz) caster sugar
1 egg
125g (4½oz) plain flour
¼ tsp baking powder
¼ tsp ground cinnamon
pinch of salt
100g (3½oz) rolled oats
60g (2oz) dried cranberries

1 Preheat the oven to 180°C (350°F/Gas 4). In a large bowl, cream together the butter and sugars with an electric hand whisk, until light and fluffy, then whisk in the egg.

2 Sift in the flour, baking powder, cinnamon, and salt, and fold to combine. Next, fold in the rolled oats and cranberries.

3 Place heaped tablespoons of the mixture, spaced well apart, on 2 non-stick baking trays and bake in the centre of the oven for 15 minutes, until they begin to brown at the edges. The centres should remain a little chewy.

4 Remove the cookies from the oven. Allow them to rest on their trays for 5 minutes before transferring them to a wire rack to cool completely.

COOK'S TIP These are delicious to eat, while still warm, with a glass of cold milk.

Dried cranberries are an
excellent alternative to raisins,
with a sweet yet tart flavour.

APPLE AND CINNAMON SNICKERDOODLES

Processing dried apple into a fine powder adds a sweet yet sharp flavour to the coating on these soft cake-like cookies.

★ **MAKES** 20

★ **PREP TIME** 10 mins, plus chilling

★ **COOK TIME** 10-12 mins

Ingredients

100g (3½oz) unsalted butter, softened

175g (6oz) caster sugar

1 egg

½ tsp vanilla extract

1 apple, peeled and coarsely grated

225g (8oz) plain flour

½ tsp baking powder

pinch of salt

For the topping

25g (scant 1oz) caster sugar

25g (scant 1oz) apple crisps or dried apples

1½ tsp ground cinnamon

1 In a large bowl, cream together the butter and sugar with an electric hand whisk until light and fluffy. Whisk in the egg and vanilla extract, then stir in the grated apple. Sift in the flour, baking powder, and salt, then fold in to combine. Cover and chill the mixture for 30 minutes. Meanwhile, make the topping. In a food processor, process the sugar, apple crisps, and cinnamon to a fine powder.

2 Preheat the oven to 200°C (400°F/Gas 6). Remove the batter from the fridge. Use a small ice-cream scoop or a tablespoon measurer to form small balls, and set them aside on a plate. Roll them briefly between your palms to even out the shape. If the batter is too soft to do this, return the plate to the fridge for a further 15 minutes to chill.

3 Now roll the snickerdoodles in the cinnamon-sugar topping, making sure that they are well covered. Flatten them slightly between your palms and place them, spaced well apart, on 2 lined baking trays. Bake in the centre of the oven for 10–12 minutes, until risen and golden brown. Remove from the oven and allow them to rest on the trays for 5 minutes before transferring them to a wire rack to cool completely.

CINNAMON CHURROS WITH CHOCOLATE CHILLI SAUCE

These cinnamon- and sugar-sprinkled Spanish snacks take minutes to make and will be devoured just as quickly.

★ **MAKES** 20
★ **PREP TIME** 10 mins, plus cooling
★ **COOK TIME** 15 mins

Ingredients

25g (scant 1oz) unsalted butter
200g (7oz) plain flour
50g (1¾oz) caster sugar
1 tsp baking powder
1 litre (1¾ pints) peanut or sunflower oil
1 tsp ground cinnamon

For the chocolate chilli sauce

50g (1¾oz) good-quality dark chocolate, broken into pieces
150ml (5fl oz) double cream
1 tbsp caster sugar
1 tbsp unsalted butter
pinch of salt
¼ tsp chilli powder or cayenne pepper, to taste

1 Measure 200ml (7fl oz) of boiling water into a jug. Add the butter and stir until it melts. Sift together the flour, half the sugar, and the baking powder into a bowl. Make a well in the centre and slowly pour in the hot butter liquid, beating continuously, until you have a thick paste; you may not need all the liquid. Leave the mixture to cool and rest for 5 minutes.

2 Pour the oil into a large, heavy-based saucepan or deep-fat fryer to a depth of at least 10cm (4in) and heat it to 190°C (375°F). Test the oil as shown in the technique on p144. Keep the correct-sized saucepan lid nearby and never leave the hot oil unattended. Regulate the temperature, making sure it remains even, or the churros will burn.

3 Place the cooled mixture into a piping bag fitted with a 2cm (¾in) star-shaped nozzle. Pipe 7cm (2¾in) lengths of the dough directly into the hot oil using a pair of scissors to snip off the ends. Do not crowd the pan, or the temperature of the oil will go down. Cook the churros for 1–2 minutes on each side, turning them when they are golden brown. When done, remove the churros from the oil with a slotted spoon and drain on kitchen paper. Turn off the heat.

4 Mix the remaining sugar and the cinnamon together on a plate and toss the churros in the mixture while still hot. Leave to cool for 5–10 minutes before serving while still warm.

5 For the chocolate chilli sauce, put the chocolate, cream, sugar, and butter in a medium, heatproof bowl over a saucepan of barely simmering water (see technique for melting chocolate on p238). Heat the mixture, stirring constantly, for 3–4 minutes until the chocolate melts and the sauce amalgamates and thickens.

6 Take the sauce off the heat and add a pinch of salt. Add the chilli powder or cayenne pepper to taste, a pinch at a time, and taste as you add it. The sauce will not immediately appear hot or spicy; the right amount of spice will be reached when it leaves a slow heat in your mouth, but does not overwhelm you. Transfer to a bowl and serve immediately with freshly made churros.

CHOCOLATE CUSTARD-FILLED DOUGHNUTS

Doughnuts are surprisingly easy to make. These are light, airy, and taste far nicer than any shop-bought varieties.

★ **MAKES** 12

★ **PREP TIME** 35 mins, plus rising and proving

★ **COOK TIME** 15-20 mins

Ingredients

150ml (5fl oz) milk

75g (2½oz) unsalted butter

½ tsp vanilla extract

2 tsp dried yeast

75g (2½oz) caster sugar

2 eggs, beaten

425g (15oz) plain flour, preferably "00" grade, plus extra for dusting

½ tsp salt

1 litre (1¾ pints) peanut or sunflower oil, for deep-frying, plus extra for greasing

caster sugar, for coating

For the chocolate custard filling

200ml (7fl oz) whole milk

2 egg yolks

4 tbsp caster sugar

1 tsp cornflour

½ tsp vanilla extract

85g (3oz) dark chocolate, finely chopped

1 Heat the milk, butter, and vanilla extract in a saucepan until the butter melts. Let it cool until tepid. Whisk in the yeast and a tablespoon of the sugar. Cover and leave for 10 minutes. Mix in the eggs.

2 Sift the flour and salt into a large bowl. Stir in the remaining sugar. Make a well in the flour and add the milk mixture. Bring together to form a rough dough. Turn the dough out onto a floured surface and knead for 10 minutes until soft and pliable. Put in an oiled bowl and cover with cling film. Keep it warm for 2 hours until doubled in size.

3 On a floured surface, knock back the dough and divide it into 12 equal pieces. Roll them between your palms to form balls. Place on baking sheets, spaced well apart. Cover with cling film and a tea towel. Leave in a warm place for 1–2 hours until doubled in size.

4 In a large, heavy-based saucepan or deep-fat fryer, heat a 10cm (4in) depth of oil to 190°C (375°F), as shown in the technique on p144. Slide the doughnuts off the sheets. Do not worry if they are flatter on one side. Carefully lower 3 at a time into the hot oil, rounded-side down. Turn after 1 minute. Remove with a slotted spoon when golden brown all over. Drain on kitchen paper, then, while still hot, toss them in caster sugar. Cool before filling.

5 For the filling, pour the milk into a saucepan over a medium heat, and heat until small bubbles form on the edge and steam rises. Do not allow the milk to boil. Using an electric mixer, whisk the egg yolks, sugar, and cornflour together until pale yellow and thick. Slowly whisk in the warm milk. Return the mixture to the saucepan and simmer, stirring continuously, over a very low heat until the sauce thickens and coats the back of a spoon. Stir in the vanilla extract, then add the chocolate and stir until it has completely melted. Remove from the heat and pour into a jug or bowl. Let the filling cool completely, then pour into a piping bag with a thin nozzle.

6 Pierce each doughnut on the side and insert the nozzle. Gently squirt in about a tablespoon of the filling, until it almost starts to spill out again. Dust the hole with a little more sugar, and serve.

BANANA AND BUTTERSCOTCH MUFFINS

Make double quantities of the butterscotch sauce as it stores well in the fridge. Gently reheat it to pour over ice cream.

- ★ **MAKES** 12
- ★ **PREP TIME** 30 mins
- ★ **COOK TIME** 20 mins

Ingredients

250g (9oz) self-raising flour
60g (2oz) caster sugar
1 tsp baking powder
pinch of fine salt
50ml (1¾fl oz) whole milk
50ml (1¾fl oz) peanut
   or sunflower oil
½ tsp vanilla extract
1 egg
2 bananas

For the butterscotch

60g (2oz) unsalted butter
100g (3½oz) dark soft
   brown sugar
150ml (5fl oz) double cream
½ tsp vanilla extract
pinch of salt

For the streusel topping

50g (1¾oz) light soft
   brown sugar
50g (1¾oz) plain flour
25g (scant 1oz) unsalted
   butter, softened
½ tsp ground cinnamon

1 First, make the butterscotch. Melt the butter in a small, heavy-based saucepan, then mix in the sugar and cook over a low heat until it is no longer granular. Add the cream, vanilla extract, and salt and whisk well to combine. Bring to the boil, reduce to a low simmer, and cook, stirring constantly, for 5 minutes until thickened. Remove from the heat and pour into a large, shallow bowl to cool quicker.

2 Meanwhile, make the streusel topping. In a small bowl or the bowl of a food processor, rub together, or pulse, all the ingredients until they resemble coarse breadcrumbs.

3 Preheat the oven to 200°C (400°F/Gas 6). Sift the flour, sugar, baking powder, and salt into a large bowl. Using a hand-held blender, process the milk, oil, vanilla extract, egg, 1 banana, and three-quarters (about 150ml/5fl oz) of the cooled butterscotch until smooth. Cut the remaining banana into small cubes.

4 Make a well in the centre of the flour mixture and mix in the liquid ingredients along with the chopped banana, being careful not to over-mix the batter.

5 Line a muffin tin with paper cases and fill each one two-thirds full with the muffin mixture. Heat the remaining butterscotch until it is runny and divide it over the surface of each muffin. You may need to do this in 2 batches.

6 Top each muffin with a heaped teaspoon of the streusel topping, making sure that the butterscotch is completely covered. Bake for 20 minutes until well risen, and when a toothpick inserted into the centre of a muffin comes out clean. Remove the muffins from the oven and allow them to cool on a wire rack.

COOK'S TIP The butterscotch can be made up to 3 days ahead and stored in the fridge until needed. Any leftover streusel topping can be stored in an airtight container in the freezer and used straight from the freezer for other recipes.

SOUTHERN-STYLE CORNBREAD

This simple bread is quick to make, and best eaten while still warm from the oven.

★ **SERVES** 8
★ **PREP TIME** 15 mins
★ **COOK TIME** 25-30 mins

Ingredients

150g (5½oz) plain flour
150g (5½oz) fine polenta
    or cornmeal
2 tsp baking powder
1 tsp salt
pinch of sugar
250ml (9fl oz) buttermilk (or
    to make your own, see p12)
1 egg, beaten
60ml (2fl oz) vegetable oil
butter, to serve, plus extra
    for greasing

1 Preheat the oven to 220°C (425°F/Gas 7). In a bowl, mix together the flour, polenta, baking powder, salt, and sugar. Stir in the buttermilk, egg, and oil, and mix until well incorporated.

2 Pour the batter into a greased 20cm (8in) round pan, spreading it evenly.

3 Bake in the oven for 25–30 minutes, or until golden brown. Allow to cool slightly and serve warm with butter as a side dish with soups or stews.

SERVE WITH

CAJUN ANDOUILLE GUMBO

SEE PAGE 112

THREE BEAN CHILLI

SEE PAGE 120

NOW TRY...

MUFFINS

Pour the batter into a greased 12-hole muffin tin to make individual **cornbread muffins** and bake for 25 minutes.

CHEESE & CHILLI

For a spicy twist, mix in 115g (4oz) grated strong **Cheddar cheese** and 1 finely chopped **jalapeño** or other mild green chilli.

BACON

Heat a greased cast-iron frying pan in the oven for 15 minutes. Remove from the oven, pour in the batter, and top with 6 **smoked streaky bacon rashers**, cut into small pieces. Return to the oven for 25 minutes.

CAYENNE CHEDDAR CHEESE STRAWS

These crisp, crumbly canapés are particularly moreish when served still warm from the oven.

★ **MAKES** 50-60

★ **PREP TIME** 20 mins, plus chilling

★ **COOK TIME** 5-10 mins

Ingredients

300g (10oz) plain flour, plus extra for dusting

1 tsp cayenne pepper

½ tsp smoked paprika or ancho chilli powder

1 tsp salt

115g (4oz) butter, cut into cubes

450g (1lb) Cheddar cheese, cut into cubes

50g (1¾oz) grated Parmesan cheese

1 Put the flour, cayenne pepper, paprika, and salt in a food processor and pulse-blend. Mix in the butter and cheeses, one half at a time.

2 Blend on high speed for 2–3 minutes, or until a soft dough forms. Wrap in cling film and chill for 1 hour.

3 Preheat the oven to 190°C (375°F/Gas 5). Roll out the dough to a 1cm (½in) thick rectangle, as shown in the technique below. Cut into 18cm (7in) long and 1cm (½in) wide strips. Transfer the strips onto a baking sheet lined with baking parchment. Bake for 5–10 minutes, or until crisp.

ROLLING DOUGH

1 Remove the cling film, turn out the dough onto a floured surface, and pat it down with your hands.

2 Using a rolling pin, roll out the dough evenly to a 1cm (½in) thick rectangle of the desired size.

WHITE CHOCOLATE AND COCONUT POPCORN BALLS

Children love to help with these easy-to-make sweet treats. Roll them in coloured sprinkles for added sparkle.

★ **MAKES** 10
★ **PREP TIME** 20 mins
★ **COOK TIME** 5 mins, plus drying

Ingredients

2 tbsp peanut or sunflower oil
100g (3½oz) popcorn or popcorn kernels
30g (1oz) unsalted butter, plus extra for greasing
60g (2oz) mini marshmallows
75g (2½oz) white chocolate chips
25g (scant 1oz) dessicated coconut, unsweetened

1 If you are making the popcorn, heat the oil over a high heat in a large, heavy-based saucepan. Add the popcorn kernels and shake the pan so they spread out into an even layer. Cover the pan and wait for 1–2 minutes until the corn starts popping. Reduce the heat to low and continue to cook, shaking the pan occasionally, until the popping noises have stopped. Transfer the popcorn to a large bowl to cool.

2 Melt the butter over a low heat in a small, heavy-based saucepan. Add the mini marshmallows and continue to cook over a low heat for 2–3 minutes, stirring constantly, until they have just melted to a thick, sticky liquid.

3 Pour the melted marshmallows over the popcorn and mix well. It should start to stick together. Add the chocolate chips and coconut and mix well to combine.

4 Lightly grease your hands with a little butter and take a handful of the mixture. Compress it between your palms to make a round, compacted ball of popcorn and place on a baking sheet to dry. Repeat until you have 10 balls. Let them dry for at least 1 hour before storing in an airtight container.

Popcorn is simple to make, only takes a few minutes, and costs very little.

CHILLI GINGER CANDIED PECANS

A bag of candied pecans makes a lovely festive gift, prettily wrapped and hand-labelled.

★ **MAKES** 225g (8oz)
★ **PREP TIME** 10 mins
★ **COOK TIME** 20 mins

Ingredients

2 egg whites
1 tsp vanilla extract
125g (4½oz) light soft brown sugar
large pinch of chilli powder
1 tbsp ground ginger
225g (8oz) whole pecans

1 Preheat the oven to 180°C (350°F/Gas 4). In a small bowl, whisk the egg whites until white, soft peaks form. Stir in the vanilla extract.

2 In a separate bowl, mix together the sugar and spices. Toss the pecans in the egg white mixture and then in the dry ingredients. Spread them out on a baking sheet lined with baking parchment. Bake for 20 minutes, or until crisp.

3 Remove the pecans from the oven and toss in the spice mixture again. Leave to cool. Serve as a snack or as a topping in salads, soups, or ice cream.

GOOEY S'MORES BARS

These s'mores bars, with a cinnamon-flavoured ganache, are an easy-to-make alternative to the traditional camping treat.

★ **MAKES** 12

★ **PREP TIME** 15 mins

★ **COOK TIME** 40 mins, plus chilling

Ingredients

115g (4oz) butter, melted, plus extra for greasing

100g (3½oz) light soft brown sugar

100g (3½oz) caster sugar

4 eggs

1 tsp vanilla extract

10 digestive biscuits

75g (2½oz) plain flour

1 tsp baking powder

300g bag mini marshmallows, for the topping

For the ganache

175g (6oz) plain or dark chocolate, broken into small pieces

1 tsp ground cinnamon

125ml (4½fl oz) double cream

1 Preheat the oven to 180°C (350°F/Gas 4). Grease and line a 23cm (9in) square baking tin.

2 Using an electric hand whisk, cream the butter and the sugars in a bowl. Add the eggs, one at a time, and the vanilla extract and whisk until light and fluffy.

3 In a food processor, process the digestive biscuits until they resemble breadcrumbs. Alternatively, place the biscuits in a plastic food bag and crush with a rolling pin. Turn out into a large bowl and add the flour, baking powder, and egg mixture. Stir to combine. Pour the batter into the baking tin and bake for 35 minutes, or until golden brown.

4 For the ganache, place the chocolate, cinnamon, and cream in a small heatproof bowl over a saucepan of simmering water (see technique for melting chocolate on p238). The bowl should not touch the water. Stir occasionally until the chocolate melts. Remove immediately.

5 Pour the ganache over the biscuit base and top with the marshmallows. Grill on a very low heat, until toasted and melted. Let it cool for 15 minutes before transferring to the fridge. Chill for 30–45 minutes; this will make it easier to slice. Cut into equal-sized bars and serve at room temperature.

CHOCOLATE MARSHMALLOW FUDGE

This recipe is ideal for children to make. It is quick, easy, and ready in the time it takes for the chocolate to set.

- ★ **MAKES** 36 squares
- ★ **PREP TIME** 5 mins
- ★ **COOK TIME** 5 mins, plus cooling

Ingredients

250g bag mini marshmallows
400g (14oz) plain or dark chocolate
450g can condensed milk
60ml (2fl oz) whole milk
1 tsp vanilla extract

1 Line a 23cm (9in) square baking tray with baking parchment. Lay out the marshmallows on the tray. In a saucepan, heat the chocolate, condensed milk, and milk over a medium heat. Cook, stirring frequently, until the chocolate melts and all the ingredients are combined.

2 Remove from the heat, add the vanilla extract, and stir to combine. Spread the chocolate mixture over the marshmallows and set aside to cool completely. When the fudge has set, cut into 4cm (1½in) squares and serve.

Marshmallows don't just belong by the camp fire – try using them in the kitchen as well.

PEAR AND CARDAMOM BUTTER

The complex flavours of pears and cardamom are an exciting twist on the more usual apple butter.

★ **MAKES** 2 x 300ml
  (10fl oz) jars
★ **PREP TIME** 15 mins
★ **COOK TIME** 1 hr, plus cooling

Ingredients
4 pears, about 400g (14oz)
  in total
150ml (5fl oz) cider vinegar
100g (3½oz) light soft
  brown sugar
½ tbsp cardamom pods, ground
pinch of salt

1 Core and peel the pears, as shown in the technique below, then roughly chop. In a saucepan, combine the pears, vinegar, 120ml (4fl oz) of water, sugar, cardamom, and salt. Bring to the boil on a high heat, then reduce the heat and simmer, uncovered, for 1 hour, or until the pears are tender. Remove from the heat and allow to cool completely for about 1 hour.

2 Blend in a food processor, or purée with a hand-held blender. Spread generously on toast and serve with hot coffee.

COOK'S TIP The spread will keep for up to 2 weeks in an airtight container.

CORING AND PEELING A PEAR

1 Use a melon baller or a teaspoon to scoop out the small core in the base of the pear.

2 Use a vegetable peeler or a small, sharp knife to pare off the skin thinly and evenly, then remove the stalk.

LAVENDER CHOCOLATE PRETZEL RODS

A small amount of lavender adds a delicate fragrance and subtle flavour to these sophisticated snacks.

★ **MAKES** 20

★ **PREP TIME** 10 mins

★ **COOK TIME** 10 mins, plus drying

Ingredients

150g (5½oz) plain or dark chocolate chips or squares

20 large, thick pretzel rods or knotted pretzels

3 tbsp dried culinary lavender

1 Melt the chocolate in a small heatproof bowl over a saucepan of simmering water, as shown in the technique below.

2 Dip two-thirds of a pretzel rod or knotted pretzel into the melted chocolate, tilting the bowl for a good coating. Carefully drip off any excess chocolate into the bowl. Continue to dip all the pretzel rods.

3 Sprinkle over the lavender sparingly and transfer the pretzel rods to a lined baking sheet to dry. You can also try topping the pretzel rods with sprinkles, crushed nuts, dried fruit, or rock candy for a delicious alternative.

MELTING CHOCOLATE

1 Put the chocolate in a small heatproof bowl over a saucepan of simmering water, making sure the bowl does not touch the water.

2 Stir occasionally with a metal spoon and remove the bowl from the saucepan as soon as the chocolate has melted.

PISTACHIO BRITTLE

Brittles are simple to make, and you can try combining different dried fruit and nuts to find your favourite combination.

★ **SERVES** 6-8

★ **PREP TIME** 5 mins

★ **COOK TIME** 18 mins, plus cooling

Ingredients

200g (7oz) caster sugar

175g (6oz) light corn syrup

125g (4½oz) shelled pistachios

30g (1oz) butter, cut into cubes, plus extra for greasing

1 tsp bicarbonate of soda

1 tsp vanilla extract

1 In a heavy-based saucepan, combine the sugar, corn syrup, and 60ml (2fl oz) water over a medium heat. Cook, stirring frequently with a wooden spoon, as shown in the technique below.

2 At this hard breaking point, add the pistachios. Continue stirring until the temperature rises to 160°C (325°F) again.

3 Remove from the heat and stir in the butter, bicarbonate of soda, and vanilla extract. Continue to stir as it foams and the butter melts.

4 Pour onto a greased 23 x 35cm (9 x 14in) baking tray and let it cool completely. Break into pieces and store in an airtight container.

COOK'S TIP If you do not have a sugar thermometer, drop a small amount of the mixture into a glass of cold water, and if the candy breaks, it is hot enough.

BOILING SUGAR

1 In a heavy-based saucepan, heat the sugar, corn syrup, and 60ml (2fl oz) water over a medium heat.

2 Cook, stirring frequently, until a sugar thermometer dipped into the liquid reads 160°C (325°F) and the sugar turns brittle and golden brown.

FRESH BERRY COMPOTE WITH VANILLA AND THYME

Cook down ripe summer berries to make this sweet, syrupy compote, perfect for serving with pancakes or ice cream.

★ **SERVES** 4
★ **PREP TIME** 10 mins
★ **COOK TIME** 20 mins

Ingredients

30g (1oz) caster sugar
1 vanilla pod, split and
    seeds scraped
sprig of thyme
150g (5½oz) blackberries
100g (3½oz) dark cherries,
    stoned and halved weight
    (see technique, below)
100g (3½oz) blueberries

1 Put the sugar, vanilla pod, thyme, and 2 tbsp water in a medium, heavy-based saucepan, stir together, and bring to the boil. Add the blackberries and cherries, reduce the heat and simmer, covered, for 8–10 minutes, until the berries start to break down and release their juices.

2 Remove the lid, add the blueberries, increase the heat, and continue to cook the compote for a further 8–10 minutes, stirring occasionally, until the sauce has thickened and reduced, and the berries are soft.

3 Remove from the heat and cool. Remove the vanilla pod and thyme before serving cold, or at room temperature.

COOK'S TIP This deliciously dark compote will keep for several days in the fridge, and is marvellous over ice cream, yogurt, or Home-made granola (see p60) for a morning treat.

STONING CHERRIES

To stone with a pitter, place the cherry in the pitter, stem-side down, and press until the stone emerges from the hole at the bottom.

If using a knife, slice the cherry lengthways in two, cutting all the way around the stone. Twist and separate the halves and remove the stone.

NO-COOK SPICY SUMMER RELISH

This fresh, vibrant relish takes seconds to make and is great in burgers, with hot dogs, or even in wraps and sandwiches.

★ **SERVES** 6-8

★ **PREP TIME** 10 mins

Ingredients

1 red pepper

1 yellow pepper

1 small red onion, roughly chopped

1 garlic clove

½ jalapeño or other mild green chilli, deseeded

3 tbsp rice wine vinegar or white vinegar

2 tsp caster sugar

salt and freshly ground black pepper

good-quality mayonnaise, to serve (optional)

1 Deseed and roughly chop the red and yellow peppers, as shown in the technique below. In a food processor, pulse the peppers, onion, garlic, and jalapeño until finely chopped.

2 Put the chopped vegetables in a non-reactive (not aluminium or cast-iron) bowl. Add the vinegar, sugar, and season well. Stir until well combined, then cover and chill for at least 4 hours.

3 To serve, drain off any excess liquid and serve as it is or stir in some mayonnaise for a creamier finish.

COOK'S TIP This relish will keep in the fridge for up to 5 days, tightly sealed.

PREPARING A PEPPER

1 Place it on its side and cut off the top and bottom. Stand on one of the cut ends and slice in half lengthways. Remove the core and seeds.

2 Lay each section flat on the cutting board. Remove the remaining pale, fleshy ribs, then roughly cut the flesh into chunks.

QUICK STOVETOP SAUERKRAUT

Traditionally, sauerkraut is fermented over several weeks. Try this almost instant version for a quick, easy alternative.

★ **SERVES** 4
★ **PREP TIME** 10 mins
★ **COOK TIME** 1½ hrs

Ingredients

1 tbsp olive oil
2 garlic cloves, crushed
1 small white onion, diced
1 head of green cabbage,
  shredded
500ml (16fl oz) cider vinegar
2 tbsp salt
1 tbsp caraway seeds

1 Heat the oil in a deep, straight-sided frying pan or Dutch oven. Add the garlic to the pan and fry over a medium heat until golden. Stir in the onion and fry for 10 minutes, or until translucent.

2 Add the cabbage to the pan along with 120ml (4fl oz) water, the vinegar, salt, and caraway seeds. Bring to the boil, reduce to a simmer, cover, and cook over a low heat for 1½ hours. Serve warm with hot dogs or sausages.

COOK'S TIP This sauerkraut is also great added to soups and stews for a healthy, warming meal.

Shredded cabbage, cooked in this way, will keep for several weeks in the fridge.

SPICY CHOW CHOW

This simple refrigerator pickle is rather like pickled coleslaw. It is delicious with cold meats and cheeses, as well as in sandwiches and wraps.

* **MAKES** 4 x 300ml (10fl oz) jars
* **PREP TIME** 20 mins
* **COOK TIME** 10 mins

For the slaw

5 green tomatoes, finely chopped
1 green pepper, deseeded and finely chopped
1 red pepper, deseeded and finely chopped
1 red onion, finely chopped
3 garlic cloves, crushed
½ head of green cabbage, shredded
1 tbsp sea salt

For the pickle

600ml (1 pint) cider vinegar
225g (8oz) light soft brown sugar
1 tbsp mustard seeds
1 tsp celery seeds
1 tsp chilli flakes
60g (2oz) sea salt

1 To make the slaw, combine the vegetables with the sea salt in a large bowl and mix well. Cover and chill in the fridge overnight.

2 Drain the vegetables and transfer them to a medium saucepan. Add the vinegar, sugar, mustard seeds, celery seeds, chilli flakes, and the sea salt. Simmer the vegetable mixture over a medium heat for 15 minutes.

3 Divide the mixture between 4 clean, sterilized jars. (To sterilize the jars, see step 1, p249.) The relish will keep for up to 2 weeks in the fridge.

SERVE WITH

BREAKFAST
BURRITOS
SEE PAGE 68

SHRIMP AND
GRITS
SEE PAGE 110

HOT PEPPER JELLY

This simple jelly is an easy introduction to preserving, without the need for traditional water-bath canning.

★ **MAKES** 4 x 300ml
(10fl oz) jars

★ **PREP TIME** 20 mins

★ **COOK TIME** 10 mins

Ingredients
400g (14oz) jalapeños or
other mild green chillies,
finely chopped

100g (3½oz) green peppers,
deseeded and
roughly chopped

2 tbsp pectin

375ml (13fl oz) cider vinegar

675g (1½lb) runny honey

1 Process the jalapeños and peppers in a food processor to make a purée. Transfer the purée to a saucepan and combine with the pectin, vinegar, and honey. Bring to the boil, then reduce the heat and let it simmer for 10 minutes.

2 Pour into 4 clean, sterilized jars and tightly screw on the lids. (To sterilize the jars, see step 1, opposite.) Leave to set for 1 hour before serving. The jelly will keep for up to 2 weeks in the fridge.

Green pepper lends
a mild, sweet flavour
to this jelly.

REFRIGERATOR PICKLES

There is nothing quite like the crunch of home-made refrigerator pickles, which are fresher than shop-bought equivalents.

★ **MAKES** 2 x 200ml (7fl oz) jars
★ **PREP TIME** 10 mins

Ingredients

50g (1¾oz) caster sugar
2 tsp salt
200ml (7fl oz) white wine
    vinegar or rice wine vinegar
freshly ground black pepper
4-5 small pickling cucumbers,
    thinly sliced
1 tbsp finely chopped
    dill fronds
½ tsp dill seeds, lightly crushed

1 Preheat the oven to 140°C (275°F/Gas 1). To sterilize the jars, wash them thoroughly and place them upside-down on a baking sheet. Put them in the oven for at least 15 minutes. Put the lids in a metal bowl and pour over a kettleful of boiling water. Leave for 5 minutes, then remove and leave to drain. Dry well with kitchen paper.

2 Put the sugar and salt in a bowl and add a little of the vinegar. Whisk until the salt and sugar dissolve, then add the remaining vinegar and a good grinding of pepper.

3 Once the jars are cold, layer the cucumbers in the jars, adding a sprinkling of chopped dill and a few dill seeds between each layer.

4 When the jars are full, pour over the vinegar mixture and seal. Shake the jars to disperse the liquid evenly and refrigerate overnight for them to get really crispy.

COOK'S TIP These pickles will keep in the fridge for up to 1 month, packed in a sterilized, sealed jar. Make sure they are always covered with vinegar.

Step-by-step preparation techniques
are in *italic*.

A

anchovy fillets
Caesar salad with seared salmon 39
Green Goddess salad dressing 48
apples
apple and blackberry cobbler 189
apple and cinnamon snickerdoodles 223
apple dumplings with vanilla ice cream
196
apple pie 184-5
granola with dried fruit compote 60
grilled cheese sandwich 91
pork chops with apple and bacon
compote 136
spiced apple and pear crisp 197
Waldorf salad 42-3
artichoke hearts: warm artichoke and
spinach dip 26-7
aubergines
Cajun andouille gumbo 113
summer vegetable Philly cheese steak
76
vegetarian po' boys 75
avocados
black bean and chipotle soup 38
breakfast burritos 68-9
Caesar salad with seared salmon 39
chunky guacamole feta salsa 11
flank steak and Cheddar burritos 79
fried chicken cobb salad 44
huevos rancheros on tortilla 62
prawn and sweet potato quesadillas 78
pulled chicken tacos 86-7
refried black beans with pico de gallo
166
shrimp, corn, and avocado salad 47
stoning and peeling 11

B

bacon
bacon, onion, and cheese hot dogs 84
black bean and chipotle soup 38
BLT with fried green tomatoes 71
Boston baked beans 146
country fried steak with pepper gravy
118
fried chicken cobb salad 44
grilled cheese sandwich 91
hoppin' John 100
New England clam chowder 34-5
pork chops with apple and bacon
compote 136
smoky bacon potato skins 14
smoky split pea soup 36
southern-style cornbread 229
sweet and smoky shrimp and grits 110
sweet potato casserole with bacon 162
waffles with bacon maple sauce 54

Waldorf salad 43
see also pancetta
baking
angel food cake with blackberry sauce
205
apple and cinnamon snickerdoodles 223
banana and butterscotch muffins 227
blueberry crumb cake 215
cayenne Cheddar cheese straws 230
chocolate and cherry devil's food cake
204
chocolate chip cookies 220-1
chocolate courgette bundt cake 218
chocolate custard-filled doughnuts 226
chocolate fudge cupcakes 214
cinnamon churros with chocolate chilli
sauce 224
cranberry oatmeal cookies 222
double chocolate brownies 206-7
lemon soured cream pound cake 219
pecan caramel cinnamon buns 202
pumpkin pie spice beignets 208
red velvet cupcakes 210
southern-style cornbread 228-9
strawberries and cream whoopie pies
211
triple-layered coconut cake 212
bananas
banana and butterscotch muffins 227
buttermilk pancakes 57
grilled banana PBJ 70
pecan and orange bananas foster 172
pound cake banana pudding 175
beef
classic burgers 126-7
country fried steak with pepper gravy
118
deli-style Reuben 80-1
dry-rub steak with chimichurri sauce
128
five alarm chilli 121
flank steak and Cheddar burritos 79
patty melt 127
slow-cooked pot roast 124
spicy grilled brisket 123
steak tacos 87
summer vegetable Philly cheese steak
76
sweet and spicy meatloaf 122
three bean chilli 120-1
beetroots: slow-cooked pot roast 124
berries
berries and cream shortcake 177
see also blackberries; blueberries;
raspberries; strawberries
black beans
black bean and chipotle soup 38
Boston baked beans 147
breakfast burritos 69
flank steak and Cheddar burritos 79
huevos rancheros on tortilla 62

refried black beans with pico de gallo
166
slow-cooked black beans 160
spicy chicken nachos with jalapeños 15
three bean chilli 120-1
tortilla chicken soup 30
black-eyed beans
hoppin' John 100
tropical Texas caviar 16
blackberries
angel food cake with blackberry sauce
205
apple and blackberry cobbler 189
Boston cream trifle 180
fresh berry compote with vanilla and
thyme 242
Waldorf salad 43
blueberries
blueberry compote 57
blueberry crumb cake 215
blueberry ripple cheesecake 192
Boston cream trifle 180
fresh berry compote with vanilla and
thyme 242
granola with dried fruit compote 60
peach and blueberry cobbler 189
bread
BLT with fried green tomatoes 71
chicken Parmesan sliders 104
chocolate bread pudding 174
curried lamb Sloppy Joes with naan
bread 88
deli-style Reuben 80-1
fried shrimp po' boys 74-5
grilled banana PBJ 70
grilled cheese sandwich 90-1
pecan and orange bananas foster 172
salami muffulettas with red peppers 82
sausage and chestnut stuffing 168
southern-style breakfast casserole 61
strawberry-stuffed French toast 55
summer vegetable Philly cheese steak
76
breakfasts
baked egg hash brown nests 66
biscuits and creamy sausage gravy 58
breakfast burritos 68-9
buttermilk pancakes 56-7
egg white, spinach, and salmon omelette
67
eggs benedict with smoked salmon
64-5
granola with dried fruit compote 60
huevos rancheros on tortilla 62
southern-style breakfast casserole 61
strawberry-stuffed French toast 55
waffles with bacon maple sauce 54
butter beans
seared tuna and creamy butter bean
pasta 115
stovetop Brunswick stew 131

buttermilk
  biscuits and creamy sausage gravy 58
  buffalo chicken wings 12-13
  buttermilk pancakes 56-7
  buttermilk ranch salad dressing 48
  fried green tomatoes with basil cream 164
  jalapeño, onion, and Cheddar hushpuppies 142
  peach cobbler 188-9
  red velvet cupcakes 210
  southern fried chicken 96-7
  southern-style cornbread 228-9
  strawberry shortcake 176-7
butterscotch
  banana and butterscotch muffins 227
  butterscotch brownies 207

C

cabbage
  Asian slaw 151
  cabbage slaw 87
  coleslaw 150-1
  quick stovetop sauerkraut 245
  spicy chow chow 246
candy
  chilli ginger candied pecans 233
  chocolate marshmallow fudge 236
  gooey s'mores bars 234
  lavender chocolate pretzel rods 238
  pistachio brittle 240
  white chocolate and popcorn balls 232
cannellini beans
  Boston baked beans 146
  three bean chilli 120-1
  white chilli 121
caramel
  caramel and chocolate crunch sundae 194
  pecan caramel cinnamon buns 202
  salted caramel 185
carrots
  Asian slaw 151
  biscuit-topped chicken pot pie 98
  cabbage slaw 87
  coleslaw 150-1
  slow-cooked pot roast 124
  smoky split pea soup 36
  spicy chorizo minestrone 32
celery
  chicken with rosemary dumplings 99
  coleslaw 150-1
  hoppin' John 100
  smoky split pea soup 36
  spicy chorizo minestrone 32
  stovetop Brunswick stew 131
  Waldorf salad 42-3
  zesty pastalaya 108
cheese
  bacon, onion, and cheese hot dogs 84
  baked egg hash brown nests 66

biscuit-topped chicken pot pie 98
biscuits and creamy sausage gravy 58
breakfast burritos 68-9
Caesar salad with seared salmon 39
cayenne Cheddar cheese straws 230
chicken Parmesan sliders 104
chunky guacamole feta salsa 11
creamed corn with basil and Parmesan 152
croque madame 91
deli-style Reuben 80-1
flank steak and Cheddar burritos 79
fried chicken cobb salad 44
fried green tomatoes with basil cream 164
grilled cheese sandwich 90-1
huevos rancheros on tortilla 62
jalapeño, onion, and Cheddar hushpuppies 142
mac 'n' cheese 138-9
mole shredded pork enchiladas 132
patty melt 127
pigs in blankets with Parmesan pastry m 19
prawn and sweet potato quesadillas 78
pretzeldogs with Cheddar and ale dip 83
rainbow potato gratin 158
salami muffulettas with red peppers 82
smoky bacon potato skins 14
southern-style breakfast casserole 61
southern-style cornbread 229
spicy chicken nachos with jalapeños 15
spicy pimiento cheese dip 28
summer vegetable Philly cheese steak 76
sweet and smoky shrimp and grits 110
sweet potato Parmesan tots 157
tomato, basil, and mozzarella pizza 102-3
warm artichoke and spinach dip 26-7
see also cream cheese
cherries
  cherry and walnut brownies 207
  chocolate and cherry devil's food cake 204
  fresh berry compote with vanilla and thyme 242
  granola with dried fruit compote 60
  lattice-topped cherry pie 187
  stoning 242
chicken
  Asian chicken and rice noodle soup 29
  baked chicken 97
  biscuit-topped chicken pot pie 98
  bourbon and brown sugar BBQ chicken 95
  buffalo chicken wings 12-13
  Cajun andouille gumbo 113
  chicken nuggets 97
  chicken Parmesan sliders 104

chicken with rosemary dumplings 99
classic burgers 127
fried chicken cobb salad 44
pulled chicken tacos 86-7
southern fried chicken 96-7
spicy chicken nachos with jalapeños 15
spicy chorizo-style dirty rice 114
stovetop Brunswick stew 131
tortilla chicken soup 30
white chilli 121
zesty pastalaya 108
chickpeas
  Boston baked beans 147
  jalapeño hummus 69
  spicy chorizo minestrone 32
  white chilli 121
chillies
  Asian chicken and rice noodle soup 29
  blackened mahi-mahi with pineapple salsa 106
  breakfast burritos 68-9
  Cajun andouille gumbo 112-13
  curried lamb Sloppy Joes with naan bread 88
  five alarm chilli 121
  flank steak and Cheddar burritos 79
  grilled peach salsa with corn chips 10
  hoppin' John 100
  hot pepper jelly 248
  huevos rancheros on tortilla 62
  jalapeño hummus 69
  jalapeño, onion, and Cheddar hushpuppies 142
  no-cook spicy summer relish 244
  pulled chicken tacos 86-7
  slow-cooked black beans 160
  southern-style breakfast casserole 61
  southern-style cornbread 229
  spicy chicken nachos with jalapeños 15
  three bean chilli 120-1
  tortilla chicken soup 30
  tropical Texas caviar 16
  vegetable fajitas with coriander cream 141
  vegetarian chilli 121
  white chilli 121

chocolate
    Boston cream trifle 180
    caramel and chocolate crunch sundae 194
    chocolate and cherry devil's food cake 204
    chocolate bread pudding 174
    chocolate chip cookies 220-1
    chocolate courgette bundt cake 218
    chocolate custard-filled doughnuts 226
    chocolate fudge cupcakes 214
    chocolate marshmallow fudge 236
    chocolate-crusted Key lime pie 178
    cinnamon churros with chocolate chilli sauce 224
    double chocolate brownies 206-7
    gooey s'mores bars 234
    lavender chocolate pretzel rods 238
    melting chocolate 238
    mole shredded pork enchiladas 132
    peanut butter ice cream sandwiches 193
    red velvet cupcakes 210
    strawberries and cream whoopie pies 211
    triple chocolate chip cookies 221
    white chocolate and popcorn balls 232
chorizo
    breakfast burritos 68-9
    southern-style breakfast casserole 61
    spicy chorizo minestrone 32
    spicy chorizo-style dirty rice 114
    zesty pastalaya 108
citrus fruit
    segmenting 169
    see also grapefruits; lemons; limes; oranges
clams
    brown ale cioppino 109
    New England clam chowder 34-5
coconut
    coconut funnel cakes 198
    granola with dried fruit compote 60
    triple-layered coconut cake 212
    white chocolate and popcorn balls 232
collard greens agrodolce 148
cornmeal and polenta
    cornbread muffins 229

cornmeal-crusted catfish nuggets 105
cornmeal-crusted fried okra 161
festive cornbread stuffing 169
fried green tomatoes with basil cream 164
jalapeño, onion, and Cheddar hushpuppies 142
southern-style cornbread 228-9
sweet and smoky shrimp and grits 110
waffles with bacon maple sauce 54
courgettes
    chocolate courgette bundt cake 218
    spicy chorizo minestrone 32
crabmeat
    extracting meat from a cooked crab 24
    lemon shallot crab cakes 22
    New England crab dip 24
cranberries
    cranberry oatmeal cookies 222
    festive cornbread stuffing 169
    granola with dried fruit compote 91
    grilled cheese sandwich 91
    pistachio and cranberry cookies 221
    spiced cranberry and orange sauce 165
cream cheese
    blueberry ripple cheesecake 192
    red velvet cupcakes 210
    strawberry-stuffed French toast 55
    warm artichoke and spinach dip 26-7
cucumbers: refrigerator pickles 249

D

deep-frying: heating oil for 144
desserts
    apple dumplings with vanilla ice cream 196
    apple pie 184-5
    blueberry ripple cheesecake 192
    Boston cream trifle 180
    caramel and chocolate crunch sundae 194
    chocolate bread pudding 174
    chocolate-crusted Key lime pie 178
    coconut funnel cakes 198
    lattice-topped cherry pie 187
    lemon and grapefruit meringue pie 182
    meringue-topped sweet potato pie 183
    peach cobbler 188-9
    peanut butter ice cream sandwiches 193
    pecan and maple pumpkin pie 186
    pecan and orange bananas foster 172
    pecan, maple, and bourbon pie 179
    pineapple upside-down cakes with basil cream 190
    pound cake banana pudding 175
    spiced apple and pear crisp 197
    strawberry shortcake 176-7
dough, rolling 230

E

edamame: warm edamame succotash 145
eggs
    baked egg hash brown nests 66
    breakfast burritos 68-9
    chocolate bread pudding 174
    croque madame 91
    deli-style Reuben 81
    devilled duck eggs with smoked salmon 18
    egg salad with celery, capers, and dill 46
    egg white, spinach, and salmon omelette 67
    eggs benedict with smoked salmon 64-5
    eggs florentine 65
    fried chicken cobb salad 44
    home-style potato salad 51
    huevos rancheros on tortilla 62
    lemon and grapefruit meringue pie 182
    meringue-topped sweet potato pie 183
    southern-style breakfast casserole 61
    strawberry-stuffed French toast 55
    whisking egg whites 67

F

figs: granola with dried fruit compote 60
fish and seafood
    blackened mahi-mahi with pineapple salsa 106
    Cajun andouille gumbo 113
    cornmeal-crusted catfish nuggets 105
    fish po' boys 75
    see also clams; crabmeat; prawns; salmon; tuna

G

garlic
    garlic and shallot mashed potatoes 156
    peeling garlic 156
grapefruits: lemon and grapefruit meringue pie 182
grapes: Waldorf salad 42-3
green bean casserole 149

H

ham
    croque madame 91
    pineapple-glazed baked ham 135
    salami muffulettas with red peppers 82
    scoring and glazing ham 135

I

ice cream
    apple dumplings with vanilla ice cream 196
    caramel and chocolate crunch sundae 194
    peanut butter ice cream sandwiches 193
    pecan and orange bananas foster 172

K

kale
hoppin' John 100
spicy chorizo minestrone 32
kidney beans
red beans and quinoa 140
three bean chilli 120–1

L

lamb
classic burgers 127
curried lamb Sloppy Joes with naan
bread 88
lemons
fried shrimp with lemon aïoli 20–1
lemon and grapefruit meringue pie 182
lemon shallot crab cakes 22
lemon soured cream pound cake 219
light bites
bacon, onion, and cheese hot dogs 84
BLT with fried green tomatoes 71
curried lamb Sloppy Joes with naan
bread 88
deli-style Reuben 80–1
flank steak and Cheddar burritos 79
fried shrimp po' boys 74–5
grilled banana PBJ 70
grilled cheese sandwich 90–1
prawn and sweet potato quesadillas 78
pretzeldogs with Cheddar and ale dip
83
pulled chicken tacos 86–7
salami muffulettas with red peppers 82
summer vegetable Philly cheese steak
76
limes
barbecued corn with lime and chilli
butter 153
blackened mahi-mahi with pineapple
salsa 106
chocolate-crusted key Lime pie 178
flank steak and Cheddar burritos 79
jalapeño hummus 69
tropical shortcake 177
tropical Texas caviar 16
vegetable fajitas with coriander cream
141

M

mains
biscuit-topped chicken pot pie 98
blackened mahi-mahi with pineapple
salsa 106
bourbon and brown sugar BBQ chicken
95
brown ale cioppino 109
Cajun andouille gumbo 112–13
chicken Parmesan sliders 104
chicken with rosemary dumplings 99
classic burgers 126–7
cornmeal-crusted catfish nuggets 105
country fried steak with pepper gravy
118
dry-rub steak with chimichurri sauce
128
garlic buttered roast turkey 94
hoppin' John 100
mac 'n' cheese 138–9
mole shredded pork enchiladas 132
pineapple-glazed baked ham 135
pork chops with apple and bacon
compote 136
seared tuna and creamy butter bean
pasta 115
slow-cooked pulled pork wraps 130
slow-cooked pot roast 124
southern fried chicken 96–7
spaghetti and herbed turkey meatballs
119
spicy chorizo-style dirty rice 114
spicy grilled brisket 123
stovetop Brunswick stew 131
sweet and smoky shrimp and grits
110
sweet and spicy meatloaf 122
three bean chilli 120–1
tomato, basil, and mozzarella pizza
102–3
twice-cooked baby back ribs 134
vegetable fajitas with coriander cream
141
zesty pastalaya 108
mangoes
tropical shortcake 177
tropical Texas caviar 16
maple syrup
collard greens agrodolce 148
granola with dried fruit compote 60
grilled cheese sandwich 91
pecan and maple pumpkin pie 186
pecan, maple, and bourbon pie 179
spiced cranberry and orange sauce
165
waffles with bacon maple sauce 54
marshmallows
chocolate marshmallow fudge 236
gooey s'mores bars 234
white chocolate and popcorn balls 232
mushrooms
breakfast burritos 69
chicken with rosemary dumplings 99
corn chowder 35
green bean casserole 149
slow-cooked pot roast 124
spicy chorizo minestrone 32
summer vegetable Philly cheese steak
76
vegetable fajitas with coriander cream
141
vegetarian po' boys 75
mussels: brown ale cioppino 109

N

noodles
Asian chicken and rice noodle soup 29
slow-cooked pot roast 124
nuts
granola with dried fruit compote 60
sausage and chestnut stuffing 168
see also peanut butter; pecan nuts;
pistachio nuts; walnuts

O

oats
cranberry oatmeal cookies 222
granola with dried fruit compote 60
spiced apple and pear crisp 197
okra
Cajun andouille gumbo 112–13
cornmeal-crusted fried okra 161
onion rings with chipotle aïoli 144
oranges
festive cornbread stuffing 169
granola with dried fruit compote 60
pecan and orange bananas foster 172
spiced cranberry and orange sauce 165
zesting an orange 165

P

pancetta
baked egg hash brown nests 66
Cajun andouille gumbo 113
collard greens agrodolce 148
slow-cooked black beans 160
warm edamame succotash 145
pasta
mac 'n' cheese 138–9
seared tuna and creamy butter bean
pasta 115
spaghetti and herbed turkey meatballs
119
spicy chorizo minestrone 32
zesty pastalaya 108
pastrami on rye 81
peaches
grilled peach salsa with corn chips 10
peach and blueberry cobbler 189
peach cobbler 188–9

peanut butter
  grilled banana PBJ 70
  peanut butter brownies 207
  peanut butter ice cream sandwiches 193
pears
  coring and peeling a pear 237
  pear and cardamom butter 237
  pear pie 185
  spiced apple and pear crisp 197
  Waldorf salad 43
peas
  biscuit-topped chicken pot pie 98
  chicken with rosemary dumplings 99
  mac 'n' cheese 139
pecan nuts
  apple pie 185
  blueberry crumb cake 215
  chilli ginger candied pecans 233
  pecan and maple pumpkin pie 186
  pecan and orange bananas foster 172
  pecan caramel cinnamon buns 202
  pecan, maple, and bourbon pie 179
  sweet potato casserole with bacon 162
  Waldorf salad 43
peppers
  Asian slaw 151
  blackened mahi-mahi with pineapple salsa 106
  breakfast burritos 68-9
  Cajun andouille gumbo 112-13
  creamy tomato soup with corn and peppers 33
  five alarm chilli 121
  flank steak and Cheddar burritos 79
  hoppin' John 100
  hot pepper jelly 248
  no-cook spicy summer relish 244
  preparing a pepper 244
  red beans and quinoa 140
  roasting and peeling peppers 82
  salami muffulettas with red peppers 82
  spicy chorizo minestrone 32
  spicy chorizo-style dirty rice 114
  spicy chow chow 246
  spicy pimiento cheese dip 28
  summer vegetable Philly cheese steak 76
  three bean chilli 120-1
  tortilla chicken soup 30

tropical Texas caviar 16
vegetable fajitas with coriander cream 141
vegetarian po' boys 75
zesty pastalaya 108
pineapple
  blackened mahi-mahi with pineapple salsa 106
  coring a pineapple 106
  pineapple upside-down cakes with basil cream 190
  pineapple-glazed baked ham 135
  tropical Texas caviar 16
pistachio nuts
  pistachio and cranberry cookies 221
  pistachio brittle 240
plum cobbler 189
popcorn: white chocolate and popcorn balls 232
pork
  mole shredded pork enchiladas 132
  pork chops with apple and bacon compote 136
  slow-cooked pulled pork wraps 130
  twice-cooked baby back ribs 134
potatoes
  baked egg hash brown nests 66
  biscuit-topped chicken pot pie 98
  breakfast burritos 68-9
  country fried steak with pepper gravy 118
  garlic and shallot mashed potatoes 156
  home-style potato salad 50-1
  New England clam chowder 34-5
  potato röstis 65
  rainbow potato gratin 158
  slicing a potato 158
  slow-cooked pot roast 124
  smoky bacon potato skins 14
  smoky split pea soup 36
  stovetop Brunswick stew 131
prawns
  brown ale cioppino 109
  Cajun andouille gumbo 112-13
  fried shrimp po' boys 74-5
  fried shrimp with lemon aïoli 20-1
  New England clam chowder 35
  prawn and sweet potato quesadillas 78
  shrimp and tequila 87
  shrimp, corn, and avocado salad 47
  sweet and smoky shrimp and grits 110
  zesty pastalaya 108
preserves
  fresh berry compote with vanilla and thyme 242
  hot pepper jelly 248
  no-cook spicy summer relish 244
  pear and cardamom butter 237
  quick stovetop sauerkraut 245
  refrigerator pickles 249
  spicy chow chow 246

prunes: granola with dried fruit compote 60
pumpkin
  pecan and maple pumpkin pie 186
  pumpkin pie spice beignets 208

Q
quinoa: red beans and quinoa 140

R
raspberries
  Boston cream trifle 180
  chocolate fudge cupcakes 214
  raspberry walnut salad dressing 48
rice
  flank steak and Cheddar burritos 79
  hoppin' John 100
  spicy chorizo-style dirty rice 114

S
salad dressings
  buttermilk ranch 48
  Catalina 48
  Green Goddess 48
  raspberry walnut 48
  Thousand Island 48
salads
  Caesar salad with seared salmon 39
  egg salad with celery, capers, and dill 46
  fried chicken cobb salad 44
  home-style potato salad 50-1
  shrimp, corn, and avocado salad 47
  Waldorf salad 42-3
  salami muffulettas with red peppers 82
salmon
  brown ale cioppino 109
  Caesar salad with seared salmon 39
  devilled duck eggs with smoked salmon 18
  egg white, spinach, and salmon omelette 67
  eggs benedict with smoked salmon 64-5
sauerkraut
  deli-style Reuben 80-1
  quick stovetop sauerkraut 245
sausages
  bacon, onion, and cheese hot dogs 84
  biscuits and creamy sausage gravy 58
  Cajun andouille gumbo 112-13
  pigs in blankets with Parmesan pastry 19
  pretzeldogs with Cheddar and ale dip 83
  red beans and quinoa 140
  sausage and chestnut stuffing 168
  see also chorizo
sides
  barbecued corn with lime and chilli butter 153

Boston baked beans 146
coleslaw 150-1
collard greens agrodolce 148
cornmeal-crusted fried okra 161
creamed corn with basil and Parmesan 152
festive cornbread stuffing 169
fried green tomatoes with basil cream 164
garlic and shallot mashed potatoes 156
green bean casserole 149
jalapeño, onion, and Cheddar hushpuppies 142
onion rings with chipotle aïoli 144
rainbow potato gratin 158
red beans and quinoa 140
refried black beans with pico de gallo 166
sausage and chestnut stuffing 168
slow-cooked black beans 160
spiced cranberry and orange sauce 165
sweet potato casserole with bacon 162
sweet potato Parmesan tots 157
warm edamame succotash 145
soups
    Asian chicken and rice noodle soup 29
    black bean and chipotle soup 38
    creamy tomato soup with corn and peppers 33
    New England clam chowder 34-5
    smoky split pea soup 36
    spicy chorizo minestrone 32
    tortilla chicken soup 30
spinach
    egg white, spinach, and salmon omelette 67
    eggs florentine 65
    fried chicken cobb salad 44
    warm artichoke and spinach dip 26-7
split peas: smoky split pea soup 36
starters
    buffalo chicken wings 12-13
    chunky guacamole feta salsa 11
    devilled duck eggs with smoked salmon 18
    fried shrimp with lemon aïoli 20-1
    grilled peach salsa with corn chips 10
    lemon shallot crab cakes 22
    New England crab dip 24
    pigs in blankets with Parmesan pastry 19
    smoky bacon potato skins 14
    spicy chicken nachos with jalapeños 15
    spicy pimiento cheese dip 28
    spicy sweetcorn fritters with salsa 25
    tropical Texas caviar 16
    warm artichoke and spinach dip 26-7
strawberries
    Boston cream trifle 180
    preparing strawberries 55
    strawberries and cream whoopie pies 211

strawberry shortcake 176-7
strawberry-stuffed French toast 55
sugar, boiling 240
sweet potatoes
    baked egg hash brown nests 66
    biscuit-topped chicken pot pie 98
    Cajun andouille gumbo 113
    home-style potato salad 51
    meringue-topped sweet potato pie 183
    prawn and sweet potato quesadillas 78
    rainbow potato gratin 158
    slow-cooked pot roast 124
    sweet potato casserole with bacon 162
    sweet potato Parmesan tots 157
sweetcorn
    barbecued corn with lime and chilli butter 153
    biscuit-topped chicken pot pie 98
    chunky guacamole feta salsa 11
    corn chowder 35
    creamed corn with basil and Parmesan 152
    creamy tomato soup with corn and peppers 33
    removing corn kernels 152
    shrimp, corn, and avocado salad 47
    spicy sweetcorn fritters with salsa 25
    stovetop Brunswick stew 131
    three bean chilli 120-1
    tortilla chicken soup 30
    tropical Texas caviar 16
    vegetable fajitas with coriander cream 141
    warm edamame succotash 145

T
tomatoes
    black bean and chipotle soup 38
    BLT with fried green tomatoes 71
    Boston baked beans 147
    breakfast burritos 68-9
    brown ale cioppino 109
    Cajun andouille gumbo 112-13
    chicken Parmesan sliders 104
    chunky guacamole feta salsa 11
    creamy tomato soup with corn and peppers 33
    flank steak and Cheddar burritos 79
    fried chicken cobb salad 44
    fried green tomatoes with basil cream 164
    grilled peach salsa with corn chips 10
    huevos rancheros on tortilla 62
    mac 'n' cheese 139
    mole shredded pork enchiladas 132
    pulled chicken tacos 86-7
    red beans and quinoa 140
    refried black beans with pico de gallo 166
    shrimp, corn, and avocado salad 47
    spaghetti and herbed turkey meatballs 119

spicy chorizo minestrone 32
spicy chow chow 246
spicy sweetcorn fritters with salsa 25
stovetop Brunswick stew 131
sweet and smoky shrimp and grits 110
three bean chilli 120-1
tomato, basil, and mozzarella pizza 102-3
tortilla chicken soup 30
warm edamame succotash 145
zesty pastalaya 108
tortillas
    breakfast burritos 68-9
    flank steak and Cheddar burritos 79
    grilled peach salsa with corn chips 10
    huevos rancheros on tortilla 62
    mole shredded pork enchiladas 132
    prawn and sweet potato quesadillas 78
    pulled chicken tacos 86-7
    vegetable fajitas with coriander cream 141
tuna
    home-style potato salad 51
    mac 'n' cheese 139
    seared tuna and creamy butter bean pasta 115
turkey
    classic burgers 127
    deli-style Rachael 81
    garlic buttered roast turkey 94
    spaghetti and herbed turkey meatballs 119

W
walnuts
    cherry and walnut brownies 207
    raspberry walnut salad dressing 48
    Waldorf salad 42-3

ABOUT THE AUTHORS

Caroline Bretherton has worked in the food industry on both sides of the Atlantic for almost 20 years. Her enthusiasm and skills led her to start her own catering company, and later a café, before going on to work consistently in television and the print media. She has already published four books with DK: *The Allotment Cookbook Through the Year*, *Step-by-Step Baking*, *The Pie Book*, and *Family Kitchen Cookbook*. She lives in North Carolina with her family, from where she continues to write about all things food related.

Elena Rosemond-Hoerr – a North Carolinian born and bred – is a writer, photographer, and author of the award-winning food blog biscuitsandsuch.com. Elena lives on the coast with her husband and dog, baking pies, gardening, and celebrating America's rich food heritage.

ACKNOWLEDGMENTS

Caroline Bretherton would like to thank: Borra Garson and all at Deborah McKenna for their work on my behalf; Peggy Vance, Dawn Henderson, Bob Bridle, and all at DK for their enthusiasm and encouragement; and Elena Rosemond-Hoerr for being such a fabulous co-author and photographer.

Elena Rosemond-Hoerr would like to thank: my sweet husband Dan for his impeccable taste-testing skills; my incredible co-author Caroline for holding my hand through the cookbook writing process; and Bob Bridle and the patient team at DK for their support and enthusiasm.

DK would like to thank: Stuart West and Elena Rosemond-Hoerr for photography; Penny Stock and Lisa Pettibone for photography art direction; Jane Lawrie for food styling; Wei Tang for prop styling; Jane Bamforth, Anna Burges-Lumsden, Sue Davie, Jan Fullwood, Chris Gates, Katy Greenwood, Anne Harnan, and Sue Harris for recipe testing; Corinne Masciocchi for proofreading; and Marie Lorimer for the index.

PICTURE CREDITS

The publisher would like to thank the following for their kind permission to reproduce their photographs: (Key: a-above; b-below/bottom; c-centre; f-far; l-left; r-right; t-top)
Jacket images: *Front*: Alamy Images: Patti McConville tr. *Back*: Alamy Images: Patti McConville tr.
All other images © Dorling Kindersley
For further information see: **www.dkimages.com**